"Just when it seemed there were no more rousing espionage stories left to tell, along comes Giles Milton with *Russian Roulette*. With his customary panache and originality, he weaves an astonishing account enlivened by a remarkable cast of characters." —**Laurence Bergreen, author of** *Columbus: The Four Voyages* **and** *Over the Edge of the World: Magellan's Terrifying Circumnavigation of the Globe.*

"Impressive . . . [An] entertaining history of spectacular, often nasty derring-do by real-life secret agents." —*Publishers Weekly*

"Milton's vivid presentation . . . will entertain aficionados of intelligence." —*Booklist*

"Wonderful . . . Very readable . . . An entertaining one-stop-shop book that introduces readers to the turbulent years of the Russian Revolution and the new 'great game' of intelligence run by the British and the Soviets." —**Tish Wells,** *McClatchy*

Acclaim from the British press:

"Giles Milton's fast-packed account of Britain's attempts to sabotage Lenin's revolution reads like a madcap thriller . . . Milton has synthesised and filleted a mass of material—old memoirs, official archives and newly released intelligence files—to produce a rollicking tale . . . which explains the long war against Russia with verve, wit and colour. It reads like fiction, but it is, astonishingly, history." —*The Times*

D0289771

RUSSIAN ROULETTE

ALSO BY GILES MILTON

Non-Fiction
The Riddle and the Knight
Nathaniel's Nutmeg
Big Chief Elizabeth
Samurai William
White Gold
Paradise Lost
Wolfram

Fiction
Edward Trencom's Nose
According to Arnold

RUSSIAN ROULETTE

How British Spies Thwarted Lenin's Plot
for Global Revolution

GILES MILTON

BLOOMSBURY PRESS
NEW YORK · LONDON · NEW DELHI · SYDNEY

Bloomsbury Press
An imprint of Bloomsbury Publishing Plc

1385 Broadway   50 Bedford Square
New York   London
NY 10018   WC1B 3DP
USA   UK

www.bloomsbury.com

BLOOMSBURY and the Diana logo are trademarks of Bloomsbury Publishing Plc

First published in Great Britain 2013 by Sceptre, an imprint of Hodder & Stoughton
First U.S. edition 2014
This paperback edition published 2015

ISBN: HB: 978-1-62040-568-0
       PB: 978-1-62040-570-3
     ePub: 978-1-62040-569-7

Library of Congress Cataloging-in-Publication Data has been applied for.

2 4 6 8 10 9 7 5 3 1

Typeset by Hewer Text UK Ltd, Edinburgh
Printed and bound in the U.S.A. by Thomson-Shore Inc., Dexter, Michigan

To find out more about our authors and books visit www.bloomsbury.com.
Here you will find extracts, author interviews, details of forthcoming events,
and the option to sign up for our newsletters.

Bloomsbury books may be purchased for business or promotional use.
For information on bulk purchases please contact Macmillan Corporate
and Premium Sales Department at specialmarkets@macmillan.com

For Alexis

'James Bond is just a piece of nonsense I dreamed up. He's not a Sidney Reilly, you know!'

Ian Fleming

CONTENTS

LIST OF CHARACTERS

BRITISH

Mansfield Cumming: Head of Secret Intelligence Service (SIS). Director of secret operations inside Soviet Russia.

Samuel Hoare: SIS bureau chief in Petrograd.

Ernest Boyce: SIS bureau chief in Moscow.

John Scale: SIS bureau chief in Stockholm.

Paul Dukes: spy (operating under aliases of Joseph Ilitch Afirenko, Joseph Krylenko, Alexander Vasilievitch Markovitch and Alexander Bankau).

Arthur Ransome: journalist and spy.

George Hill: spy (operating under alias of George Bergmann).

Sidney Reilly: spy (operating under aliases of Konstantine Markovich Massino, Mr Constantine and Sigmund Relinsky).

Augustus Agar: special agent.

Somerset Maugham: special agent (operating under name of Somerville).

Oswald Rayner: special agent.

Frederick Bailey: spy employed by government of British India (operating under aliases of Andrei Kekechi, Georgi Chuka and Joseph Kastamuni).

Wilfrid Malleson: army general and spy-master employed by government of British India.

Robert Bruce Lockhart: diplomat.

RUSSIAN

Vladimir Ilyich Lenin: Russia's revolutionary leader.

Leon Trotsky: revolutionary and leader of Red Army.

Felix Dzerzhinsky: Director of the Cheka, Russia's secret police.

Karl Radek: Vice-Commissar for Foreign Affairs.

Yakov Peters: Deputy Chairman of the Cheka.

Grigori Zinoviev: Head of the Comintern.

Evgenia Shelepina: Trotsky's secretary and Arthur Ransome's lover.

Maria Zakrveskia (Budberg), known as Moura: Robert Bruce Lockhart's lover.

INDIAN

Manabendra Nath Roy: Indian revolutionary and leader of the 'Army of God'.

ACKNOWLEDGEMENTS

Much of the research material for *Russian Roulette* is housed in two depositories of archives: The India Office Records, now kept at the British Library, and the National Archives at Kew.

Special thanks are due to the ever-helpful staff of the India Office Records. They proved invaluable in guiding me through the 751 files of Indian Political Intelligence. They also provided access to Frederick Bailey's photographic collection: two of his photographs are reproduced in the plate section of this book.

The staff of the National Archives proved helpful in locating key documents. The pictures of the M Device, also reproduced in the plate section, were found in one of the National Archive's many files concerning the development of chemical weapons.

Thank you to the Institute of Historical Research.

The librarians of the London Library, where much of this book was written, have proved as helpful for *Russian Roulette* as they were for all my previous books.

A full list of sources is provided at the end of this book but special mention must be made of one author whose works have proved particularly inspiring. The doyen of Great Game specialists is Peter Hopkirk, whose books combine serious scholarship with page-turning narrative. Although new material has come to light in recent years, they remain a standard (and invaluable) reference for the subject of the struggle for control of Central Asia.

I am indebted to those spies who elected to publish their experiences, risking costly law suits for doing so. 'There is scarcely a page . . . that does not damage the foundation of secrecy upon which the Secret Service is built up.' So reads a Secret Intelligence Service memo concerning the publication of Compton Mackenzie's book *Greek Memories*, with its account of Mansfield Cumming.

First-hand accounts must be treated with caution: my aim throughout was to corroborate and balance the sometimes exuberant stories of the spies' undercover adventures with the more sober tone of their intelligence reports.

Thank you to my literary agent, Georgia Garrett, for her hard work and ever-helpful advice; and to her team at Rogers, Coleridge and White.

Thank you, equally, to my editor, Lisa Highton, for her excellent advice, encouragement and supportiveness, and for seeing the project through from inception to publication.

Thanks are also due to Federico Andornino, Juliet Brightmore (for her work on the plate section) and Tara Gladden, who copy-edited the book.

I would like to single out my French editor, Vera Michalski, for special mention. She embraced the project from the outset and bought the French (and Polish) rights long before the book was completed.

Thank you, also, to the other foreign editors who will be publishing the book, notably Peter Ginna at Bloomsbury USA and Sindbad editors in Russia.

Lastly, a fanfare of thanks must be sounded for the home team: Alexandra, who read countless versions of the manuscript yet still managed to provide excellent (and much-needed) advice; and to Madeleine, Héloïse and Aurélia for reminding me that there is life outside the world of espionage, skull-duggery and dirty tricks.

Magny, spring 2013.

MAPS

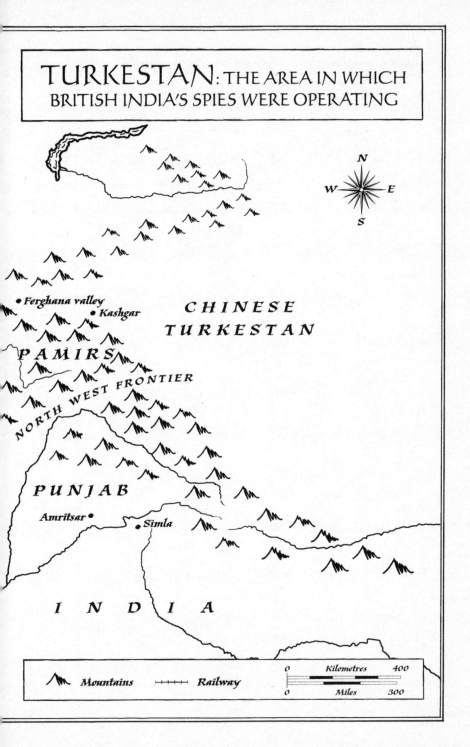

TURKESTAN: THE AREA IN WHICH BRITISH INDIA'S SPIES WERE OPERATING

- Ferghana valley
- Kashgar

CHINESE TURKESTAN

PAMIRS

NORTH WEST FRONTIER

PUNJAB

Amritsar •
• Simla

INDIA

⋏⋏ Mountains   ┼┼┼┼ Railway

0   Kilometres   400
0   Miles   300

RUSSIA: THE AREA IN WHICH MANSFIELD
CUMMING'S SPIES WERE OPERATING

NORWAY

Barents Sea

Murmansk

N
W   E
S

0   Kilometres   400
0   Miles   200

White
Sea

Archangel

Torneå

SWEDEN

Area of attack by
chemical weapons

FINLAND

Terijoki

Helsingfors   Kronstadt

Stockholm   Vologda

PETROGRAD

Tallinn
(Reval)

Gulf of Finland

Baltic Sea

MOSCOW

Riga

Kaunus

RUSSIA

GERMANY

Brest–Litovsk

Warsaw

Kharkov

Kiev

UKRAINE

Rostov–on–Don

Vienna

Budapest   Odessa

Ekaterinodar

AUSTRIA–HUNGARY

Black Sea

CENTRAL MOSCOW: SAFE HOUSES AND ESPIONAGE HEADQUARTERS

① Kremlin, where Robert Bruce Lockhart was imprisoned.

② Cheka headquarters, where Sidney Reilly was buried.

③ American Consulate, where the spies planned their coup against Lenin (Novinskiy Boulevard).

④ Headquarters of George Hill's courier operations (Degtyarny Street).

⑤ George Hill's hired rooms for meetings with couriers.

⑥ Tramble Cafe, Tverskoy Boulevard: Sidney Reilly's favourite place for secret meetings.

⑦ George Hill's secret espionage headquarters (Pyatnitskaya Street).

⑧ Sidney Reilly's Moscow headquarters (Cheremeteff Pereulok). Raided by Cheka, 1918.

⑨ George Hill's rooms for secret meetings and recruiting couriers.

⑩ George Hill's safe house, 11 miles east of central Moscow, at Kuskovo.

⑪ Bolshoi Theatre, where Sidney Reily intended to carry out his coup d'etat.

⑫ Sidney Reilly's safe house, Tverskaya Street.

THE VILLAIN

Shortly before dusk on 16 April 1917, three Englishmen could be seen loitering in the shadows of Finlyandsky Station in the Russian city of Petrograd.

They were not spies – at least, not yet. But they had all been drawn to the station for the same reason. They had been informed that something unusual, and possibly dangerous, was due to happen that very evening. And they wanted to be there to witness it.

They had already been waiting several hours, for the train they were hoping to meet was running extremely late. When it at last pulled alongside the platform, it let out a valedictory hiss of steam, as if to remind passengers of its tiresome trek across Northern Russia. Then the carriage doors started to bang open, as the passengers flung them against the side of the train.

From one of these doors emerged a most peculiar-looking individual. His beard was clipped to a sharp point and his protruding forehead was accentuated by his felt homburg. In the gloom of a Petrograd twilight, he had the air of a Scandinavian goblin.

This newly arrived stranger looked from left to right as his beady eyes adjusted themselves to the darkness. The long years of war meant that only a few of the station's gaslights were working.

As he called to his comrades who were still on the train, there was the loud snap of a carbide lamp. Suddenly, dramatically, the station's shadows were cut through by a thick shaft of light. The mystery figure was bathed from head to foot in dazzling brightness.

It was a scene of operatic grandeur, or so it seemed to the small group that had gathered on the station concourse. As a hastily assembled band pumped out the 'Marseillaise', Vladimir Ilyich Ulyanov – better known as Lenin – turned to acknowledge the crowd. He was returning to Russia after ten years in exile.

The group of armed revolutionaries who had gathered to greet Lenin unfurled their red and gold banners and shone more of their lights onto their beloved leader. As they did so, Lenin clambered onto the bonnet of an armoured car and made his first historic address on Russian soil. He declared that the political turmoil afflicting Russia was no local affair: it was the beginning of a worldwide revolution that was certain to engulf the democracies of Western Europe and North America.

'Dear Comrades, soldiers, sailors and workers! I greet you as the vanguard of the worldwide proletarian army.' Lenin's opening words prompted a wild fanfare from his supporters. As the cheering increased in volume, he launched into a fiery and uncompromising speech, promising to unleash 'a civil war throughout Europe' that would rip the continent apart. 'Long live the worldwide Socialist revolution!'

Lenin was entirely ignorant of the fact that his arrival was being monitored by three Englishmen. One of these men was Arthur Ransome, a journalist with the *Daily News*. Ransome was not impressed by this bald-headed revolutionary, with his outdated clothes and caustic tongue. He did not even mention Lenin in that evening's despatches.

Paul Dukes, a courier working for the British Embassy, was similarly underwhelmed. He described Lenin as a 'little man with Asiatic features who was totally unknown to the general populace'.

Yet there was something about Lenin's turn of phrase that grabbed his attention. It was gripping – magnetic, even – and he was sufficiently disturbed by his gospel of world revolution to send a warning to the Foreign Office in London. His telegram was widely treated as a joke. 'Some of my colleagues laughed,' said Dukes. 'They pooh-poohed the idea of Lenin's having any significance.'

The third in the trio of Englishmen at the station, William Gibson, left the fullest account of Lenin's arrival. 'An ugly bald man below medium height, with eyes like daggers, he regarded the crowd with an indescribable look of insolent mastery.'

Gibson watched in appalled fascination as Lenin commanded silence with a flick of his hand. Everyone instantly obeyed. 'Without one word,' wrote Gibson, 'this seemingly wretched little figure made his presence felt to the onlookers in a way they had never before experienced in their lives.'

Gibson felt repulsed and fascinated in equal measure by this enigmatic character. 'Whatever he was, he seemed alike superhuman and inhuman; ready to bathe in blood to gain the glorious realisation of his mighty dream.' It was as if Lenin was a new Messiah, albeit one preaching violent revolution rather than peace.

'There was something sinister, terrifying, in the air, and yet one felt drawn towards him.' Lenin's hypnotic charm worked an immediate spell on its audience.

★

William Gibson had been right to fear this revolutionary oddball. Everything that Lenin predicted seemed to come to pass. Like an Old Testament prophet, his words were miraculously transformed into reality.

People scoffed when he vowed to sweep away the old order in Russia. Yet he did just that within months of arriving back in the country. Few believed that he would pull Russian forces out of the First World War and even fewer that he would have Tsar Nicholas and his family murdered in cold blood. Yet both of these things came to pass.

Very soon after Lenin seized power, the world awoke to the fact that it was facing a new and terrible threat. The British ambassador, Sir George Buchanan, was the first to alert London to the fact that a dark force was emerging in Russia – one quite unlike any other regime in existence. He warned that Lenin had not only brought revolution to Russia, but was determined 'to overthrow all the so-called imperialistic governments.' He first intended to direct all his energies into the struggle against Britain. Then, he would turn his attentions to the rest of the world.

Scarcely had Buchanan's message been received in London than Lenin tore up the Anglo-Russian Convention of 1907. This was an agreement of vital strategic importance to Britain: it set out spheres of influence in Central Asia and protected British India's northern frontiers from attack by Russia. Suddenly, those frontiers looked very vulnerable.

Lenin's nullification of the treaty was accompanied by an uncompromising message; one that sent the first shiver of alarm through Whitehall. He issued a rallying cry to Asia's oppressed millions, urging them to follow the lead of the Bolsheviks and cast off the yoke of colonial rule.

His rhetoric soon became even more fiery. India, the jewel in Britain's imperial crown, was to be snatched away by the Bolsheviks. 'England is our greatest enemy,' he thundered. 'It is in India that we must strike them hardest.'

The timing of Lenin's call to arms could not have been worse for the rulers of British India. Civil unrest was on the rise and revolutionary violence was greatly feared by the authorities, especially given the paucity of British troops in the subcontinent.

At the outset of war, India's viceroy, Lord Hardinge, had spoken of 'the risks involved in denuding India of troops.' But the soldiers of British India had been urgently required in both Europe and Mesopotamia and they were transferred en masse. Hardinge feared the worst. 'Our position in India is a bit of a gamble at the present time,' he warned.

This was an understatement. By the time Lenin seized power in Russia there had been such an exodus of British troops that not a single battalion remained on Indian soil, with the exception of the eight permanently stationed on the volatile North-West Frontier. Even these were hopelessly ill-equipped. 'The recruiting barrel has been scraped to the bottom,' conceded their commander, Lieutenant-General George Molesworth.

Lenin had long argued that the Bolshevik movement should fund and assist Indians 'in their revolutionary war against the imperialist powers that oppress them.' Now, the Bolshevik Council of People's Commissars voted to invest the enormous sum of two million gold roubles in exporting their revolution.

Ambassador Buchanan was appalled by what he was hearing. 'Mr Lenin spoke of us as rapacious extortioners and plunderers,' he said, 'while he incited our Indian subjects to rebellion.' He added that it was quite extraordinary 'for a man who claims to direct Russian policy to use such language to a friendly and allied country.'

But Lenin did not see Britain as a friendly and allied country. He had long viewed it as his most bitter enemy, one whose empire needed to be violently dismantled.

Ambassador Buchanan feared that Lenin was intent on launching a whole new chapter of the Great Game – the struggle for political mastery in Central Asia. He also believed that Russia's Bolshevik rulers would stop at nothing to push revolution deep into British India.

This was indeed Lenin's goal. But his revolutionary vision had an even wider sweep. He had long been convinced that if Britain lost her prized imperial possession, with its cheap labour and raw materials, then revolution in the motherland would surely follow. This would then spark a wave of revolutions throughout Western Europe and North America, causing the world's greatest democracies to topple like dominos.

The old order was already haunted by the spectre of revolution by the time Lenin seized the reins of power in Russia. There was a very real fear that it would only take one extra push for the Western world to come crashing down.

★

Thus began an exhilarating game of Russian Roulette in which the stakes could not have been higher. The world was at a tipping point and no one could predict which way the balance would fall.

The most obvious way to counter the Bolshevik revolutionaries would have been to launch a full-scale military intervention in Russia before the new rulers had consolidated their grip on power. This was indeed contemplated. But Britain simply did not have the resources to land a sufficiently large army in Russia while it was still at war with Germany. Indeed, it was struggling to survive a catastrophic conflict that had claimed millions of young lives.

The threat posed by Lenin was so unpredictable and relentless that it was to call for a wholly new approach, one in which the rules of the game were to be forever changed.

With military intervention an impossibility, there was no other option but to rest the fate of the Western world upon the shoulders of a small but highly trained group of secret agents. They would have to risk everything to infiltrate Russia's revolutionary government and sabotage Lenin's strategy from within.

They would be working in the shadows, in a murky world of espionage, treachery and double-dealing. Some would be sneaked into Moscow. Others would spearhead a daring mission into Central Asia, where they were to play a devious game of cat and mouse in the sun-baked citadels of Turkestan. All knew that human lives were going to have to be placed at risk if they were to have any hope of success.

In the highly dangerous battle of wits that was to follow, these British agents had one advantage over their Bolshevik adversaries: they had already been working inside Russia for more than three years. Long before Lenin brought his revolutionary ideas to Petrograd, they already knew how to break the rules.

The team was led by an English gentleman named Samuel Hoare, and it was to make the first of many daring strikes in the winter of 1916.

PART ONE

SHOOTING IN THE DARK

TOP SECRET

CHAPTER ONE

MURDER IN THE DARK

TOP SECRET

S amuel Hoare eased himself from his chair and wandered over to the window of his office in the Russian War Ministry.

In the parade ground below, hundreds of young conscripts were rehearsing an attack through a quagmire of straw and mud. Icy rain was pouring from a gunmetal sky, turning the ground to liquid. Yet the conscripts seemed oblivious to the autumn chill as they advanced on their bellies towards imaginary German trenches.

Hoare stared at them for a moment before returning to the huge pile of documents that had just been delivered to his desk. Secret reports of battle failures; secret accounts of deserting troops; secret tales of disaster and mutiny. It did not take a genius to realise that Russia was losing the war on the Eastern Front.

Samuel Hoare was head of the Russian bureau, a seventeen-strong team of British intelligence officers working in Petrograd, capital of the Russian Empire. He had arrived in the city in the spring of 1916, excited and not a little bemused by his unexpected summons to join Britain's intelligence service.

It had all happened so quickly: a private meeting in Whitehall, some questions about his fluency in Russian and then an offer of employment, swiftly concluded with a handshake. 'In the space of a few seconds,' he later recalled, 'I was accepted into the ranks of the Secret Service.'

He was an unlikely candidate for espionage. An English baronet of the old school, he had been the Conservative Member of Parliament for Chelsea since 1910. Well-spoken, well-mannered, well-heeled, he was solidly conventional. Harrow and Oxford, old chap. Double first.

But he had taught himself conversational Russian and this had earned him the notice of the Secret Intelligence Service. He was to be sent to Petrograd in order to forge links with Russian generals and monitor the fighting on the Eastern Front.

It was not a question of spying on the enemy: Russia was a key member of the Triple Entente (Britain, France, Russia) fighting against Germany in the First World War. However, Hoare's role was certainly of vital importance. The conflict on the Eastern Front was tying down huge numbers of German troops that could otherwise be transferred to the Western Front. A sudden influx of battle-hardened soldiers to Northern France would spell disaster for the British Tommies struggling to hold their entrenched positions in Picardie and Champagne.

Hoare was hoping to be initiated into a world of glamour, duplicity and deception when he first arrived in Petrograd. He had been given a rudimentary training in eavesdropping and ciphering and was looking forward to using his new skills.

However, his work at the Russian War Ministry proved monotonous and exhausting, with twelve-hour days and no holidays. Far from infiltrating subversive meetings, he found himself helping to supply Russian ministries with much needed supplies. On one occasion, he was asked to procure thousands of beeswax candles for the Holy Synod of the Orthodox Church.

His evenings were no less tedious – a succession of champagne soirées with highly decorated generals whose knowledge of battlefield strategy was lamentable. 'Incompetent, idle, self-indulgent, irresponsible,' was Hoare's opinion of the Minister of War.

Teamwork meant everything to Hoare. He played according to the rules – taking pride in being firm but fair – and he expected his men to do the same. He was unaware that they didn't all agree with his very British approach to espionage. Nor did he realise that there was a far more nefarious side to the activities of the bureau that he directed. Among those serving in his team was a young Oxford graduate named Oswald Rayner. Along with a handful of others, Rayner had established a clandestine inner circle that members referred to as the 'far-reaching system'.

This 'system' aimed to act in absolute secrecy, spearheading underground missions that left no trace of their involvement. These dangerous operations, of which Hoare had no knowledge, were to become a hallmark of the Russian bureau.

Oswald Rayner's 'far-reaching system' was to make the first of many spectacular strikes in the winter of 1916. It was to leave a fingerprint so faint that it would remain undetected for nine decades.

★

The bitter chill of December 1916 brought a heightened sense of gloom to the city of Petrograd.

'For us,' wrote Hoare, 'it made the ordinary routine of life difficult and irritating, but for the hundreds of thousands of working women who, badly clothed and miserably housed, stood hour after hour in queues amidst the snow and sleet of a Petrograd winter, and often went home with nothing for their families, it was a grim tragedy that led inevitably to bloodshed and revolution.'

Hoare's weekly intelligence reports revealed that poor leadership and inadequate weaponry had led to Russian war fatigue. 'I am confident that Russia will never fight through another winter,' he wrote that December.

The imperial splendour of the Marinsky Theatre offered the only possibility of escape. Oblivious to the steady disintegration of the Russian Army, it continued to stage exquisitely choreographed ballets. Tsar Nicholas himself no longer attended, yet the royal box still sparkled with candlelight throughout the performances. '[It] seemed to many of us to symbolise a capital that the Emperor seldom visited and a society that the Emperor never saw,' wrote Hoare.

The tsar's absence only fuelled the rumours that he was no longer in charge of the country. The British ambassador, Sir George Buchanan, concurred with the many who said he was under the baleful influence of the tsarina. Others claimed that the affairs of state were being manipulated by the tsarina's 'holy' advisor, Grigori Rasputin.

As the tsarina grew increasingly alarmed about the health of her haemophiliac son, so she became increasingly dependent on Rasputin. He seemed blessed with semi-magical powers that brought temporary relief to the young tsarevich, heir to the Russian imperial throne.

Rasputin had many enemies. Licentious and dissolute, he was widely (if erroneously) believed to belong to the extremist Khlyst sect. Its practitioners held that boundless debauchery was the best way of suppressing lust and they engaged in orgiastic rituals while invoking the name of the Holy Spirit.

Rasputin's lifestyle was widely criticised in the press. The tsarina was also much maligned, albeit more obliquely. Born into the Hesse-Darmstadt dynasty, she was suspected of having pro-German sympathies. It was not long before she and Rasputin were being viewed as a monstrous duo that was secretly sabotaging the Russian war effort in the hope of a German victory.

As the food crisis worsened, people spoke euphemistically of 'Dark Forces' at work in the Petrograd palaces. 'Each and every calamity or inconvenience was in the public mind due to the "Dark Forces", wrote Hoare.

Rasputin was eventually named as the leader of these 'Forces' and his removal from the court was demanded by the Duma, the legislative assembly. A succession of parliamentary speakers denounced his dangerous hold over the imperial family.

Hoare summed up these speeches in a single sentence: 'Let the Emperor only banish this man and the country would be freed from the sinister influence that was striking down its natural leaders and endangering the success of its armies in the field.'

He was convinced that Russia's problems would be instantly solved if only Rasputin were to be removed from the capital. But no one, it seemed, had the power or authority to rid the country of the tsarina's favourite.

★

An icy wind was whipping off the Gulf of Finland.

The River Neva was frozen to a pewter crust and fine wisps of snow were rasping its surface. The city of Petrograd was shivering in a deep winter chill.

Shortly before midnight on 29 December 1916, a lone car swung into the courtyard of the Yusupov Palace. The car's yellow headlamps cast a brief glare on the palace's colonnaded gateway. The vehicle then made a circular sweep of the snow-covered courtyard and came to a halt by the side entrance of the building.

Three people were seated inside the car, all of them from very different walks of life. At the wheel was Doctor Lazovert, an army doctor on leave from his duties at the battlefront. He was dressed in disguise, masquerading as the chauffeur of the Yusupov family.

Behind him sat Prince Feliks Yusupov, an elite member of the imperial *Corps des Pages*. He was heir to the richest dynasty in the Russian Empire and celebrated as one of the most decadent aristocrats in Petrograd. He was also one of the most handsome. His almond eyes and delicate cheeks might have looked effeminate were it not for the compensation of a strong aquiline nose.

The third person in the car was Grigori Rasputin, the Russian tsarina's confidant. He usually wore the simple garb of an Orthodox monk but on this particular night he was dressed for a party.

'He wore a silk blouse embroidered in cornflowers with a raspberry-coloured cord as a belt,' recalled Yusupov in his account of the evening. 'His velvet breeches and highly polished boots seemed brand new.'

Rasputin's beard, usually a wiry tangle, had been neatly combed: Yusupov had never seen him look so immaculate. 'As he came near to me,' he wrote, 'I smelt a strong odour of cheap soap.'

Rasputin was visibly agitated. He confessed to Yusupov that he had been warned that hidden enemies were plotting to kill him. His close friendship with the tsarina and his perceived influence over the tsar had indeed earned him many foes.

Rasputin's reputation may have been tarnished in the eyes of the public at large, but it had done him no harm amongst the aristocratic ladies of the Imperial court. His attraction was so magnetic – hypnotic, even – that women lost all sense of propriety when they were in his presence. One English eyewitness looked on in horrified astonishment as a succession of princesses queued up to suck his fingers after he had finished eating his meal with his hands.

The death threats against Rasputin had not stopped him from accepting an invitation to the Yusupov Palace. He had been lured there by the promise of a debauched midnight rendezvous with Prince Feliks's wife, Irina.

Marital infidelity was not unusual amongst the more decadent sections of Petrograd's aristocratic elite. Yusupov knew that offering his wife to another man would raise few eyebrows amongst those in his own dissolute social circle. He was himself almost certainly bisexual and he was also ambiguous in his gender. He confessed in his memoirs to spending his evenings disguised as a lady and consorting with the gypsy musicians of the Neva Delta.

For Rasputin, the chance of a few snatched hours with Princess Irina was not to be turned down lightly. She was blessed with both a wistful beauty and an impeccable pedigree: she was the tsar's niece. As Yusupov knew all too well, his wife was most alluring bait.

Dr Lazovert stepped out of the car and opened the side door to the palace, standing aside to allow Yusupov and Rasputin to enter the marbled atrium. The sound of echoed laughter could be heard coming from Yusupov's study and the gramophone was playing a scratchy version of 'Yankee Doodle Went To Town'.

The merriment unnerved Rasputin and he asked what was going on. 'Just my wife entertaining a few friends,' said Yusupov. 'They'll be going soon.'

Neither of these statements was true. Yusupov's wife was more than 2,000 miles away at the family's country estate in the Crimea. And the guests had no intention of leaving. Grand Duke Dmitri, the tsar's first cousin, had arrived a few hours earlier, along with a flamboyant monarchist named Vladimir Purishkevich. There was also a Russian officer named Captain Sergei Soukhatin in the palace that night. Unbeknown to Rasputin, all of these men were conspirators. They were planning to murder him before the first light of dawn broke through the winter sky.

It was to be a night not just of murderous intent, but of spectacular deceit. Nothing was quite as it seemed in the Yusupov Palace on that December evening. Nothing would happen exactly as it was recorded. When the perpetrators came to set down their stories, it was as if the entire evening had been reflected in a distorting mirror that twisted and obscured reality.

The principal eyewitness account was written by Prince Feliks himself. It makes for a compelling, if disturbing, read. He recalled that Rasputin paused momentarily in the atrium before the two of them descended into the palace basement where there was a private dining room.

It was rarely used by the family, for it was a grim vaulted cellar with chiselled stone walls and granite flagstones. But it had one distinct advantage over all the other rooms in the building: it was deep underground and hidden from the eyes and ears of the world. Anything could happen down here and no one would ever know.

Yusupov had decked out the room with antiques to make it look as if it was in daily use. Rugs had been spread across the flagstones and on the red granite mantelpiece there stood golden bowls, antique majolica plates and figurine sculptures carved from ivory.

Rasputin's eye was drawn not to the rock-crystal crucifix, as Yusupov had expected, but to a small wooden cabinet studded with little mirrors. '[He] was particularly fascinated by the little ebony cabinet,' recalled the prince, 'and took a childish pleasure in opening and shutting the drawers, exploring it inside and out.'

Rasputin spoke once again of the supposed plot to kill him. 'There have been several attempts on my life,' he said, 'but the Lord has always frustrated these plots. Disaster will come to anyone who lifts a finger against me.'

Yusupov's account of what happened next is extremely detailed, but it omitted several important facts. He claimed that he had four accomplices, and that one of their number, Dr Lazovert (the fake chauffeur), had supplied the poison that was to be used to murder Rasputin, lacing the cakes and dainties that the target was known to enjoy.

'Doctor Lazovert put on rubber gloves and ground the cyanide of potassium crystals to powder,' wrote Yusupov. 'Then, lifting the top of each cake, he sprinkled the inside with a dose of poison which, according to him, was sufficient to kill several men instantly.' Concerned that Rasputin might decline the cakes, he dusted the wine glasses with cyanide as well.

Yusupov recalled how Rasputin chatted with him for more than an hour in the underground dining room. Then, finally, he ate two of the poisoned cakes in quick succession. They had no effect.

'I watched him horror-stricken,' wrote Yusupov. 'The poison should have acted immediately but, to my amazement, Rasputin went on talking quite calmly.'

The monk then knocked back several glasses of Madeira, but once again the cyanide proved ineffectual. 'His face did not change, only from time to time he put his hand to his throat as though he was having some difficulty in swallowing.'

Almost two and a half hours had by now passed since Yusupov and Rasputin arrived at the palace. As the clock struck three, the prince heard his fellow conspirators in the room above. A drowsy Rasputin raised his head and asked what was happening. 'Probably the guests leaving,' said Yusupov. 'I'll go and see what's up.'

Yusupov rushed upstairs and broke the news that the poison had not worked. He asked to borrow Grand Duke Dmitri's pocket Browning and then returned to the basement. He was preparing himself for the kill.

If Yusupov is to be believed, Rasputin was examining the crystal crucifix when he re-entered the room armed with the Browning. 'A shudder swept over me: my arm grew rigid, I aimed at his heart and pulled the trigger. Rasputin gave a wild scream and crumpled on the bearskin.'

The gunshot brought Yusupov's friends rushing into the room, all of them anxious to see the dead Rasputin. 'His features twitched in nervous spasms,' wrote Yusupov, 'his hands were clenched, his eyes closed.'

Within moments, his corpse stiffened and all movement ceased. Dr Lazovert examined the body and declared that the bullet had killed him instantly.

The conspirators lingered for a few more minutes before leaving the room in order to discuss the disposal of the corpse.

But Yusupov did not stay with them for long. He made his way back downstairs in order to check on his dead victim. And as he peered at Rasputin's waxen face, his blood ran cold. 'All of a sudden, I saw the left eye open . . . A few seconds later his right eyelid began to quiver, then opened.'

Yusupov was transfixed by the bodily resurrection that was taking place in front of him. 'I then saw both eyes – the green eyes of a viper – staring at me with an expression of diabolical hatred.'

And then, dramatically, all hell broke loose. 'Rasputin leaped to his feet, foaming at the mouth. A wild roar echoed through the vaulted rooms and his hands convulsively thrashed at the air.'

Yusupov would later recall being seized with terror; as well he might. 'He rushed at me, trying to get at my throat, and sank his fingers into my shoulder like steel claws. His eyes were bursting from their sockets, blood oozed from his lips. And all the time he called me by name, in a low, raucous voice.'

The demonic Rasputin then clasped his way up the stairs and made his escape through one of the doors that led into the courtyard. 'He was crawling on hands and knees, gasping and roaring like a wounded animal.'

Yusupov screamed at Vladimir Purishkevich, telling him to shoot. Seconds later, he heard two shots ring out, and then another two. When he finally made his way outside, he found Purishkevich standing over Rasputin's corpse. The tsarina's holy advisor was finally dead.

The body was wrapped in a shroud of heavy linen and bundled into the boot of a waiting car. The men then took it to Petrovski Island, where it was tipped over the edge of the high bridge. They watched it tumble into a section of the River Neva that had yet to freeze.

Yusupov's account details not only his own role in the murder, but also that of Grand Duke Dmitri, Vladimir Purishkevich and Dr Lazovert, as well as Captain Sergei Soukhatin. However, in the days that followed, there were rumours of a sixth conspirator in the palace. Someone else was said to have been present that night – a professional assassin who was working in the shadows.

What Yusupov was at pains to conceal was that Oswald Rayner, a key member of the Russian bureau's secret inner circle, had also been there that night. His critical role in the killing might have remained a secret for all time had it not been for a fatal mistake on the part of the murderers.

The mistake occurred in the aftermath of the murder, when the plotters were disposing of the body. Yusupov and his friends had assumed that the corpse would sink beneath the ice and be flushed out into the Gulf of Finland. There, trapped under the ice for the rest of the winter, it would be lost forever. What they had never expected was that Rasputin's corpse would be found and plucked from the icy waters.

★

Rasputin's corpse was spotted in the Neva River on the second full day after his death. A river policeman noticed a fur coat lodged beneath the ice and ordered the frozen crust to be broken. The body was carefully prised from its icy sepulchre and taken to the mortuary room of Chesmenskii Hospice. Here, an autopsy was undertaken by Professor Dmitrii Kosorotov.

The professor noted that the corpse was in a terrible state of mutilation: 'his left side has a weeping wound, due to some sort of slicing object or a sword. His right eye has come out of its cavity and falls down onto his face ... His right ear is hanging down and torn. His neck has a wound from some sort of rope tie. The victim's face and body carry traces of blows given by a supple but hard object.' These injuries suggest that Rasputin had been garrotted and repeatedly beaten with a heavy cosh.

Even more horrifying was the damage to his genitals. At some point during the brutal torture, his legs had been wrenched apart and his testicles had been 'crushed by the action of a similar object.' In fact, they had been flattened and completely destroyed.

Other details gleaned by Professor Kosorotov suggest that Yusupov's melodramatic account of the murder was nothing more than fantasy. Yet it was fantasy with a purpose. It was imperative for Yusupov to depict Rasputin as a demonic, superhuman figure whose malign hold over the tsarina was proving disastrous for Russia. The only way he could escape punishment for the murder was to present himself as the saviour of Russia: the man who had rid the country of an evil force.

The story of the poisoned cakes was almost certainly an invention: the postmortem included an examination of the contents of Rasputin's stomach: 'The examination,' wrote the professor, 'reveals no trace of poison.'

Professor Kosorotov also examined the three bullet wounds in Rasputin's body. 'The first has penetrated the left side of the chest and has gone through the stomach and liver,' he wrote. 'The second has entered into the right side of the back and gone through the kidney.' Both of these would have inflicted terrible wounds. But the third bullet was the fatal shot. '[It] hit the victim on the forehead and penetrated into his brain.'

It was most unfortunate that Professor Kosorotov's postmortem was brought to an abrupt halt on the orders of the tsarina. But the professor did have time to photograph the corpse and to inspect the bullet entry wounds. He noted that they 'came from different calibre revolvers.'

On the night of the murder, Yusupov was in possession of Grand Duke Dmitrii's Browning, while Purishkevich had a Sauvage. Either of these weapons could have caused the wounds to Rasputin's liver and kidney. But the fatal gunshot wound to Rasputin's head was not caused by an automatic weapon: it could only have come from a revolver. Forensic scientists and ballistic experts agree that the grazing around the wound was consistent with that which is left by a lead, non-jacketed bullet fired at point-blank range.

They also agree that the gun was almost certainly a British-made .455 Webley revolver. This was the favourite gun of Oswald Rayner, a close friend of Yusupov since the days when they had both studied at Oxford University.

At first glance, Rayner was unlikely material for espionage and subversion. The son of a Birmingham draper, he grew up with neither money nor prospects. But he found employment as an English teacher in Finland (then an autonomous grand duchy of the Russian Empire) and taught himself Russian.

He then returned to England to read Modern Languages at Oxford University. It was a move that would transform his life.

Rayner's fluency in Russian, French and German did not escape official notice when he sought to join the army at the outbreak of war. Such linguistic ability was of great use in wartime. Rayner was sent to Petrograd in November 1915, with the task of co-ordinating the censorship of telegrams. It was not long before he found himself playing a far more dangerous game.

Yusupov is circumspect when he writes in his memoirs about his old friend from Oxford. He mentions bumping into him on the day after the murder of Rasputin but presents their meeting as a chance encounter.

'As I went down to dinner,' he wrote, 'I met my friend Oswald Rayner, a British officer who I had known at Oxford. He knew of our conspiracy and had come in search of news.'

Yusupov may well have met Rayner on the evening that followed the murder and Rayner was certainly with Yusupov when he fled Petrograd by train. But Rayner had not needed to 'come in search of news'.

Rayner would later admit to his family that he was present in the Yusupov Palace on that night in December, information that would eventually find its way into his obituary. And Yusupov himself confessed that his Oxford friend knew of the murder in advance, although he stopped short of saying that Rayner was in the palace at the time.

Surviving letters from Rayner's fellow agents also reveal his involvement. 'A few awkward questions have already been asked about wider involvement,' wrote one. 'Rayner is attending to loose ends and will no doubt brief you on your return.'

It was the tsar himself who made enquiries as to whether or not Rayner had been involved in the killing. He had picked up rumours that were circulating around the palaces of Petrograd – rumours of British involvement in the plot. Anxious to know more, he went so far as to summon the ambassador, Sir George Buchanan, and ask him whether or not 'Yusupov's Oxford University friend' had a hand in the murder of Rasputin.

The ambassador was wholly ignorant of the affair and discreetly asked Samuel Hoare for information. Hoare robustly denied that any of his men had been involved. An 'outrageous charge', he told the ambassador, and 'incredible to the point of childishness.' Buchanan did not probe any further. He said he would 'solemnly contradict it to the Emperor at his next audience.'

Whether or not Hoare knew the truth of what took place remains unclear. He was certainly aware of a plot to 'liquidate' Rasputin for he had been told about it by Vladimir Purishkevich, one of the conspirators. He claims not to have believed it. 'I thought his words were symptomatic of what everyone was thinking and saying, rather than the expression of a definitely thought out plan.'

Although Hoare may have been ignorant of his agent's involvement in the murder, he was remarkably quick to learn of Rasputin's death. He sent the news to London several hours before it was publicly known in Petrograd.

'In the early morning of Saturday, December 30th,' begins his report, 'there was enacted in Petrograd one of those crimes that by their magnitude blur the well-defined rules of ethics and by their results change the history of a generation.'

The report was sent directly to London, where it landed on the desk of 'the Chief', or 'C', as he was known to his agents. He was the man ultimately in charge of the Russian bureau. He also ran the London headquarters of an organisation that was to operate under a number of names, but would eventually become known as the Secret Intelligence Service (MI6).

Nameless, faceless and working from a secret location in Whitehall, C was to be in charge of all of the boldest under-cover operations in Russia for the next six years.

CHAPTER TWO

THE CHIEF

The Chief sat in his office, his back to a glazed dormer window. A broad shaft of sunlight spilled through the glass behind him, lighting the secret inks that stood on his desk in slim glass phials.

The positioning of his chair by the window was no accident: it meant that visitors were momentarily dazzled by the light. For the first few seconds they saw only a silhouette.

The identity of the head of the Secret Intelligence Service was one of the most strictly guarded secrets in Whitehall. Even his trustworthy agents had no clue as to who he was. They knew him by his initial, C, and only in exceptional circumstances did they get to meet him.

'A pale, clean-shaven man, the most striking features of whose face were a Punch-like chin, a small and beautifully fine bow of a mouth and a pair of very bright eyes.' So wrote Compton Mackenzie, author of *Whisky Galore*, who worked for C during the First World War.

C's chin was indeed Punch-like (one visitor described it as 'like the cut-water of a battleship') and his eyes were piercing.

Few interviewees would ever forget them, not least because his penetrating stare was accentuated by a gold-rimmed monocle.

The monocle was used to theatrical effect; C would let it drop from his eye as a sign of disapproval. But his gruff exterior was offset by an underlying warmth of spirit. With favoured colleagues, that stern countenance would slowly melt into a grin and those sharp eyes sparkle in amusement.

The Chief rarely looked up from his paperwork when visitors entered his office. 'He remained bent over the table, perusing through a pair of dark, horn-rimmed spectacles some documents,' wrote Mackenzie of his nerve-wracking first meeting. Finally, C glanced up and inspected his visitor. '[He] took off his glasses, leant back in his chair and stared hard at me for a long minute without speaking. "Well?" he said finally.'

Mackenzie introduced himself and reminded C that he was just returned from a long stint abroad.

' "And what have you to say for yourself?" he asked, putting in an eyeglass and staring at me harder than ever.'

The ice was soon broken and the ensuing meeting went well: C even suggested that they dine together at the Savoy. 'I intended to make myself extremely unpleasant to you,' he later admitted, 'but I said that when I saw you I should probably find a man after my own heart and fall on your neck.'

C often whisked newly appointed agents to lunch at one of his London clubs. He would drive them there at breakneck speed in his magnificent Rolls-Royce, as if he wished to initiate them into a new and more reckless world.

★

Those in C's inner circle would eventually get to know his real name: it was Mansfield George Smith Cumming (the Cumming was adopted from his wife). He was a naval commander by profession, but suffered from such acute seasickness that he was retired from active service and posted to Southampton where he worked on the harbour's boom defences.

Cumming was fifty and in semi-retirement when he received an unexpected letter from the Admiralty. 'Boom defence must be getting a bit stale . . .' it read. 'I have something good I can offer you and if you would like to come and see me on Thursday about noon, I will tell you what it is.'

The letter was signed by Rear Admiral Alexander Bethell, director of Naval Intelligence, and dated 10 August 1909. It was to mark the beginning of an illustrious new career for Mansfield Cumming.

The offer was a startling one. The government had decided to establish a wholly new organisation called the Secret Service Bureau, with two separate but connected divisions. One was to deal with domestic intelligence, the other exclusively with foreign.

Cumming was to head the latter division, charged with gathering military, political and technical intelligence from overseas. His task was to recruit agents, train them and then send them into foreign countries in order to report on the threat they posed to Britain.

The establishment of the Secret Service Bureau was not the first government foray into foreign espionage. The navy had set up an intelligence department in the 1880s and the War Office also had an Intelligence Branch. These were preoccupied with military espionage. Now, the increasingly tense international situation called for the creation of a new, more professional organisation, with a far wider reach.

Cumming accepted the job offer with alacrity, reasoning that it would be a wonderful opportunity to do good work 'before I am finally shelved.'

His organisation would eventually expand until it operated across the globe, but it had very modest beginnings. Cumming's first day at work, on 7 October 1909, did not begin well. 'Went to the office,' he wrote in his diary, 'and remained all day but saw no one, nor was there anything to do.'

He was denied access to War Office files, an essential starting point for his new bureau, and had virtually no equipment.

A week later, he was still complaining of having nothing to do. 'Office all day,' he wrote. 'No one appeared.'

In a letter to Rear Admiral Bethell, who had offered him the job, he vented his frustration. 'Surely we cannot be expected to sit in the office month by month doing absolutely nothing?' He soon realised that the success of his new bureau would be entirely dependent upon his own initiative.

Cumming's first office was established in London's Victoria Street, opposite the Army and Navy Stores, where it was to operate under the guise of a detective agency. The location was not ideal, largely because C kept bumping into friends who wanted to know what he was doing there.

To preserve his anonymity, he rented a private flat in Ashley Mansions on Vauxhall Bridge Road and moved most of his operations to this unassuming new headquarters. An office, he would say, arouses interest and curiosity, 'but a private dwelling calls for no comment.'

He would later move again, to the eaves of an Edwardian mansion at Number Two, Whitehall Court. This was a labyrinthine collection of offices close to the centre of government. Potential agents were led up six flights of stairs before entering a warren of corridors, passageways and mezzanines.

Nothing was quite as it appeared. There were mirrors and blind corners and doors that seemed to lead to nowhere. Many recruits felt as if they were wandering through an optical illusion. One of them noted that by the time he reached C's door, he had the distinct impression that he was back in the same place as when he had first arrived on the sixth floor.

Cumming referred to his Whitehall Court staff as his 'top mates' while the spies themselves were 'rascals' and 'scally-wags'. He had no qualms about hiring men of dubious repute, so long as they were up to the job. One potential spy recalled the Chief swivelling around in his chair and saying: 'I know all about your past history. You are just the man we want.'

Yet Cumming's attitude was the exception to the norm. Many in the government and army viewed espionage as both immoral and disreputable. Britain's pre-war military attaché in Berlin had baulked at the idea of sending intelligence back to London. 'You will not have forgotten when we talked this matter over some months ago, that I mentioned how distasteful this sort of work was to me.'

Cumming viewed things rather differently. 'After the War is over, we'll do some amusing secret service work together,' he told Compton Mackenzie. 'It's capital sport.'

The author-turned-spy, Valentine Williams, described Cumming as 'cunning as an old dog fox, as *rusé* and as full of guile as a veteran sergeant major.' He would sit behind his vast desk and await the delivery of some secret report from the hands of his secretary.

'Were it favourable, he would chuckle, "Ha!" while a grimly roguish smile, boding no good to someone, would slowly spread over the broad face.'

★

Mansfield Cumming was soon engaged in work of vital importance to national security. The naval arms race with Germany and the First World War dominated the early years of his tenure. He despatched agents to France, Belgium and Germany, from where they sent back information on troop movements and naval manoeuvres.

He spent long hours at the office, working through weekends and public holidays. He only occasionally saw his wife, May, who lived for much of the time at their country house at Bursledon in Hampshire. A prim and rather demure Scottish lady, May had grown used to her husband's long absences.

During the early years of his tenure as the Chief, Cumming undertook espionage missions in person, disguising himself with toupee, fake moustache and an outfit that even he described as 'rather peculiar'. In preparation for one important assignment, he hired clothes from William Berry Clarkson's theatrical costume shop in Soho. The disguise, he declared, was 'perfect . . . its existence not being noticeable even in a good light.'

He delighted in showing visitors a photograph of himself pretending to be a heavily built German. '[He] was entranced when I failed to recognise the party in question,' wrote Valentine Williams. 'It was himself, disguised for the purposes of a certain delicate mission he once undertook on the Continent before the war.'

One of these foreign missions came very close to killing him. It also revealed a dogged, obsessive determination that was to become the hallmark of his working life.

In the summer of 1914, he had headed to France in the company of his only son, Alistair. They were driving at high speed through woodland in Northern France when Alistair lost control of the wheel. The car spun into a roadside tree and flipped upside down. Alistair was flung from the vehicle and landed on his head. Cumming was trapped by his leg in a tangle of smouldering metal.

'The boy was fatally injured,' wrote Compton Mackenzie in his account of the incident, 'and his father, hearing him moan something about the cold, tried to extricate himself from the wreck of the car in order to put a coat over him; but struggle as he might, he could not free his smashed leg.'

If he was to have any hope of reaching his son, there was only one thing to do. He reached for his pocket knife and hacked away at his mangled limb 'until he had cut it off, after which he had crawled over to the son and spread a coat over him.' Nine hours later, Cumming was found lying unconscious next to his son's dead body.

His recovery was as remarkable as his survival. He was back at his desk within a month, brushing aside any outer shows of mourning for his son. Cumming had the ramrod emotional backbone that so typified the gentlemen of his social class and era. Just a few months after his accident, one of his operatives visited him at his offices on the top floor of Whitehall Court.

Cumming, who had not yet received his artificial leg, was inching his substantial frame down six flights of stairs: 'two sticks, and backside, edging its way down one step at a time.' Little wonder that his friends described him as 'obstinate as a mule.'

The spy, Edward Knoblock, recalled that when Cumming did finally acquire a prosthetic limb made of wood, he used it to theatrical effect. He would terrify potential recruits by reaching for his sharp letter knife and raising it high in the air. He would then slam it through his trousers and into his wooden leg, 'concluding, if the applicant winced, "Well, I am afraid you won't do." '

★

Mansfield Cumming kept in daily touch with Samuel Hoare during his long months in Russia. Hoare was a diligent head of bureau and could usefully have remained at his post until the end of the war. But he was disenchanted with life as a spy and left Petrograd shortly after Rasputin's murder. He had been hoping for danger and excitement: all he got was bureaucracy and paperwork.

The rest of Hoare's team remained in the city, including Oswald Rayner. He was lucky to escape censure or worse for his role in the murder of Rasputin. Although the tsar had voiced his suspicions, Rayner was neither apprehended nor even questioned by the Russian police. He spent the day after the murder chatting with Yusupov in his private chambers, making a hasty exit when Grand Duke Nicholas arrived to interrogate the prince.

At the time, Yusupov vehemently denied playing any role in the murder and used his formidable network of connections to ensure that he was never put on trial. The tsar banished him to his country estates in South-West Russia, a lenient punishment for someone widely believed to have orchestrated the murder of the tsarina's favourite.

Whatever Yusupov and his conspirators may have hoped, Rasputin's death made little change to the defeatist atmosphere on the streets of Petrograd. Daily hardships were on the increase and people began openly protesting about the regime. On 10 March 1917, the Petrograd correspondent of the *Daily News*, Arthur Ransome, took a stroll around the city and sensed that events were starting to spin out of control.

'A rather precarious excitement,' he wrote, 'like a Bank Holiday with thunder in the air.'

The number of protestors on the streets had increased dramatically by the following morning. 'Crowds of all ages and conditions made their way to the Nevsky,' recalled Robert Wilton, correspondent for *The Times*. But the mood was still good-humoured and there was no inkling of the violence to come.

Accounts vary as to where and when the first shots were fired. Wilton was close to Moscow station at 3 p.m. when he heard the crack of gunfire. By the time he reached the scene, the crowd had been dispersed and the snow 'was plentifully sprinkled with blood.'

Cumming's team in Petrograd was by now seriously alarmed. There had been political demonstrations in the past and even open condemnation of the tsar. But the outbreak of large-scale violent protest was a worrying new development.

Unrest rapidly spread to other parts of the city. Later that afternoon, police armed with machine-guns began firing on the crowd in Znamenskaya Square. Some fifty protestors were shot dead.

In a telegram to the *Daily News*, Arthur Ransome reported that the bloodshed was of a different order to anything that had come before. The city, he noted, was 'like a pot of porridge coming slowly to the boil, with bubbles, now here and now there, rising to burst on the surface.' He felt that it was the beginning of a revolution.

On the following day, a Monday, angry demonstrators broke into the notorious Krestovsky Prison and released all the political prisoners. They then ran amok in the streets, smashing shop windows and attacking gendarmes.

'Their faces had taken on a fanatical look,' wrote one English eyewitness. 'They were out for business and they carried crowbars, hammers and lengths of weighted, tarred and knotted rope.' Among the rioters were many soldiers who had abandoned their regiments in order to protest against the tsar.

To many onlookers, there was a palpable sense that the old order was about to be engulfed in catastrophe. Russia was sliding towards an unknown future in which society was to be polarised. The aristocracy and intellectual elite for which pre-war St Petersburg had been so famous now stood jeopardised by the forces of revolution.

An Englishman, William Gibson, was witness to a direct confrontation between these two incompatible worlds. While of no consequence in itself, it provided him with a graphic illustration of the troubles to come.

He had been watching the street mob systematically ransack the mansions and palaces of the elite and he knew they would soon reach the marbled residence of his mother-in-law, the formidable Madame Schwartz-Ebehard. She was a pillar of the old order; 'a massive woman of fifty-five, with tight lips and eyes which could turn to steel . . . a veritable tower of strength, both physically and morally.'

Gibson made his way to her house and warned her to flee before it was sacked by the mob. But Madame Schwartz-Ebehard remonstrated in the strongest terms. She was determined to defend her mansion against the illiterate thugs outside. Gibson was shamed into remaining as well.

When the mob finally smashed their way in, Madame Schwartz-Ebehard was ready for them. 'Seizing the gong-stick from the brass Chinese gong which filled a corner, she had boomed out a peremptory tattoo.'

The men were stopped in their tracks. 'Madame had drawn herself to her full height and had stared the rabble up and down.' She pointed at her highly polished marble floor and then glared at the thugs.

'Your boots are filthy,' she declaimed coldly. 'You should clean them before you come in here. You are spoiling the floor. Besides, you were not invited.'

She haughtily informed them they were *moujiki-bordiaji* – 'scum of the gutters' – and ordered them out. She had no intention of being intimidated by revolutionaries.

The men lifted their rifles and pointed them at her, but Madame Schwartz-Eberhard swept them aside. 'Calmly and deliberately she had smacked the face of one desperado after another.' Then, after flinging the ringleader backwards, she kicked them out and locked the door.

Madame Schartz-Eberhard was fortunate to escape with her life. In her glacial haughtiness, she personified the social grandeur of the old regime. In mansions such as hers, the old ways and manners had been kept alive. Now, those ways were in danger of being trampled underfoot.

Within hours of her foolhardy stand, the revolution was fully under way. The Preobrazhensky and Volynsky Regiments mutinied and soldiers from the Pavlovsky Regiment began firing on the police.

Colonel Alfred Knox, military attaché at the British Embassy, realised the situation was now desperate. A meeting with three senior Russian generals confirmed his conviction that the old regime was doomed. The only hope of quashing the revolution was for troops to be brought in from the countryside. But when these soldiers arrived, they greeted the crowds with warm affection and 'in extreme brotherly love handed over their rifles.'

As the battle for the streets intensified, a political battle was also under way. The Duma or legislative assembly had been officially dissolved by the tsar. Now, it reconvened itself and established a Temporary Committee with one member for each party. When journalist Harold Williams entered the parliamentary chamber, he found it awash with soldiers listening to fiery orators 'who had suddenly appeared from obscurity.'

Williams' wife was meanwhile attending a rival gathering that seemed, to her eyes, to have sprung from nowhere. The Council of Workmen's Deputies, better known as the Petrograd Soviet, was a body of revolutionary activists that was far more in tune with the mood on the streets.

It began issuing its own decrees, including the controversial Order No. 1, which instructed army units to obey the Duma only if its orders did not contradict those of the Petrograd Soviet. A power struggle was already under way.

Colonel Knox was by now seriously alarmed: the behaviour of the Petrograd Soviet was the clearest possible signal that the revolution had entered a new and more unpredictable phase. 'Leaflets were distributed advocating the murder of officers,' wrote Knox. 'The outlook was very black on the evening of the 15th.'

The guardians of the old order were shortly to receive the greatest shock of all. On the same day that Colonel Knox wrote his report, Tsar Nicholas II announced his abdication. 'We have thought it well to renounce the Throne of the Russian Empire and lay down the supreme power,' he told the nation.

A new Provisional Government was formed on the following day, with Prince Lvov as prime minister and the charismatic Alexander Kerensky as Minister of Justice.

'Only those who know how things were but a week ago can

understand the enthusiasm of us who have seen the miracle take place before our eyes . . .' wrote Arthur Ransome. 'It is as if honesty had returned.'

The Provisional Government moved swiftly to agree an eight-point programme with the Petrograd Soviet. Point One in this programme offered the 'immediate amnesty for all political prisoners, including terrorists.'

In distant London, Mansfield Cumming had long ago expressed his belief that 'Russia will be the most important country for us in the future.' He was about to be proved right. The amnesty for Russian political prisoners was to have consequences that were both dramatic and unforeseen.

CHAPTER THREE

THE PERFECT SPY

TOP SECRET

ansfield Cumming's network of agents inside Russia expanded rapidly during the long years of war. As well as his team working at the Petrograd bureau, he also had men based at many of Russia's key frontier posts.

These agents were ostensibly working as military control officers, helping their Russian allies to man the country's vast borders. But they were also secretly collecting information on who was travelling in and out of the country.

One of these officers, Harry Gruner, was serving at the snowbound outpost of Torneå, a frontier village nestled on the border between Sweden and Finland. Few travellers would ever have come to Torneå were it not for the fact that it was also a railway junction with an onwards connection to Helsingfors (Helsinki) and Petrograd. Ever since the revolutionary upheaval of four weeks earlier, a stream of political exiles had been using this route to cross back into Russia.

Shortly before nightfall on Saturday, 15 April 1917, Gruner heard the muffled hiss of horse-drawn sleighs approaching the little border cabin. It was an unusually chill evening and the air was spiked with frost. Spring had yet to arrive in this frozen slice of the country and the wooden cabin was covered in a shroud of snow.

Gruner stepped into the darkness to greet the travellers and immediately saw that they were Russian. He also noticed that they were jumpy when asked to show their papers. There was good reason for their nervousness: among their number was the notorious revolutionary firebrand, Vladimir Ilyich Lenin.

Lenin had been living in exile for almost a decade, preaching the gospel of class warfare and radical social upheaval. He had also been demanding Russia's immediate withdrawal from the war. There were many inside the country who viewed him as a dangerous troublemaker.

Lenin appeared 'outwardly calm' as Gruner interrogated him. According to one of those in his party, the fellow revolutionary, Grigori Zinoviev, he was 'most of all interested in what was happening in far off Petersburg.' Yet he was also concerned that this young border guard would try to prevent him from crossing the frontier.

Gruner hoped to do just that: Lenin was a prize catch, one that would earn him plaudits in London. But he found himself in a dilemma. Russia's new government had sanctioned the return of all political refugees, regardless of the threat they might pose. Lenin was clearly more dangerous than most, but Gruner had no obvious justification in preventing him and his party from crossing the frontier.

Reluctant to let his quarry slip so easily back onto Russian soil, he sent a telegram to Petrograd informing the government of Lenin's arrival at Torneå. He also asked 'whether a mistake had not been made in permitting him to return.'

While he awaited the reply, he submitted all the travellers to a humiliating strip search.

'We were undressed to the skin,' recalled Zinoviev's wife indignantly. 'My son and I were forced to take off our stockings . . . All the documents and even the children's books and toys my son had brought with them were taken.'

Lenin, too, was searched and once again interrogated. Gruner asked him why he had left Russia and why he was going back. Lenin said nothing incriminating, much to Gruner's disappointment. He knew he could not detain the group of Russians indefinitely. He made a meticulous search of Lenin's luggage in the hope of finding seditious literature. There was none.

One of the Russians noticed Lenin chuckling with delight as the search finally came to an end. 'He broke into happy laughter and, embracing me, he said: "Our trials, Comrade Mikha, have ended." ' He was confident that the Provisional Government would oblige Gruner to allow them to cross the frontier.

This was exactly what happened. Gruner received a telegram reminding him that 'the new Russian Government rested on a democratic foundation. Lenin's group should be allowed to enter.'

Gruner had no option but to allow them to proceed. He stamped their papers and let them continue on their journey. It was a decision he would later regret. One of his colleagues recalled that he was teased mercilessly for having set Lenin free.

'You're a bright lad,' they would say to him. 'Locking the stable door when the horse was out, or, rather, in.'

Another of them joshed that if Gruner had been Japanese, 'he would have committed hara-kiri.'

He might have wished he had done so. Within a few months he would be arrested on Lenin's orders and held under sentence of execution.

★

Four thousand miles away in Halifax, Nova Scotia, a tip-off from British intelligence had led to the arrest of Leon Trotsky, another of Russia's most notorious revolutionary exiles.

Trotsky had been living in New York since the beginning of 1917, delivering fiery lectures on his hopes of destroying Russia's new Provisional Government. He even urged the workers of Manhattan to bring down their own political masters, overthrowing them by way of violent revolution. 'It's time you did away with such a government once and forever,' he told them.

Trotsky's activities had not gone unnoticed by Mansfield Cumming, who was receiving regular reports from his principal spymaster in New York, William Wiseman.

Wiseman, a maverick baronet, had been sent to New York in the previous year. He had established an espionage bureau based in the British Consulate at 44 Whitehall Street, Manhattan. Its principal task was to monitor Indian and Irish revolutionaries living in the city. But Wiseman also kept a close eye on Trotsky, sending agents to infiltrate his meetings and keep tabs on his revolutionary collaborators.

In the last week of March, Wiseman received a tip-off that Trotsky was planning to return to Russia with a group of fellow activists. They were carrying a large sum of money, more than $10,000, which was to be used to finance a new wave of revolutionary activity, one far more violent than the unrest that had swept the tsar from power.

The revolutionaries boarded the SS *Kristianiaford* in New York, unaware that Wiseman's agents were tracking them.

Trotsky assumed that the voyage would be trouble-free; he was to get an unpleasant surprise when the vessel made a brief refuelling stop in Halifax, Nova Scotia. The port was manned by British naval officials, for Canada was still a dominion of the British Empire, and these officials had been ordered to arrest Trotsky and his men.

'These are Russian socialists leaving for the purpose of starting revolution against the Russian government,' read the telegram sent to Halifax.

Trotsky lost all his dignity when informed that he was being detained. According to one observer, he 'crouched and whined and cried in abject terror' – perhaps because he feared that the British would kill him. But when he realised he was not going to be executed, 'his bluff returned and he protested violently.'

He was held under lock and key for the next four weeks and proved a most troublesome prisoner. He spent his waking hours preaching revolution to the German prisoners of war that had also been interned on Nova Scotia.

'[Trotsky] is a man holding extremely strong views and of most powerful personality,' wrote the British commandant, 'his personality being such that after only a few days stay here he was by far the most popular man in the whole camp.'

In distant Petrograd, the Provisional Government was growing increasingly alarmed by the number of dangerous political exiles returning to Russia. When it learned of Trotsky's internment, it asked the British to hold him indefinitely.

This proved a gift to revolutionary agitators in Petrograd, who were infuriated by Trotsky's detention. They hinted that British nationals in Russia would be targeted unless he was immediately released.

For a few short days in the spring of 1917, British intelligence achieved the singular coup of holding both Trotsky and Lenin, the principal architects of the future Bolshevik revolution.

But as it was with Lenin, so it was to prove with Trotsky. In the third week of April, he was released and allowed to continue on his journey. Within a few days, he was aboard a new ship, the *Helig Olaf*, and bound for Petrograd.

★

As revolutionary figures returned to Petrograd in ever-increasing numbers, Mansfield Cumming began to consider how best to arrange his Russian operations. He was looking to the future, aware that his agents might soon have to work undercover in a country that was no longer an ally.

He jotted a number of notes on what he considered to constitute the 'perfect spy': someone who could enter a country under a fake identity and live there clandestinely for many months. One man who fitted the archetypal profile was George Hill, a British officer of exceptional talent.

A member of the Royal Flying Corps, Hill had been sent to Russia to help in the training of pilots on the Eastern Front. But he was also working for British military intelligence with the codename Agent IK8. He proved so good at infiltrating secret meetings that he was soon poached and given employment by Mansfield Cumming.

Hill had lived in numerous different cities, including London, Hamburg, Riga, St Petersburg, Tehran and Krasnovodsk. A broad-beamed individual with a potato-shaped face, he had a military gait and public-school buffoonery that left no one in any doubt as to his nationality. Yet he showed a remarkable talent for blending into foreign cultures.

In part, this was due to his skills as a linguist. 'I had half a dozen languages at the tip of my tongue,' he wrote, '[and] had learned to sum up the characteristic qualities and faults of a dozen nationalities.'

Hill knew that fluency in the language was only the first step to perfecting an undercover existence. A spy could live incognito for a sustained period of time only if he learned to adopt 'the habits and ways of thoughts of the people among whom his field of operations lies'. He also needed 'a brain of the utmost ability, able to draw a deduction in a flash and make a momentous decision in an instant.'

According to Hector Bywater, an expert in professional espionage, the perfect spy could only make such decisions if he kept an icy detachment from the pressures of work.

'Steady nerves were, of course, a great asset, for the Secret Service man was liable at any moment to find himself in an awkward situation which demanded perfect coolness and presence of mind.'

A photographic memory was also vital, as future operations in Russia were to demonstrate. Agents would often find themselves with only a few minutes to study crucial documents, maps and military plans.

Above all, a talent for organising – what Hill called 'the office work of espionage' – was absolutely essential. 'Nine out of ten spies who are caught have faulty organisation or communication to blame for their arrest,' he wrote.

Arrest for Cumming's men in the months ahead would spell certain death. No one was so aware of the high stakes as Hill himself. He had witnessed the execution of two Bulgarian spies in the Balkan city of Monastir and left a graphic description of them being killed by firing squad.

'The wall behind, white a moment before, was scarred by bullet marks and bespattered with blood, just as if a paint brush had been dipped into a pot of red paint and flicked on the wall.'

The grotesque spectacle got the better of him. 'I hurried off to find a spot where I could be sick without disgracing myself.'

Mansfield Cumming had started training programmes for his spies in or around 1915. When Samuel Hoare had been recruited into the Secret Service, he had been enrolled on an intensive four-week espionage course. He was not at liberty to reveal any more than the barest outlines of what was taught.

'One day it would be espionage or contre-espionage', he wrote, 'another coding and ciphering, another, war trade and contraband, a fourth, postal and telegraphic censorship.'

Other agents recalled Cumming himself giving twice-weekly lectures on spy-craft, the details of which are sadly lost.

George Hill was also given a rudimentary training in espionage in the weeks before he left London. 'Experts from Scotland Yard lectured me on shadowing [people] and recognising the signs of being shadowed,' he wrote. 'I was taught the methods of using invisible inks. I learned a system of codes and was primed with all the dodges which are useful to spies.'

Codes, invisible inks and mechanical gadgets were stock in trade to Cumming. In the rare moments when he was not at his desk, he would invariably be found bent over a lathe in the workshop that he had installed at Whitehall Court. It was equipped with drills, chisels and other instruments, brought specially from his country house in Bursledon.

Long after the office staff had gone home for the night, Cumming could be found in his workshop knocking together one of the speciality homespun contraptions that he liked to devise for his agents in the field.

He had heavy hands and sausage fingers, yet he must have had a delicate touch for he was capable of building precision instruments, including a long-case clock made out of phosphor bronze and chromium steel. It stands in the headquarters of MI6 to this day.

'He had a passion for inventions of all sorts,' recalled one of his agents, Edward Knoblock, 'and being a rich man, he often bought the rights to them, such as strange telescopes, mysterious mechanisms with which to signal in the dark . . . rockets, bombs etc.'

Secret inks held a particular fascination for Cumming, with good reason. The ability to transmit messages in disappearing ink had proved extremely important during the war. It would be even more important for his agents working in revolutionary Russia.

Cumming hired the services of the distinguished physicist, Thomas Merton, who conducted ink experiments with many different chemical solutions. These included potassium permanganate, antipyrine and sodium nitrate. One reliable ink was made with a blend of sodium thiosulphate and ammonia solution, which could then be developed with gold chloride.

'Secret inks were our stock in trade and all were anxious to obtain some which came from a natural source of supply.' So wrote Frank Stagg, who had joined Cumming's headquarters at the outbreak of war. 'I shall never forget C's delight when the Chief Censor, Worthington, came one day with the announcement that one of his staff had found out that semen would not respond to iodine vapour.'

As Cumming chortled into his cravat, Stagg told him 'that he had had to remove the discoverer from his office immediately as his colleagues were making life intolerable by accusations of masturbation.'

Cumming expressed concern that his female spies might not have a ready access to semen. He 'asked Colney Hatch [a lunatic asylum] to send [a sample of] female equivalent for testing.' Whether or not they obtained any is alas not recorded.

Semen was certainly used by some of Cumming's spies, to the great displeasure of those on the receiving end. 'Our man in Copenhagen, Major Holme, evidently stocked it in a bottle,' wrote Stagg, 'for his letter stank to high heaven and we had to tell him that a fresh operation was necessary for each letter.'

Information obtained illicitly was to be transmitted in secret code as well as invisible ink. Cumming had a highly skilled team of cipher men in London who were constantly changing the codes in order to minimise the chance of them being decrypted. George Hill would later write about one of the codes he used while working in Russia.

'It had been invented by a genius at the Secret Service headquarters in London and of the many I have seen [it] was the easiest and safest for a secret service man to carry.'

He was not allowed to provide any details, except to say that it required only a pocket dictionary and the key to the cipher, 'which was on a tiny card and could easily be hidden.'

George Hill would carry many additional items during his time in Russia and they were to serve him well in times of danger. 'I had always found the value of including in my kit a certain amount of good plain chocolate, half a dozen pairs of ladies' silk stockings and two or three boxes of the more expensive kind of Parisian toilet soap,' he recalled. 'My experience was that, presented at the right psychological moment, they would unlock doors which neither wine nor gold would open.'

Hill hinted at an extensive range of gadgets available to Cumming's agents. 'Secret inks, tiny cameras the size of half a crown and not much thicker, photographs reduced so that their films can be concealed in a cigarette . . .'

But he warned his readers that such items were of no use 'unless one has the essentials – will, wit and determination to carry out the task which is set.'

★

Hill had little previous experience in intelligence work when he arrived in Petrograd in the aftermath of the first revolution that had swept the tsar from his throne. The principal menace at this point came not from Lenin's Bolsheviks but from the Germans, who had insinuated numerous enemy agents into Russia. These agents were working hard to undermine the new government and force Russia's withdrawal from the war.

Hill became acquainted with a lady known as Madame B who was running a network of Russian double agents, all of whom were working secretly for Germany. What none of them knew was that Madame B was herself an agent provocateur whose job was to expose their activities.

Hill attended one of Madame B's meetings in order to eavesdrop on their conversations. When he left at the end of the evening, he realised that he was being followed by two of the men from the gathering.

'Just as they were about to close with me I swung round and flourished my walking stick. As I expected, one of my assailants seized hold of it.'

He was in for an unpleasant surprise. 'It was a swordstick, which had been specially designed by Mssrs. Wilkinson, the sword-makers of Pall Mall, and the moment my attacker had the scabbard in his fist, I drew back the rapier-like blade with a jerk and with a forward lunge ran it through the gentleman's side.'

His would-be assailant let out a scream and then collapsed onto the pavement in a pool of blood. As his comrade ran off, Hill fumbled for his revolver. But by the time he was ready to fire, the man had disappeared.

Hill returned to the Bristol Hotel, where he was staying, and went straight to his room, 'examining the blade on the stairs, anxious to know what it looked like after its adventure. I had never run a man through before.'

He was surprised by the cleanness of the blade. 'It was not a gory sight. There was only a slight film of blood half-way up the blade and a dark stain at the tip'.

★

Lenin's Bolsheviks were one of the smallest of the numerous political groups in Petrograd but they quickly made their mark. On the morning after Lenin's arrival at Finlyandsky Station they broke into the vacant mansion belonging to the celebrated ballerina, Mathilde Kschessinskaia. There was no respect for the fact that it was private property.

When the British ambassador's daughter, Muriel Buchanan, opened her curtains and gazed across the street, she saw 'an enormous scarlet flag fluttering above the walls.' She was surprised that the revolutionaries had dared to occupy Madame Kschessinskaia's house, but was not unduly alarmed by their presence. 'Nobody took them seriously,' she wrote. 'They were just another lot of fanatics.'

Lenin's supporters were the most unruly element in the Petrograd Soviet, the revolutionary assembly established to represent the city's workers. On 3 May, Lenin demanded 'all power to the Soviets' – the numerous councils and assemblies that had sprung up across Russia – and argued that the Provisional Government had far too much authority. His demand fell on deaf ears: for the moment, the Provisional Government felt secure enough to ignore the Bolsheviks.

Lenin's supporters were to be dealt a harsher blow some two weeks later when the Provisional Government's brightest talent, Alexander Kerensky, was put in charge of the War Office and Admiralty.

Kerensky's appointment delighted the Entente governments. A gifted orator with a deep sense of purpose, he was a safe pair of hands. Russia was unlikely to implode into violence so long as he remained at the helm.

Kerensky was also vigorously in favour of continuing the fight against Germany. 'There is no Russian front,' he said in one highly publicised speech. 'There is only one united Allied front.'

Kerensky and Lenin were each regarded by their supporters as great orators. Yet to one detached observer, Kerensky stood head and shoulders above his political rival. The journalist Morgan Philips Price listened to both men debating a confidence motion in the Provisional Government. Lenin lambasted the ministers he detested, taunting them for running scared of the workers and peasants of Russia.

'One sat spellbound at his command of the language and the passion of his denunciation,' wrote Price. 'But when it was all over, one felt inclined to scratch one's head and ask what it was all about.' Like so many people, Price underestimated Lenin's magnetism until it was too late.

Next to his feet was Kerensky, who was determined to humiliate Lenin in public. 'There was a hush in the hall as there rose up a short, thickset man with a square face and close-cropped hair . . . his face was pale with nervous tension and his eyes blazed like fiery beads.'

Kerensky began his speech in quiet, measured tones, clinically dissecting Lenin's argument. He then launched a scornful attack on Lenin's dream of a second revolution. 'You say that you want to strengthen our new-won freedom,' he said as he jabbed his finger at Lenin, 'and yet you propose to lead us the way of France in 1792. Instead of appealing for reconstruction, you clamour for further destruction. Out of the fiery chaos that you wish to make will arise, like a Phoenix, a dictator.'

Price turned his head towards Lenin as he listened to the speech. '[He] was calmly stroking his chin, apparently wondering whether the words of Kerensky would come true, and on whose shoulders the cloak of dictatorship, if it came, would rest.'

The motion of confidence in the Provisional Government won the day: Lenin's revolutionary Bolsheviks were roundly defeated. Yet they were not downhearted. Every setback seemed to reinvigorate them and their confidence grew to such an extent that Cumming's agents at the Russian bureau became seriously alarmed.

It was imperative to keep Kerensky in power, since he was held to be the only political leader who could impose his will on the army. Yet there was a growing fear that his grasp on power was weakening and that his eventual downfall was inevitable. This would spell disaster not just for Britain, but also for the United States, which had become a fellow combatant less than a month after the February revolution.

To avert such a catastrophe, ministers in Whitehall asked Mansfield Cumming to set up a joint Anglo-American intelligence mission to Russia. Its aim was to supply Kerensky's pro-war government with money, extra resources and more vigorous anti-German propaganda.

Cumming immediately contacted his man in New York, William Wiseman, who had forged close links with his opposite number in American intelligence. Wiseman knew that American officials also viewed Russia's continued role in the war as imperative. It did not take much to persuade them to back the joint mission.

The British government supplied Wiseman with $75,000. The money, destined for Russia's Provisional Government, was wired into his J.P. Morgan and Co. account in New York. A similar sum was received from the Americans. All Wiseman now needed was an agent who could be relied upon to deliver the money to Kerensky without raising any suspicions.

Secrecy was imperative: both the Germans and the Bolsheviks could make a lot of political capital out of such blatant intervention in Russian politics.

Wiseman thought long and hard before selecting his man. Agent Somerville, better known as the writer, Somerset Maugham, had already proved his worth in Switzerland. He had been sent there two years previously to act as a link man for Cumming's agents working inside enemy Germany.

'If you do well you'll get no thanks,' he had been told on his departure from England, 'and if you get into trouble you'll get no help.'

Maugham was on holiday on Long Island when he received Wiseman's unexpected summons at the beginning of July 1917. Intrigued, he made his way to Wiseman's Lower Manhattan offices.

Wiseman briefed Maugham on the necessity of keeping Kerensky at the helm of the Russian government. He also spoke of the importance of supporting Russia's fight against Germany on the Eastern Front.

'The long and the short of it,' wrote Maugham, 'was that I should go to Russia and keep the Russians in the war.'

Maugham was daunted by the prospect of undertaking such a mission, especially when he was told that the British and American governments were determined that it should succeed.

'I was staggered by the proposition,' he later admitted. 'I told Wiseman that I did not think I was competent to do the sort of thing that was expected of me.'

He asked for forty-eight hours to think it over. He was in the early stages of tuberculosis, had a high fever and was coughing up blood. But he was excited by the prospect of working again for British intelligence and decided to accept Wiseman's proposal.

The weeks that followed were taken up with meticulous planning. Maugham was introduced to key contacts who would be able to facilitate his journey across a country that was rapidly descending into chaos. Among those charged with helping him was Emanuel Voska, an American secret agent who was to travel with him to Petrograd.

Agent Voska had also been briefed about what needed to be done: his instructions were similar to those given to Maugham. 'Keep Russia in the war,' he was told. 'We will stand you any expense. So far as we are concerned, you may have the greatest freedom of action.'

By the end of July, Maugham was fully prepared. He had one last question for Wiseman before he left New York: he asked if he would be paid for his mission. He said that his operations in Switzerland had been undertaken as a gentleman amateur, 'and found afterwards that I was the only man working in the organisation for nothing and that I was regarded not as patriotic or generous but merely damned foolish.' Wiseman took the hint and offered both a salary and expenses.

Maugham left for San Francisco carrying $21,000 of the money for Kerensky in cash. It was concealed in a belt hidden under his shirt. He was accompanied by Emanuel Voska, three American diplomats and three Czech emissaries. Once inside Russia, Maugham was to travel alone and incognito.

'The Czechs and I should appear to be entire strangers to one another,' he wrote, 'and communicate, if necessary, only with precaution.' If anyone asked his occupation, he was to say that he was a journalist being sent to Petrograd to cover the unfolding revolution.

Maugham would later write several accounts of his mission to Russia, including an intimate portrait of a nameless secret agent working for the Americans. It is almost certainly the wily Emanuel Voska, who seemed to have many of the facets required by the perfect spy.

'Ruthless, wise, prudent and absolutely indifferent to the means by which he reached his ends,' wrote Maugham. '[There was] something terrifying about him ... he was capable of killing a fellow creature without a trace of ill-feeling.'

Maugham and his fellow travellers travelled by boat to Vladivostok before boarding the Trans-Siberian Express for Petrograd. By the time they were approaching the Russian capital, in August 1917, Kerensky's position had been seriously weakened.

In mid June, his Provisional Government had launched a massive offensive against the German Army. After initial success, the Russians suffered a catastrophic counter-attack that resulted in the slaughter of half a million men. In the wake of defeat came more political unrest. Ministers wrangled among themselves, leading to the eventual collapse of the government. In the political vacuum that followed, Lenin's revolutionaries took their protest to the streets.

'On the Nevsky Prospekt, about ten o'clock, the shooting began,' wrote the journalist, Harold Williams. 'Who began it is not clear, but men on motor-lorries with machine-guns began firing indiscriminately into the crowd.'

The situation was precarious but Kerensky eventually managed to restore order. A heavily disguised Lenin slipped away to Finland while Trotsky was temporarily arrested, along with a number of other key activists. Few doubted that the political unrest would continue.

'The feeling of Petrograd,' wrote the journalist Arthur Ransome, 'is rather like that of a person half awake and not quite sure whether he has been visited by a burglar or a bad dream.'

This was the city in which Somerset Maugham arrived in August 1917. He checked into the Hotel Europe – 'a stamping ground for Allied agents' – and then went for a stroll along the Nevsky Prospekt. He was disappointed in Russia's imperial capital, finding it 'dingy and sordid and dilapidated'.

On the morning after his arrival, he presented himself at the British Embassy for a meeting with the ambassador, Sir George Buchanan. He was hoping that Buchanan would provide him with assistance in making contact with Kerensky. He was quickly disabused of this notion.

Buchanan was studiously late for the meeting and when he did at long last arrive, he treated Maugham with glacial disdain, speaking to him in the manner of an Edwardian headmaster admonishing a wayward pupil.

Buchanan was always frosty with people who worked for Mansfield Cumming. He was outraged that British agents were allowed to operate on what he considered to be his patch. The fact that they conducted their affairs without any reference to him only served to further offend him.

A few months earlier he had telegraphed London and demanded that all of Cumming's agents in Russia be placed under his personal control. This was met with a swift (but private) snub from the War Office. An internal memo said that 'Secret Service was not a matter with which amateurs could be trusted.' It added that Cumming was financing the Russian bureau and should therefore have full control over its operations.

Buchanan was indignant to learn that Agent Somerville was 'on a confidential mission' of which he was to remain wholly ignorant. Maugham did not help matters by his extreme nervousness. 'I was conscious that I made a very poor impression on him,' he wrote. 'I was nervous and stammered badly.'

Buchanan grew even more offended when he learned that he was expected to place the embassy's cable-transmitters at Maugham's disposal, even though he was not to be privy to the contents of the cables being sent to London. They were to be written in a secret code known only to Maugham.

'He looked upon it as a grave affront,' wrote Maugham. 'I realised that I could not count on much help in that quarter.'

Maugham had other contacts in Petrograd who proved rather more than willing to assist. Among them was Alexandra Lebedev, née Kropotkin, with whom he had once had a brief love affair. She was a friend of Kerensky and promised to provide Maugham with an introduction, as well as setting up meetings with other senior ministers in the government.

Maugham was taken aback when he finally met the Russian leader. 'What struck me most was his colour,' he wrote. 'One often reads of people being green in the face with fright and I had always thought it an invention of novelists. But that is exactly what he was.'

The man upon whom the Western democracies were pinning their hopes appeared indecisive, nervous and sick. 'He seemed fearfully on edge. Sitting down and talking incessantly, he took hold of a cigarette box and played with it restlessly, locking and unlocking it, opening and shutting it, turning it round and round.'

Maugham had heard a great deal about the Russian leader's strengths and qualities. Now, sitting face to face with him, he found himself talking to a shadow. 'His personality had no magnetism. He gave no feeling of intellectual or of physical vigour.'

Maugham's task was not to judge Kerensky but to do business with him. To this end, he staged a series of meetings with him and his ministers at Mjedved restaurant, the finest in town. 'I provided my guests with quantities of caviare at the expense of the two governments who had sent me to Petrograd, and they devoured it with relish.'

They discussed how the British, Americans and French could best support the Russian Government, with Maugham's friend Alexandra Lebedev acting as interpreter.

Maugham also had several meetings with Boris Savinkov, the feisty Minister of War. Here, at last, was someone with whom he could do business. He described Savinkov as 'the most remarkable man I met.'

His fascination was due, in part, to the fact that Savinkov had been personally responsible for the assassination of a number of senior imperial officials in the years before the war. Maugham found it hard to picture such a genial individual killing people in cold blood. 'He had,' he wrote, 'the prosperous look of a lawyer.'

As the champagne flowed and the party grew increasingly merry, Maugham plucked up the courage to quiz Savinkov about the assassinations. 'When I asked him if it wasn't rather nervous work, he laughed and said: "Oh, it's just business like another."'

Savinkov was disarmingly frank when telling Maugham about the dangers posed by the Bolshevik revolutionaries. He warned that they were bent on annihilating all who did not share their radical views. 'He said to me once in his casual way: "Either Lenin will stand me up in front of a wall and shoot me or I shall stand him in front of a wall and shoot him."'

Maugham reported every detail of his conversations back to Wiseman in America. Wiseman, in turn, forwarded the information to Mansfield Cumming. As a precaution against the Germans intercepting these telegraphic messages, Maugham wrote in code, with special signifiers for each letter of the alphabet and previously agreed names for all the principal players.

Kerensky was Lane, Lenin was Davis and Trotsky was Cole. Three governments also had codenames: the British were Eyre and Co., the Americans were Curtis and Co., and the Russians were Waring and Co.

When Maugham later came to write his Ashenden spy novels – semi-fictional versions of his own experiences – he gave an account of the time and effort it took his hero to write his despatches. '[The code] was in two parts, one contained in a slim book and the other, given him on a sheet of paper and destroyed by him before he left allied territory, committed to memory.'

Decoding was even worse. 'Ashenden deciphered the groups of numbers one by one ... his method was to abstract his mind from the sense till he had finished, since he had discovered that if you took notice of the words as they came along, you often jumped to a conclusion and sometimes were led into error.'

Maugham's cables made for sombre reading in London and Washington. He expressed his belief that the Russian government was doomed and that more serious unrest was inevitable.

'Perhaps if I had been sent to Russia six months earlier I might have done something,' he wrote. 'The condition of things is much more serious than appears on the surface . . . the situation [is] entirely out of hand.'

Maugham worked hard at fulfilling his brief, despite the atmosphere of gloom. His key task was to establish how best Britain and America might support Kerensky's government. He thought that anti-German propaganda needed to be given a far higher profile. The Germans, he noted, were masters of political manipulation, 'with a vast, well-organised Secret Service covering all chief Russian centres.'

Maugham had the idea of setting up a propaganda bureau that could vigorously support Kerensky's government. He said it would require an annual budget of $500,000, a vast sum of money that raised surprisingly few eyebrows in Whitehall. He was told that ministers were prepared to spend more if the organisation proved effective. But the proposed bureau was outrun by events and the money was never needed.

Maugham's intelligence reports were carefully scrutinised by William Wiseman in New York. 'I am receiving very interesting cables from Maugham,' he informed Mansfield Cumming in London. 'He asks if he can work with British intelligence officers at Petrograd, thereby benefiting both and avoiding confusion. I see no objection . . . He is very discreet.'

Maugham spent his evenings 'coding my sombre impressions.' Then, when the work was done, he would take himself off to the Hotel Europe and swill goblets of brandy with English and American journalists.

'[We] caught the Russian mood – '*Nitchevo!*' [It doesn't matter],' wrote one of those journalists. '[We] managed to enjoy ourselves and forget the revolution.'

On one occasion, Maugham had lunch with Louise Bryant, the partner of John Reed who would later write his celebrated account of the revolution, *Ten Days that Shook the World*.

'You won't reveal you had lunch with a British secret agent, will you?' joshed a well-lubricated Maugham at the end of the meal. Bryant erupted into a peal of laughter. 'It couldn't have been funnier if he'd said he was an ambassador of the Pope,' she wrote.

The situation in Petrograd was by now so troublesome that Maugham saw no future for Kerensky's government. 'The Germans were advancing; the Russian soldiers at the front were deserting in droves, the navy was restless and there were stories bruited that officers had been cruelly butchered by their men.'

The stories were true. Bolshevik gangs were taking advantage of the unrest to murder and pillage.

In the first week of October, a desperate Kerensky summoned Maugham to a private meeting. He had a message that he wished Maugham to relay to Britain's prime minister as soon as possible. It was 'so secret that he would not put it in writing.'

Maugham agreed to deliver it to Lloyd George in person and left Petrograd that very day. But he was obliged to write the message down, for he was worried that his uncontrollable stammer would ruin his delivery of it once he was in the prime minister's presence.

Kerensky's secret proposal was an audacious political manoeuvre that had two principal objectives: to keep Russia in the war and simultaneously undermine the Bolsheviks. He wanted Lloyd George to make an offer of immediate peace with Germany, but on such stringent terms that Germany would have no option but to refuse.

A German refusal, argued Kerensky, would enable him to reinvigorate the Russian war machine. He could instil in the army a renewed sense of purpose. 'I can go to my soldiers and say: "You see, they don't want peace." Then they will fight.'

Kerensky's idea was bold but wholly unrealistic. Maugham knew that the British government would never agree to his proposition. He also knew that he was dealing with a broken man. Kerensky's last words to Maugham were a testimony to his failure as a political leader.

'When the cold weather comes I don't think I shall be able to keep the army in the trenches,' he said lamely. 'I don't see how we can go on.'

Maugham found it all very sad. 'The final impression I had was of a man exhausted. He seemed broken by the burden of power.'

Maugham left for London that very day, taking a train to Oslo and then a boat to England. He debriefed the prime minister about his mission and repeatedly tried to relay the message from Kerensky, proposing that Britain make an offer of peace to Germany. But each time he started speaking, Lloyd George cut him short.

'I received the impression, I don't exactly know for what reason, that he had an inkling of what I had to say to him and was determined not to let me say it.'

In the end, Maugham grew so frustrated that he thrust his handwritten account of Kerensky's proposition into the prime minister's hands.

'He read it and handed it back to me.

' "I can't do it," he said.

'It was not my business to argue.

' "What shall I tell Kerensky?" I asked.

' "Just that I can't do it." '

Maugham left the prime minister's office wondering how he would break the news to Kerensky. He was dreading returning to Russia, especially as his tuberculosis had returned with a vengeance. But scarcely had he began planning his trip than it was suddenly cancelled.

'[There] came the news that the Bolsheviks had seized power and Kerensky had been overthrown.'

The days of friendly co-operation were at an end. Russia had become the enemy.

CHAPTER FOUR

KNOW THY ENEMY

TOP SECRET

Mansfield Cumming's Russian bureau was still housed in the Petrograd War Ministry at the time of the second revolution of 1917 that swept the Bolsheviks to power.

The agents who had previously worked under Samuel Hoare continued to send intelligence back to Whitehall Court, although it was becoming increasingly difficult to form a clear picture of what was taking place in those turbulent times.

News also reached London from regular diplomatic channels. Ambassador George Buchanan was still at his post, but his tenure in Russia was rapidly coming to an end. Conventional diplomacy was soon to become an irrelevance.

On the evening of 7 November, Buchanan happened to glance out of the embassy window and was surprised by what he saw. 'Armoured cars took up positions at all points commanding the Winter Palace,' he noted in his diary.

Buchanan knew that Kerensky's ministers were inside the building and he feared for their safety. The 2,000-strong garrison had dwindled over the previous few days and the building's defence was now entrusted to three squadrons of

Cossacks, a handful of volunteers and a company from the Women's Death Battalion. Their numbers were so small that only a few of the palace's numerous entrances could be guarded at any one time.

Ambassador Buchanan had a second unwelcome surprise at 9.45 p.m. when the cruiser, *Aurora*, fired her famous blank shot. It was a signal for the Bolshevik revolution to begin. Soon afterwards, Buchanan saw live shells fired on the Winter Palace from the Peter and Paul fortress. By midnight, a mob of Bolshevik revolutionaries had surrounded the building and was intent on sacking this tangible symbol of the old regime.

When they finally broke into the building at around 1 a.m. they met with little resistance. The image of the Winter Palace being stormed by force was a piece of later propaganda.

'Three rifle shots shattered the quiet,' wrote the American journalist Bessie Beatty who was at the scene. 'We stood speechless, awaiting a return volley; but the only sound was the crunching of broken glass spread like a carpet over the cobblestones. The windows of the Winter Palace had been broken into bits.'

As Beatty stood there waiting to see what would happen next, there was a loud cry. 'It's all over,' shouted a Bolshevik sailor. 'They have surrendered.'

Kerensky's ministers inside the palace had taken refuge in the famous Malachite Room. According to an account later written by the British military attaché, Sir Alfred Knox, they experienced a tense few hours as they awaited the arrival of the mob. One of the ministers kept spitting on the ground. Another walked up and down 'like a caged tiger.' A third sat on a sofa 'nervously pulling up his trousers till they were finally above his knees.' All knew that the endgame was near and that Russia was heading into an uncertain future.

The ministers were still hiding in the Malachite Room when the revolutionaries burst in and arrested them. They were marched off through hostile crowds to the Peter and Paul fortress. All except Kerensky, who had fled the city. There were rumours that he would soon be returning at the head of an anti-Bolshevik army.

By 3 a.m., the corridors of the Winter Palace were packed with an unruly crowd of revolutionary activists. The American journalist, John Reed, witnessed scenes of total disorder as the mob embarked on an orgy of looting.

One man was 'strutting around with a bronze clock perched on his shoulder; another found a plume of ostrich feathers, which he stuck in his hat. The looting was just beginning when someone cried: "Comrades! Don't take anything. This is the property of the People!" '

Reed himself appropriated a jewelled sword that he tucked inside his winter coat. His sympathies with the Bolshevik revolutionaries did not preclude him from filching public property.

It was not until the following morning that Ambassador Buchanan was brought the most unwelcome news of his entire tenure in Russia. He received confirmation that Lenin's revolutionary Bolsheviks had seized power. Kerensky's Provisional Government had been swept away, along with the last vestiges of law and order.

Events now gathered apace. That very evening, 8 November, Lenin made his first public address at the Smolny Institute, a cavernous building with classical façade on the eastern fringes of Petrograd. It had previously been an elite finishing school for daughters of the nobility, but the powdered young ladies and their governesses had been evicted by a detachment of Red Guards. Now, it was the headquarters of the new revolutionary government.

Lenin read out a proclamation calling for the transfer of all privately owned land into the hands of the Peasants Soviets – local councils – that had sprung up across Russia. He then demanded an immediate end to Russia's participation in the First World War and made a dramatic call for revolution in the Western democracies. It was a portent of things to come.

When Lenin had finished speaking, Trotsky took to the rostrum and harangued the crowd. 'There are only two alternatives,' he shouted. 'Either the Russian revolution will create a revolutionary movement in Europe, or the European powers will destroy the Russian revolution.'

Both men were already viewing the Western democracies as a far more dangerous enemy than the German Kaiser.

★

George Hill was still in Petrograd when the revolutionary upheaval occurred. He was not yet working for Mansfield Cumming: he was still employed as a military advisor to the Russian armed forces.

But he was increasingly drawn to unofficial intelligence work, gathering information on anything that seemed of relevance. When he learned that the Smolny Institute had become the temporary home of the new government, he immediately headed there and talked his way inside in order to see Lenin in person.

He found the Bolshevik leader 'a strong and simple man of less than middle height with a Slavonic cast of countenance, piercing eyes and a powerful forehead.'

In a characteristically bold move, Hill stepped forward to shake Lenin's hand. 'His manner was not friendly, nor could it be said to be hostile; it was completely detached.'

He found something chilling about Lenin, something that he was unable to pinpoint at the time. It was as if he was determined to push ahead with his revolutionary ideals, whatever the cost in human blood.

Hill held out the vain hope that the Bolsheviks would keep Russia in the war. He also hoped that the new leaders would allow him and his colleagues to remain in Petrograd as military advisors to the Russian armed forces. But his visit to the Smolny Institute made him realise that this was most unlikely: the new regime looked certain to cut all its ties with the Entente governments. The Bolsheviks, he wrote, were 'ruthless, ignorant, pig-headed, seeking to conduct affairs on a strict adherence to a few second-hand phrases.'

The Bolshevik revolution rapidly consolidated itself, or so it seemed to outward observers. Revolutionary councils had sprung up across the length and breadth of Russia over the previous months. Now, representatives from these councils converged on Petrograd and met at the Smolny Institute as the All-Russian Congress of Soviets. The congress ratified the revolutionary transfer of power into Bolshevik hands, with Lenin at their head. Although there were many political battles to come, there was to be no turning back.

Trotsky, the new People's Commissar for Foreign Affairs, was keen to meet the ambassadors of the most important foreign powers, including Britain's Sir George Buchanan. He asked that they call on him at the Smolny Institute.

The ambassadors, schooled in convention, were indignant at being summoned in such a fashion. They disdainfully reminded Trotsky that there was a strict protocol to such visits. The customary procedure was for new ministers to inform the ambassadors by letter of their assumption of office.

It was a formality that infuriated Trotsky. 'He said that such a procedure was all very well under the old regime, but hardly suited present circumstances.' If they were not prepared to play by the new rules, then he was not interested in meeting them.

Ambassador Buchanan sent a series of stark messages to London warning that Lenin presented a new and formidable threat to the world. His fiery speeches about crushing the democracies of the West were delivered with a conviction that appalled Buchanan.

He particularly feared for the future of the Raj, especially when Lenin announced that he was tearing up the Anglo-Russian Convention of 1907. This annulment was more than symbolic: it left the scant defences of India's northern frontier vulnerable and exposed.

Buchanan's warning was one of his last acts as ambassador: he left the country soon afterwards, along with many of his staff. He was not sorry to bid farewell to Russia. He had suffered what was tantamount to a nervous breakdown over the previous two weeks and felt like a relic in the new Russia.

His closest acquaintances, the grand dukes and duchesses, had taken stock of their dramatic change in fortunes and were now fleeing the capital. When Buchanan bid farewell to his friend Grand Duke Michael, he must have suspected that he would never see him again.

★

Mansfield Cumming's operations had steadily expanded during the course of the war. He had more than a thousand agents in the field, most of them gathering intelligence on the Western Front.

Now, with the apparent success of Lenin's revolution, Cumming needed to turn his attentions to Russia. Whitehall

Court was to focus increasingly on events in Petrograd and Moscow.

Cumming had recruited many new employees at his London headquarters in the months that preceded the Bolshevik revolution. There were now more than sixty secretaries, typists and technical staff working at Whitehall Court; they spent their time collating reports arriving from agents around the globe.

The work was hard, with long hours and few holidays, but it was enlivened by the antics of Cumming's unofficial deputy, an affable young jester named Colonel Freddie Browning.

Cumming had personally summoned the sharp-witted Colonel Browning to an interview. The two men bonded immediately and Cumming offered him a key position at Whitehall Court.

Browning proved extremely capable, helping Cumming to restructure his fast-growing organisation. He also introduced an element of merry mayhem to the office. 'Gay, witty, with an acute sense of humour,' recalled one member of staff, '*la joie de vivre* was in his blood.'

Browning knew that people worked best when they were enjoying themselves. He kept the office ladies amused with a stream of anecdotes while his after-work soirées were relished by all, especially Cumming. 'He brought happy evenings to the old man by having gay parties with all the stage beauties that he had at call.'

So wrote Frank Stagg, another key member of the team. Stagg added that the colonel would bring together 'those who knew what was what in any particular line.' Whether he meant sex, spying or something entirely different is unclear.

Cumming was a man of his era: although married, he spent an inordinate amount of time cavorting with his 'top mates', the office staff, and there were long spells where he can have seen little of Mrs C. He certainly had an eye for pretty secretaries: when one of them was sent to Egypt, Cumming offered her a monthly dress allowance that was considerably more generous than her salary.

There was an occasion when he stood accused of having too much 'partiality with the typists', but that did not stop him employing a lady 'chauffeuse' to drive his Mercedes. He liked his ladies in uniform and went so far as to personally arrange for her to be properly attired in a smart driver's suit.

Colonel Browning was no less attentive to the needs of the secretaries. Ever the gallant, he was 'distressed at the way the female element on the staff had [only] buns for lunch'. He installed a first-class canteen in Whitehall Court, employing an army chef to produce decent meals procured through the Savoy's suppliers.

The jovial atmosphere at Whitehall Court was occasionally disturbed by the unwanted intrusion of senior civil servants. Officials at the War Office, motivated by professional rivalry, frequently suggested that Cumming's organisation should be subsumed into their own espionage operations.

Cumming reacted angrily when these changes were first mooted. The War Office dealt exclusively with military intelligence, whereas his agents covered a range of espionage operations, including political, economic and technical targets.

'Ever since the war started, my Bureau has been subjected to attacks which have disorganised and almost destroyed it,' he wrote in one tetchy memorandum. He claimed that short-sighted actions by the War Office had already compromised his work in a number of countries, including Russia.

Cumming managed to fend off the War Office for almost two years, but in 1917 he found himself facing a more formidable foe. George Macdonogh had recently been appointed as Director of Military Intelligence at the War Office: his new position made him one of the biggest guns in Whitehall.

A taciturn Scot with a chilling gaze, General Macdonogh would tell people that his sole interest in life was his work. Few doubted this assertion. He was a socially awkward individual driven by ambition, and went by his nickname, Blitz. He soon had Cumming in his sights.

Macdonogh launched his first strike in February 1917, at the time of the first Russian revolution. He declared himself overall master of all wartime intelligence operations and accused Cumming of 'empire building'. More alarmingly, he demanded that Cumming accept the status of 'being under my orders in all military intelligence matters'.

Cumming's initial response was magnificently aloof: he simply ignored the general. He was fortunate that General Macdonogh was distracted by more urgent matters and unable to press home his attack. But it was a stark warning of the troubles to come.

Macdonogh's second offensive came in October 1917, when Russia was entering a more unpredictable period of revolutionary activity. The timing could scarcely have been worse for Cumming. At the very moment when he needed to devote all his energies to Russia, his efforts were seriously undermined by an enemy on home turf.

Macdonogh sent a curt message to Cumming informing him that 'he was going to take over the whole S[ecret] S[ervice].' Cumming's organisation was to be demoted to a subordinate role.

This time, the general meant business. He set out a plan of how intelligence gathering should be structured (with himself at the helm) and then summoned a meeting of his military staff in order to start implementing the changes. Cumming was allowed to attend the meeting as an observer but was not permitted to take part in the discussions.

Cumming acted swiftly to prevent his organisation being swallowed. He instigated a major structural reorganisation in order to accommodate Macdonogh's most pressing demands. He then solicited heavy-gun support from Charles Hardinge, Permanent Under-Secretary at the Foreign Office.

Hardinge gave his wholehearted backing to Cumming. He reminded Macdonogh that Cumming answered first and foremost to the Foreign Office. He also expressed his dismay at any scheme 'which diminished the authority of the man at the top'. Cumming was to be 'master in his own house.'

General Macdonogh was not the first to try to usurp Cumming's position and nor would he be the last. Yet Cumming was quietly confident that he could see off other pretenders to his throne. As one of his agents later recalled, 'C always used to boast that as he had three masters, [the Foreign Office, Admiralty and War Office] he had not got one at all, as he could always set the other two against any objector.'

★

Once Cumming had dealt with Macdonogh he could turn his attentions back to Russia. The departure of Sir George Buchanan had left the British Embassy with a skeletal staff which had to adjust to life in a country that had gone from friend to foe in a matter of days.

The few remaining diplomats assumed that they would also be recalled to England and that the embassy would be formally closed. They were therefore surprised to learn of the appointment of a new member of staff, one whose role, from the very outset, was as controversial as it was ambiguous.

Robert Bruce Lockhart had been sent to Russia with the ostensible task of keeping open a channel of communication with Lenin's revolutionary government. British ministers did not wish to cut all their ties with Russia, even though Lenin's hostility could not have been clearer. Lockhart was charged with meeting the new leaders and establishing unofficial relations with them.

But Lockhart was also to play a far more secretive role, helping to co-ordinate the future activities of Cumming's agents inside Russia. This work was to prove highly dangerous in the months ahead.

On the face of it, Lockhart was well suited to the job for which he had been appointed. He spoke good Russian and had previously served as Consul General in Moscow. Thirty years of age and in the prime of life, he was affable, colourful and endlessly entertaining.

He described himself as 'broad-shouldered and broken-nosed, with a squat stumpy figure and a ridiculous gait.' Yet he proved a magnate for the high-society women of Petrograd, for whom wit and gallantry were more of a draw than looks.

Lockhart had many failings and he wrote about them with disarming honesty. His lack of discretion would have been a handicap in any employment, but it was doubly alarming in a diplomat. Not for nothing would he later find employment as a gossip writer for London's *Evening Standard*.

His insatiable appetite for women was another drawback. He had first got into trouble when living in Malaya a decade earlier. He had fallen hopelessly in love with a young Malay princess called Amai, thereby provoking the wrath of the local sultan.

Lockhart was repeatedly warned that 'the crow does not mate with the bird of Paradise,' but this did nothing to dampen his ardour. He installed Amai in his colonial bungalow and embarked upon a torrid affair. 'The rest of the story,' he wrote, 'is all tragedy or all comedy.' Death threats, poisoned food and life-threatening malaria brought their affair to an abrupt end: at great risk to his life, Lockhart was smuggled out of Malaya and forced to abandon his lover to an uncertain fate.

His next public indiscretion, a scandalous extramarital affair, had led to him being sacked from his previous post in the Moscow consulate. 'I had made myself talked about,' he admitted. 'The Ambassador sorrowfully but firmly decided . . . that I must go home to England for a rest.'

Lockhart's return to Russia in early 1918 did not bring about a change to his lifestyle: he continued to frequent the decadent cabaret acts staged in the underground bars of the Okhotny Ryad. There were also nights when he would clamber into his horse-drawn troika and drive to the grounds of the Strelna Palace. Here, with stinging cheeks and icicles in his hair, he would carouse with the gypsy singers like the celebrated Maria Nikolaievna.

'The cynic will say that her task in life was to collect foolish and preferably rich young men, to sing to them, and to make them drink oceans of champagne until their wealth or their father's wealth was transferred from their pockets to her own,' he wrote.

Lockhart was never one of the cynics. He would guzzle his way through Maria's champagne until the drink and the music left him in a state of blissful intoxication.

Lockhart's posting to Russia was to bring gaiety to many and misery to one. Oliver Wardrop was a humourless career diplomat who had served diligently as British Consul for some years and had remained in the country in the aftermath of Ambassador Buchanan's departure. He was dismayed to learn of Lockhart's appointment and telegraphed London to enquire as to his rank in the diplomatic hierarchy.

The reply was evasive. 'Mr Lockhart will on arrival in Moscow continue to act as unofficial British agent to the Bolshevik government.'

None the wiser, Wardrop pressed on with his work, but found himself continually distracted by Lockhart, who behaved with complete disregard to the conventions of diplomacy.

'Position of Lockhart is unique,' complained Wardrop in a sniffy letter to London. 'He is variously described in official and inspired press as "Ambassador", "Envoy", "Official Representative", "Consul General" and so on.'

What really irked Wardrop was the fact that Lockhart worked in secrecy. 'He has a staff of some six persons, exact nature of whose duties I am unaware but nevertheless with my ready consent uses my staff for ciphering and deciphering.'

Wardrop was fearful of being sidelined and sent another telegram to the Foreign Office, asking for clarification as to whether or not he was still the 'senior British official in what used to be called Russia.'

The reply merely thanked him for his 'loyal attitude'. The unpalatable truth was that Lockhart had been given carte blanche to act in whatever way he saw fit.

★

Robert Bruce Lockhart and his little team at the embassy were not the only British nationals based in Russia at this time. Among the small number of Englishmen who had made their homes in Petrograd was one who had more experience of Russia than most.

Arthur Ransome had, by this time, been working as a *Daily News* correspondent for several years and was well acquainted with both senior Russian politicians and the British expatriate community.

'A tall, lanky, bony individual,' was how George Hill described Ransome, 'with a shock of sandy hair, usually unkempt, and the eyes of a small inquisitive and rather mischievous boy. He really was a lovable personality when you came to know him.'

But Ransome had become increasingly irritable in the months before the Bolshevik revolution, partly because of his inadequate diet. The lack of fruit and vegetables had begun to affect his health and his recurring haemorrhoids had become so inflamed that he found it impossible to work.

'I can't cross a room without nearly collapsing,' he had written in a letter to his mother, 'and the day before yesterday I fainted in the street.'

He was eventually forced into the operating theatre, where he went under the knife with only a cocaine paste to dull the agony of having the haemorrhoids cut out and the bleeding veins cauterised. 'VIOLENT AND ABOMINABLE PAIN,' he wrote on the day after the operation. For the next sixty hours, the pain remained so excruciating that he could not sleep.

Ransome had returned to England after the operation, intent on taking a fishing holiday that would give him the chance to regain his strength, far from the stresses of Russia. He was joined in Wiltshire by his wife Ivy – with whom he was trapped in a deteriorating relationship – and his young daughter, Tabitha.

The much-needed holiday did not last for long: Ransome's perch fishing was abruptly interrupted by news of the Bolshevik revolution. By the second week of November he was once again writing for the *Daily News*, not as an eyewitness to the unfolding events but as a London-based commentator with knowledge of many of the key players.

Ransome might have expected a summons to Mansfield Cumming's offices at this critical juncture. He was, after all, an acknowledged expert on Russia. He also knew many of the men working for the Russian bureau. But instead of being called to Whitehall Court, Ransome was invited to the Foreign Office, where he had several meetings with the Permanent Under-Secretary for Foreign Affairs, Lord Robert Cecil.

Ransome never felt comfortable in the presence of patrician grandees and he did not warm to Lord Cecil. 'He stood in front of the fireplace, immensely tall, fantastically thin, his hawkish head swinging forward at the end of a long arc formed by his body and legs.' He seemed to personify the aloofness of the ruling elite.

Yet Lord Cecil recognised Ransome as an expert on Russian affairs and expressed a keen interest in hearing his opinions about the new revolutionary rulers. He also solicited information on the forces that opposed the Bolsheviks. When the meeting at long last drew to a close, Ransome surprised Lord Cecil by offering to return to Russia as an unofficial envoy, playing a similar role to that of Robert Bruce Lockhart.

Lord Cecil was by no means averse to the idea: Ransome, after all, could prove extremely useful in reporting on the rapidly changing situation inside Russia. He gave his consent and despatched a telegram to Petrograd alerting the remaining diplomatic staff to Ransome's appointment.

But just a few hours after sending the telegram, he countermanded it. 'In view of Athens telegram No. 2191 about Mr Ransome,' he wrote, 'if the allegations made against him there are true, he would obviously not be a suitable agent.'

The contents of 'Athens telegram No. 2191' are not known and the allegations against Ransome remain a mystery. But they almost certainly painted him as a revolutionary sympathiser, someone whose radical views meant that he could not be trusted.

There was some truth in this. Ransome sincerely hoped that the Bolshevik revolution would sweep away the many injustices of the old regime and offer a brighter future to the country's downtrodden poor. His political views did not correspond with those of British ministers.

Lord Cecil eventually gave Ransome the benefit of the doubt and agreed to facilitate his return to Petrograd.

'He gave me his blessing,' wrote a relieved Ransome, 'and made things easy for me, at least as far as Stockholm, by entrusting the diplomatic bag for me to deliver to the legation.'

Ransome was back in Petrograd on Christmas Day, crossing the border into Russia with the assistance of the Bolshevik representative in Stockholm. His heavy luggage preceded him, having been forwarded to Petrograd and delivered to the new Commissariat for Foreign Affairs, where it fell into the hands of Karl Radek, a senior Bolshevik commissar in charge of Western propaganda. He was also one of the most devious characters in the revolutionary inner circle.

Radek immediately opened the luggage to see what was inside. He found an eclectic mix: 'a Shakespeare, a folding chess-board and chessmen and a mixed collection of books on elementary navigation, fishing, chess and folklore.' Intrigued, he expressed a desire to meet the person 'who was interested in subjects that seemed incompatible.'

Ransome was summoned to the Commissariat for Foreign Affairs and introduced to the irascible Radek. The two men got along famously from the outset, swapping gossip and continually trying to wrongfoot each other.

Radek spoke in Russian with Ransome, 'but loved to drag in sentences from English books, which I sometimes annoyed him by being slow to recognise.' His favourite quotation was 'Marley was as dead as a doornail' from *A Christmas Carol*. 'He loved to apply it to politicians and to political programmes that had been outstripped by events.'

Ransome enjoyed Radek's irreverent wit, describing him as 'a little light-haired spectacled revolutionary goblin of incredible intelligence and vivacity.'

Others were less generous. Robert Bruce Lockhart found him 'a grotesque figure' whose Norfolk suit 'with knickers and leggings' could have been borrowed from the wardrobe of Mr Toad. 'A little man with a huge head, protruding ears, clean-shaven face . . . with spectacles, and a large mouth with yellow tobacco-stained teeth, from which a huge pipe or cigar was never absent.'

Both Lockhart and Ransome recognised that Radek could provide them with a direct link to the Bolshevik inner circle and they courted him assiduously.

'Almost every day he would turn up in my rooms,' wrote Lockhart, 'an English cap stuck jauntily on his head, his pipe puffing fiercely, a bundle of books under his arm, and a huge revolver strapped to his side. He looked like the cross between a professor and a bandit.'

Radek was particularly fond of Ransome and set up meetings for him with the most important players in the regime, including Trotsky and Lenin. Ransome, wearing his journalistic hat, was keen to introduce the new revolutionary leaders to a British audience. He produced lively pen-portraits of men like Radek and Lenin, bringing them vividly to life.

Unlike most foreign observers, one of whom dismissed Lenin as a 'provincial green grocer', Ransome stressed the vital appeal of Russia's new revolutionary leader.

'[He] mingled jest and argument in language that tasted of Russian tobacco and the life of the Russian peasantry. It was natural to hear him talk of the principle of his international revolution in the language of the Volga peasants, and in his mouth political theory seemed in no way out of tune with the peasant proverbs.'

Ransome was working principally as a journalist in the early months that followed the revolution. But he was already supplying information to the British government about the Bolshevik leaders and their political goals. This information would prove so valuable that he would eventually find himself on Mansfield Cumming's payroll. Ransome the revolutionary sympathiser was to become a key agent working inside Russia.

His friendship with Radek, coupled with the widely held belief that he was a closet Bolshevik, was already gaining him access to high-level meetings. He was permitted to attend both the Bolshevik's Executive Committee and the Third All-Russian Congress of Soviets.

'My position was immediately behind and above the presidium, looking down on Trotsky's muscular shoulders and great head and the occasional gestures of his curiously small hands,' he wrote. 'Beyond him was that sea of men: soldiers in green and grey shirts, workers in collarless ones, or jerseys, others dressed very much like British workmen, peasants in belted red shirts and high top boots.'

Ransome quickly gained the trust of Trotsky, who never imagined that he was passing information back to the British government.

'My complete lack of any political past was a help not a hindrance,' wrote Ransome, 'and I was soon getting a view of what was happening from much nearer than any regular journalist or politician could approach.'

Alone among the Westerners in Petrograd, he was on intimate terms with the Bolshevik leaders. He saw them 'every day, drinking their tea, hearing their quarrels, sharing with them such sweets as I had.'

As he penetrated their inner circle, he formed a very different view of their political skills to his English compatriots. He also strongly disagreed with the sentiments of the anti-Bolshevik news-sheets that were being produced in increasing numbers by their enemies.

'Meeting all these people as human beings, I could not believe the rubbishy propaganda that was being poured out by other Russians who, hoping for their destruction no matter by whom, pretended that they were German agents.'

Ransome was soon so close to the leading revolutionaries that Western diplomats began to wonder if he had 'unusual channels of information.' This he did. Unbeknown to anyone in London, he had fallen in love with Trotsky's personal secretary, Evgenia Shelepina, and was seeing her on a daily basis.

Their relationship was to transform the information he received from the regime: it was Shelepina who typed up Trotsky's correspondence and planned all his meetings. Suddenly, Ransome found himself with access to highly secretive documents and telegraphic transmissions.

He had first set eyes on Evgenia when he interviewed Trotsky on 28 December 1917, but he did not speak to her until later that evening, when he visited the Commissariat for Foreign Affairs. He poked his head into a room and, amid a group of unfamiliar faces, immediately recognised her.

'This was Evgenia,' he would write, 'the tall, jolly girl whom later on I was to marry and to whom I owe the happiest days of my life.'

Ransome had been looking for the official censor to stamp his despatch: Evgenia offered to help him find the right person. She also said she would try to find them both some food in the censor's office. 'Come along,' she said, 'perhaps he has some potatoes. Potatoes are the only thing we want. Come along.'

They eventually found both the censor and his potatoes: the latter were in the process of burning on an overheated primus stove. Evgenia rescued them from the pot and shared them out.

Ransome, trapped in his unhappy marriage with Ivy, was smitten by Evgenia. She was no beauty; she was tall, ungainly and big-boned. 'She must have been two or three inches above six feet in her stockings,' wrote George Hill, who preferred his women to be petite, young and sexually alluring. Yet even Hill eventually accepted that feminine charm was not all about surface beauty.

'At first glance, one was apt to dismiss her as a very fine-looking specimen of Russian peasant womanhood, but closer acquaintance revealed in her depths of unguessed qualities.'

The Americans in Petrograd called her 'The Big Girl' because, explained one, 'she *was* a big girl'. She played an important role in the months that followed the revolution for she controlled the visitors who wished to get Trotsky's ear. She was far more than a secretary; she could provide (or deny) access to all of the Bolshevik leaders.

'She was methodical and intellectual,' wrote Hill, 'a hard worker with an enormous sense of humour. She saw things quickly and could analyse political situations with the speed and precision with which an experienced bridge player analyses a hand of cards.'

She was ruthlessly efficient in her work. 'I do not believe she ever turned away from Trotsky anyone who was of the slightest consequence, and yet it was no easy matter to get past that maiden unless one had that something.'

Ransome took the new Bolshevik leadership very seriously and his reports on their activities – often sympathetic – caused him increasing difficulties with officials in London. His relationship with Evgenia did not help matters. In the British Embassy in Petrograd, there were whispered rumours that far from serving the British government, he was actually working as a double agent.

Ransome did little to discourage these rumours for they only served to boost his credentials amongst the leading Bolsheviks. Besides, he shared some of the views of the revolutionary leaders and genuinely hoped that Lenin and Trotsky would drag Russia into a brighter future.

★

Mansfield Cumming was quick to realise that the change of regime in Russia required a whole new approach to espionage. His team of agents were no longer working in a friendly country. The new government was overtly hostile and it was extremely likely to expel all those who had previously been working for the Russian bureau. If Cumming were to retain an intelligence-gathering team inside the country, it would have to change its modus operandi.

A Secret Service booklet produced in the aftermath of the revolution tackled the difficulties of agents having to work undercover in a hostile land. Entitled 'Notes on Instruction and Recruiting of Agents', it covered many aspects of spy-craft, from writing in code to the adoption of disguises.

This latter point was to prove of great importance to Cumming's agents. The 'Notes' warned that the adoption of a wholly new persona carried considerable dangers and had to be completely believable if it was not to be unmasked. The guise of commercial traveller was recommended, but the 'Notes' warned that this was 'a hopeless business unless the agent really knows & understands the article he is supposed to sell and also really transacts business in such article.'

The 'Notes' also provided information on infiltrating enemy organisations, notably their secret services. This, it confessed, was 'one of the most fascinating branches of S[ecret] S[ervice] work.' It said that 'clever agents' could cause immense damage and 'lead to the complete disorganisation of the service against which they are working.'

The most important instruction was for agents not to compromise their fellow spies in the event of them being captured. 'If you do get caught, keep your mouth shut and don't give anybody away.'

The remnants of Samuel Hoare's team had been allowed to remain in Petrograd in the weeks that followed the Bolshevik revolution, although they were no longer able to work at the Russian War Office. Cumming now took the bold decision to place his Russian headquarters outside the country. It would henceforth be based in Stockholm, at arm's length from Lenin's Bolsheviks. The bureau was to be run by an ex-army officer named Major John Scale, one of the men implicated in the murder of Rasputin.

'Tall, handsome, well-read, intelligent,' wrote one who knew him, 'with a debonair manner which endeared him to everyone.' Major Scale was to prove an efficient operator in the months ahead.

He was given ostensible employment as British attaché to Sweden, but this was merely a cover for his work as the Stockholm bureau chief. He was tasked with providing Cumming's agents inside Russia with money, information and logistical support.

Cumming also needed a link man in Moscow, someone who could simultaneously be in contact with both John Scale and the agents working undercover inside the country. This job was to be performed by Ernest Boyce, a silver-haired lieutenant with considerable experience in military sabotage.

The idea of creating bureaux outside the frontiers of Russia was a good one. It was to work so well, indeed, that the system was soon expanded with offices in Helsingfors (today's Helsinki), Riga and Libau (in Latvia), Kaunas (in Lithuania) and Reval (in Estonia).

There were also smaller offices at various frontier posts on Russia's borders with the Scandinavian countries. The men who worked at these posts had intimate knowledge of the local area and were able to help Cumming's agents smuggle themselves in and out of Russia.

They also supplied his men with the necessary forged papers and stamps, thereby increasing their chances of reaching Petrograd or Moscow without risk of arrest.

★

At the same time as Cumming was restructuring his Russian operations, Lenin was creating his own Bolshevik intelligence service.

The Cheka (the All-Russian Extraordinary Commission for Combating Counter-Revolution and Sabotage) was established within six weeks of the Bolsheviks seizing power. From the outset, it was viewed as a means of ruthlessly crushing dissent, whether it came from Russian citizens or from the agents of foreign powers.

Cheka agents would soon become the deadly rivals of Cumming's men in Russia and would devote much of their time to tracking them down and unmasking them. With all the resources of the state at their disposal, they were to prove a formidable foe.

'It is war now – face to face, a fight to the finish,' said Felix Dzerzhinsky, the first chief of the Cheka. He was known to his comrades as Iron Felix, with good reason. Lenin's chief henchman was ruthless and devoid of pity: indeed, he seemed to be devoid of any human emotion whatsoever.

'A man of correct manners and quiet speech,' wrote Lockhart, 'but without a ray of humour in his character.' He had a sallow face with a thick black moustache and his jet hair was worn *en brosse*.

'The most remarkable thing about him was his eyes. Deeply sunk, they blazed with a steady fire of fanaticism. They never twitched. His eyelids seemed paralysed.'

His chilling appearance struck fear into all who met him. In both manner and temperament he could not have been more different from the avuncular Mansfield Cumming.

Dzerzhinsky's name would later become a byword for terror and he would leave the streets of Russia awash with blood. Yet his early life betrayed no inkling of what was to come. He was neither Russian and nor was he a member of Lenin's much vaunted proletariat. Rather, he was the son of a Polish nobleman and was brought up in a devout Catholic household.

Dzerzhinsky loved the fervour of the faith and his early dream was to become a Catholic priest. When he eventually came to revolt against his background, he did so with equal fervour. By the time the Bolsheviks came to power, he had spent more than a decade in Siberian prisons. Now, he saw the chance of having his revenge. He would become the Bolshevik's most assiduous executioner.

The charter of the new Cheka made it clear that it would strike against any enemy of Bolshevism, even if that enemy came from abroad. Its goal was 'to suppress and liquidate all attempts and acts of counter-revolution and sabotage throughout Russia, from whatever quarter.'

The Cheka was to function as secret service with a military wing attached; it would rapidly expand as the enemies of Bolshevism became more numerous. In the first few weeks of its existence, it had just a handful of staff and its entire records fitted into Dzerzhinsky's briefcase. By mid January 1918, the staff had already topped one hundred and its powers had been extended to include the right to conduct the summary trial and execution of suspected counter-revolutionaries.

It was also given a contingent of Red Guards to undertake the liquidation of enemies. By the time the Cheka's headquarters moved to Moscow, which was made the new Bolshevik capital in March 1918, staffing levels had risen to 600.

On the night of 11 April, the Cheka gave a dramatic display of its ruthlessness. Dzerzhinsky had long been wanting to strike against the anarchist activists in the city: they had seized a number of key Moscow buildings and were terrorising the streets. After a careful monitoring of their twenty-six strongholds, Dzerzhinsky sent in his agents, reinforced with armed guards. They were sanctioned to use all necessary force and proved themselves to be extremely efficient. By the time the operation came to an end, forty anarchists were dead and five hundred more were under arrest.

Dzerzhinsky allowed Lockhart to see the properties he had captured from the anarchists, perhaps to serve as a warning that he meant business. 'The filth was indescribable,' wrote Lockhart as he toured their former strongholds. 'Wine stains and human excrement blotched the Aubusson carpets . . . the dead still lay where they had fallen.'

In one house, the Cheka had interrupted an orgy. 'The long table which had supported the feast had been overturned and broken plates, glasses, champagne bottles, made unsavoury islands in a pool of blood and spilt wine.'

A woman lay on the floor, a single bullet hole in her neck. '*Prostitutka*,' said Dzerzhinsky's assistant, who was acting as Lockhart's guide. 'Perhaps it is for the best.'

Lockhart was appalled by the violence. 'It was an unforgettable scene,' he wrote. 'The Bolsheviks had taken their first step towards the establishment of discipline.'

The Cheka would not find all their targets so easy to kill. For at the same time as Dzerzhinsky was tightening his grip on Moscow, Cumming was interviewing new agents to send into Russia. Among them was one who was to become a legend in the world of espionage.

His name was Sidney Reilly, but he would be known to both friend and foe as Reilly, Ace of Spies.

PART TWO

MASTERS OF DISGUISE

TOP SECRET

CHAPTER FIVE

THE MAN WITH THREE NAMES

TOP SECRET

Sidney Reilly emerged from the Savoy Hotel into the bright spring sunshine. He was accustomed to taking the occasional luncheon in the Savoy's dining rooms whenever he was in London. There was a club-like atmosphere that perfectly suited his persona. He liked to play the role of a well-bred English gentleman.

Reilly stepped into the Strand and awaited a passing taxi, not pausing to look around at the people in the street. He had no reason to expect anything suspicious or untoward on this beautiful March afternoon in 1918.

But had he glanced over his shoulder, he might have noticed that he was being followed. Someone had been tracking him and making notes on his movements for several hours. His pursuer had even questioned the Savoy's staff about his behaviour.

The man following Reilly was an agent from MI5 – the Home Intelligence Service – and he had been charged with gathering information on the places that Reilly frequented.

Mansfield Cumming himself had asked for Reilly to be tailed. He was on the point of offering him employment as a spy and wanted to be absolutely sure that Reilly could be trusted. He needed to know that he had the right man for an espionage mission whose aim was to gather intelligence from the heart of the new regime in Russia. It was certain to be both difficult and dangerous.

Cumming had found himself with no shortage of recruits for his Secret Intelligence Service over the previous four years. Espionage offered a welcome break for bright young officers weary of the monotony of war.

'There was from the outside point of view, a glamour, an air of romance and adventure about the whole idea which led dozens of young men to think they would try their hands at it,' wrote the espionage expert, Hector Bywater.

Cumming had started to pay increasingly close attention to the agents he intended to employ for his operations in Russia. The time would surely come when the remaining members of Samuel Hoare's bureau would be expelled from the country, along with Arthur Ransome, George Hill and the other British military officers who had been posted to Russia. Cumming needed to find agents who would be able and willing to work undercover.

An obvious recruiting ground was the British expatriate community of Petrograd. The families who had established businesses in the city were fluent Russian speakers and they also had good connections. A number of them would indeed become actively involved in espionage. But Cumming began to cast his net wider, looking for anyone who spoke perfect Russian and could blend into the crowd. His search for potential candidates had led him to Sidney Reilly, a flamboyant entrepreneur with a polyglot background and a seductive charm.

Reilly had spent much of the war in New York where he had set up business as an arms dealer and amassed a fortune of at least two million dollars, selling munitions to the Imperial Russian Army.

His moneymaking eventually preyed on his conscience – or so he claimed – and he decided to offer his services on the battlefront. According to Norman Thwaites, one of Cumming's operatives in New York, Reilly had approached him in the autumn of 1917 and said that 'he felt that he ought to be doing his bit in the war.'

Thwaites would later confess to having been bowled over by Reilly's imposing character and striking good looks. 'His appearance was remarkable,' he wrote. 'Complexion swarthy, a long straight nose, piercing eyes, black hair brushed back from a forehead suggesting keen intelligence.' To Thwaites, he was 'a man that impressed one with a good deal of power.'

Reilly's mastery of languages amazed all who met him, as did his ability to change identity at the flick of a switch. He could pass himself off as both a native Russian and a native German and he was able to blend seamlessly into a crowd. 'Not only had he charming manners,' wrote Thwaites, 'but he was a most agreeable companion with a fund of information in many spheres.'

Reilly was already being tipped as a possible agent when he was brought to the attention of Major John Scale, Cumming's bureau chief in Stockholm. Scale, in turn, proposed him to Mansfield Cumming, suggesting that Reilly might be just the sort of person needed for work inside Russia.

Cumming was cautiously enthusiastic; before offering Reilly employment he asked for a full briefing from his operatives in New York. He soon found himself with a picture of Reilly that was very different from the one drawn by Thwaites. Those who had known Reilly during the early years of the war described him as unscrupulous, disloyal and greedy.

'[He] has made money since the beginning of the war through influence with corrupted members of the Russian purchasing commissions,' read one report. 'We consider him untrustworthy and unsuitable to work suggested.'

A second telegram from New York described Reilly as 'a shrewd businessman of undoubted ability but without patriotism or principles and therefore not recommended for any position which requires loyalty as he would not hesitate to use it to further his own commercial interests.'

Cumming was so unsettled by this information that he decided to have Reilly trailed by MI5 in the days prior to their meeting at Whitehall Court. The officers who observed his movements were able to reveal little new information. Reilly always travelled by cab and his would-be pursuers kept losing him in the city traffic.

Even if they had managed to stay on his trail, it would have revealed little of interest. Reilly rarely strayed beyond the Savoy, the Ritz and Solomons in St James's Street, where he bought his daily buttonhole.

Reilly's chimerical nature was perfectly encapsulated in the contradictory nature of the surviving MI5 reports. One described him as 'very respectable, pays bills quite regularly and dines at the Savoy and Berkeley hotels'. The other concluded that he was 'one of a gang of confidence men of an international character.' It added that he was 'believed to have been born in Russian Poland.'

Reilly's place of birth was a subject of much speculation, partly because Reilly himself had invented numerous stories about his origins. He claimed at various times to have been fathered by an Irish sea captain, an Irish clergyman and a Russian aristocrat. His first wife had been told a rather different tale: she believed him to be descended from a wealthy family of landowners in Russian Poland.

Reilly was not, in fact, from Russian Poland and nor was his original name Reilly. He was born in 1874 in Odessa, in Southern Russia, and given the name Sigmund Georgievich Rosenblum. Both his parents were Jewish, although they had converted to Catholicism.

Rosenblum fled Odessa in his late teens for reasons that remain obscure. No less obscure are the next two decades of his life. He would later spin tales about how he had been a cook, a dockworker, a railway engineer in India and a brothel doorman in Brazil, but there is no certainty that he did any of these jobs. He was also said to have worked as a spy for the Japanese government and there are many unverified stories of his early forays into espionage.

At dinner parties with friends he would enliven the evening with derring-do accounts of a British Army expedition that he had accompanied into the steaming Amazonian rainforest. When natives ambushed the party, Reilly had single-handedly fought them off and saved all of the officers' lives. Like so many of Reilly's stories, it is almost certainly exaggerated and quite possibly untrue.

He was in London by the summer of 1899; he married his first wife, Margaret, at Holborn Register Office. It was from her that he took the name Reilly, discarding once and for all his birth name, Rosenblum.

When war broke out, Reilly took himself to New York where he lived with the first of his bigamous wives, Nadine Massino. (Margaret, who had taken to drink, was shipped back to England.)

All accounts agree that he had a seductive charm, loving women as he loved himself. A string of mistresses would fall under his spell. Monogamy did not come naturally to Reilly and although he was usually fastidious in his choice of women, it did not prevent him from cavorting around London on one of his visits with a common tart named Plugger. How she acquired her *nom de travail* can only be imagined.

Reilly's third wife, the vaudeville actress Pepita Burton, recalled being mesmerised by his languid chestnut-brown eyes when she first met him in the Hotel Adlon in Berlin. 'For a moment his eyes held mine and I felt a delicious thrill run through me.' She, like so many others, was instantly hooked.

But there was a darker side to Reilly's personality, one that was to haunt Mansfield Cumming for many years. He was a compulsive gambler and a reckless one to boot. He spent his money with great ostentation, staking all on a hand of cards.

What struck everyone was Reilly's vaunting ambition. He detested the Bolsheviks and was already dreaming of toppling Lenin's government. When he had come to consider who might replace Lenin, he looked no further than the mirror.

'Behind all Reilly's efforts lay the conviction that some day he was destined to bring Russia out of the slough and chaos of Communism,' wrote Norman Thwaites. 'He believed that he would do for Russia what Napoleon did for France.'

Reilly had long identified himself with Napoleon. It was an alarming comparison in one who was preoccupied with turning fantasy into reality. Such was his fascination with his historical hero that he amassed a large collection of memorabilia – a collection he would eventually sell for the considerable sum of $100,000.

Cumming had been fully briefed on Reilly's dubious background when he called him in for a meeting on 15 March 1918. His interviews with potential agents were usually cordial but perfunctory and there is no reason to doubt that his meeting with Reilly was any different. He must surely have asked him about his contacts in Russia and his political affiliations, but the content of their conversation remains unknown for Cumming recorded only a brief mention of their encounter in his diary. He found Reilly charming, yet he clearly had concerns. 'Very clever,' he wrote, 'very doubtful – has been everywhere and done everything.'

His resourcefulness was an important point in his favour: Reilly was exceptionally good at adapting himself to unfamiliar surroundings. Hector Bywater said that 'the good intelligence man had to dig himself in and stick it, bearing loneliness and fear and excitement and triumph in complete silence.'

Reilly fitted this mould so exactly that Cumming was prepared to turn a blind eye to Reilly's defects and send him into Russia, although he confessed that employing him was 'a great gamble'.

'[He] will take out £500 in notes and £750 in diamonds, which are at a premium,' wrote Cumming in his diary.

The British government were playing with high stakes: Reilly was being given the modern equivalent of £50,000.

★

Ten days after his meeting with Mansfield Cumming, Reilly – now bearing the codename ST1 (the ST stood for the Stockholm bureau) – was en route to Bolshevik Russia. The plan was for him to enter the country at the port of Archangel and then make his way overland to Moscow, the new capital.

Cumming contacted his operatives in Vologda, 300 miles to the south of Archangel, and informed them of the imminent arrival of Reilly. '[A] Jewish-Jap type,' was how he described him, 'brown eyes very protruding, deeply lined sallow face, may be bearded, height five foot nine inches.'

Cumming added that he 'carries code message of identifica-tion ... ask him what his business is and he will answer: "Diamond Buying." ' This bogus occupation was rendered more believable by the fact that he was carrying sixteen large diamonds.

Reilly was not travelling incognito on the first stage of his journey. Shortly before leaving London, he had been issued with an official business visa by Maxim Litvinoff, the Bolshevik government's sole representative in London. He was one of a small group of émigrés who had remained in England after the two Russian revolutions of 1917. Now, he found himself playing a role similar to that of Robert Bruce Lockhart.

Litvinoff was wholly ignorant of the fact that Reilly was being sent to Russia as a spy. Nor did he know that Reilly detested Lenin's new regime. He took Reilly at face value and believed his claim to be a bona fide businessman who was keen to serve the new Bolshevik government.

Reilly's independent spirit got the better of him before he even arrived at his destination. Instead of disembarking at Archangel, as Cumming had requested, he left the ship at Murmansk. He may have done this because he knew there was a direct train to Petrograd, but it meant that he immedi-ately drew attention to himself. The port was being guarded by a small team of British marines who had been sent to prevent the stockpile of Allied munitions from falling into German hands. These marines promptly arrested Reilly and locked him up in HMS *Glory* until they had completed their investigations.

It was fortunate that another of Cumming's operatives, Stephen Alley, happened to be in Murmansk at the time. The soldiers summoned Alley on board and asked for his opinion of this strange new arrival. 'His passport was very doubtful and his name was spelt REILLI,' wrote Alley. 'This, together with the fact that he was obviously not an Irishman, caused his arrest.'

But Reilly was able to provide proof of his status. He uncorked a bottle of medicine and produced a minuscule message written in code. Alley immediately recognised it as a code of the Secret Intelligence Service and Reilly was released. He was free to continue his onward journey.

Alley himself was travelling in the other direction, returning to London under something of a cloud. He had been fired by Cumming for reasons that remain obscure: Alley would later make the sensational claim that he had been sacked for failing to carry out an order to assassinate Joseph Stalin, already a member of Lenin's inner circle.

'I didn't always obey orders,' he admitted. 'Once I was asked to rub out Stalin. Never did like the chap much . . . [but] the idea of walking into his office and killing him offended me.'

Reilly was supposed to head directly to Moscow. Instead, he took the train to Petrograd in order to make contact with a number of old friends who might prove of use to him. He had not visited the city since 1915 and found that much had changed. War and revolution had left deep scars on the population and an air of decay hung like a stinking pall over the city's imperial boulevards.

'The streets were dirty, reeking, squalid. Houses here and there lay in ruins. No attempt was made to clean the streets, which were strewn with litter and garbage.

When Reilly had visited three years previously, queues for bread had been a fact of daily life. 'Now . . . the bread queues were still there, but there was no food at all.'

More alarming was the presence of the newly founded Cheka, whose officers seemed to lurk on every street corner.

'There was no police except for the secret police,' wrote Reilly, 'which held the country in thrall.' It was testimony to Dzerzhinsky's efficiency as head of the Cheka that it was already a malign presence in everyone's lives, despite having been established just three months earlier.

Reilly took care not to draw attention to himself, for the last thing he wanted was to make his presence known to Lenin's secret police. He made his way to the house of an old friend, Yelena Boyuzhovskaya, hoping that he was not yet being tracked. He confessed to being in a 'cold bath of perspiration' when he finally reached her apartment.

'Watching that I was not observed, I slipped into the house. It might have been a necropolis I entered, and my footfall awoke a thousand echoes.' He was delighted to find Yelena at home; she gave him a friendly welcome.

Reilly had equipped himself for many different eventualities during his time in Russia. He had entered the country on a genuine passport and intended to remain as Sidney Reilly for as long as was possible. But he was also prepared to change his identity and live in disguise if and when that became necessary.

He began perfecting several different personas while staying at Yelena's apartment. He was to have two principal identities, one for Moscow and one for Petrograd. In Petrograd, he would pose as a Levantine merchant named Konstantine Markovich Massino. The Massino name was adopted from his second wife, Nadine: it perfectly suited the polyglot merchant he was pretending to be.

He was so proud of this Massino disguise that he had himself photographed for posterity. With his luxuriant beard and oil-slicked hair he looked the picture of a prosperous Levantine entrepreneur.

In Moscow, Reilly was to adopt a different identity. Here, he became Mr Constantine, a successful Greek businessman who gave his address as 3 Sheremetevsky Lane. This was the home of the actress Dagmara Karozus, the niece of one of his oldest friends.

Reilly knew that the moment of greatest danger would come when he switched from one persona to another. It was imperative that the Cheka should never make the link between Constantine, Massino and Reilly.

He decided that the safest place to change both costume and disguise would be on the train between Petrograd and Moscow. He would leave the former city as Monsieur Massino, decked in his Levantine business garb, and emerge in Moscow as Mr Constantine.

Other British spies would later follow suit, constantly switching identities in order to keep one step ahead of the Cheka.

Reilly spent four weeks in Petrograd, renewing acquaintances with people that could prove of use to him in the future.

'I had many friends in the city,' he wrote. 'I knew where I could go when I arrived there. I knew upwards of a score of people on whose co-operation I could implicitly rely.'

These trusted friends were to provide Reilly with places of refuge when he found himself in trouble: without them, his undercover operations would have been impossible.

Among his most important contacts was the distinguished lawyer, Alexander Grammatikov, a close associate of Lenin. Senior Bolsheviks trusted Grammatikov as one of their most loyal supporters: Lenin himself had intervened to protect him from allegations that he had previously worked for the tsarist secret police.

Unbeknown to the Bolsheviks, these allegations were true. Grammatikov was secretly hostile to the new regime and was prepared to do everything in his power to undermine it.

'[He] gave me a very graphic and terrible account of the position of affairs in Russia,' wrote Reilly. 'The new masters were exercising a regime of blood-thirstiness and horror hardly equalled in history.' Grammatikov expressed his belief that Russia 'was in the hands of the criminal classes and of lunatics released from the asylums.'

Grammatikov was to prove a conduit to some of the most senior Bolsheviks in the new government. He was on particularly friendly terms with General Mikhail Bonch-Bruevich who sat on the Bolshevik's Supreme Military Council. The general was a fellow bibliophile and had recently been in touch with an eye to buying some of Grammatikov's books.

Grammatikov saw this as an opportunity to get Reilly from Petrograd to Moscow, a train journey that could only be undertaken with a special pass. He informed the general that he would bring the books in person, but only if he could have two passes for travel. The general issued the passes without asking any awkward questions. A few days later, on 7 May, Grammatikov and Reilly stepped off the train in Moscow.

★

Sidney Reilly had many flaws in his character but one of the most alarming was his emotional hatred of Bolshevism.

It was true that many of Mansfield Cumming's spies detested Lenin's ideology, and even went so far as to form a Bolshevik Liquidation Society that met regularly to discuss the nature of the threat.

But most of these men viewed Bolshevism with the same clinical detachment that a surgeon might have when operating on a patient's growth: seeing it as something to be cut out.

Reilly was more passionate in his hatred: he found it hard to keep a distance between himself and the enemy. 'Bolshevism,' he wrote, '. . . had been baptised in the blood of the bourgeoisie.' Its leaders were 'criminals, assassins, murderers, gunmen, desperadoes.'

The disgust felt by Reilly towards Russia's new ruling elite was due, in part, to the fact that he was a social and intellectual snob. He viewed society as a hierarchical pyramid in which his own position was extremely close to the top. He particularly disliked the fact that the Bolsheviks had inverted the pyramid, welcoming into their ranks all the most downtrodden elements of society. Often, this was purely on the grounds that their grievance against the old regime was assured. 'A man who could read and write was eyed askance; the illiterates were obviously of the oppressed, and now their time had come.'

Although the placing of so many poorly educated people in positions of authority was distasteful to Reilly, it was to prove of considerable benefit during his first months in Russia. He was travelling around the country with papers that were, as he himself confessed, 'something more than dubious, and which were frequently scanned with an air of great knowingness by Commissars who could neither read nor write.' Even in Moscow, many of the lower ranking commissars were illiterate and unable to tell whether or not the various passes and visas were genuine.

Reilly was appalled by the state of the new Bolshevik capital. It had suffered considerable damage in the street fighting that led to the Bolsheviks seizing control and evidence of the bloodshed still lay all around.

'A city of the damned,' he wrote. 'There had been looting at first, but now there was nothing left to loot. The rabble had been riotous, full of the lust of blood and destruction. Now, the rabble was cowed and frightened, except for the few that were Bolsheviks.'

Reilly was also struck by the pervading sense of fear that was already blighting people's lives. It was as if everyone was undertaking their daily lives in silence, scuttling through back streets in order to avoid the unwanted attentions of the secret police. 'Over all, silent, secret, ferocious, menacing, hung the crimson shadow of the Cheka,' wrote Reilly. 'The new masters were ruling in Russia.'

Reilly had experimented with living under his fake persona while in Petrograd, testing it in the city's squares and markets. He played the role of Massino with aplomb and was confident that he could fool even the most observant of Cheka agents. But he was reticent to shed his real identity just yet. In an act of customary boldness, he first intended to present himself at the Kremlin as Sidney Reilly, an official emissary of the British prime minister. He wanted to see if he could bluff his way into a face-to-face meeting with Lenin.

Exactly what he hoped to achieve by this high-wire strategy remains unclear. He may simply have wanted to see with his own eyes the man he was determined to destroy. He certainly thrived on dangerous games and always relished the idea of entering the lion's den. Whatever his reasons, it was characteristically audacious and self-centred. Reilly informed no one of his plan, not even Mansfield Cumming. He preferred to work as a lone operator, reliant upon no one but himself.

On this occasion, all began well. Reilly marched up to the Kremlin gates in full dress uniform and informed the sentries that he was the personal emissary of Prime Minister David Lloyd George. He demanded to see Lenin.

It must have been a convincing act, for he was immediately granted entry and taken to meet one of Lenin's senior aides. However, no sooner was he inside the building than the Bolshevik officials manning the gates immediately began investigating the identity of this uninvited emissary.

Reilly's presence in Moscow was as yet unknown to the skeleton staff of the British Embassy. Robert Bruce Lockhart was taken by surprise when, at six o'clock that evening, he received a telephone call from Lev Karakhan, the Deputy Commissar for Foreign Affairs.

The commissar had an extraordinary story to recount. 'That afternoon,' he told Lockhart, 'a British officer had walked boldly up to the Kremlin gate and had demanded to see Lenin.'

Karakhan provided Lockhart with a few more details before asking if the man was an impostor. Lockhart was as perplexed as the commissar and asked to know more. He was told that the man's name 'was Relli'.

This meant nothing to Lockhart. 'I nearly blurted out that he must be a Russian masquerading as an Englishman, or else a madman.'

But he knew that Mansfield Cumming was intending to send new agents into Russia and he chose to bite his tongue. 'Bitter experience . . . had taught me to be prepared for almost any surprise and, without betraying my amazement, I told Karachin [sic] that I would inquire into the matter.'

There was only one man who could tell him more. Ernest Boyce was now working as Cumming's principal agent in Moscow and he was also the link man with the main Stockholm bureau. Lockhart was sure that he would know the identity of this mystery individual.

Boyce was nonplussed when Lockhart recounted the story of Reilly's visit to the Kremlin. He calmly replied that, 'the man was a new agent, who had just come out from England.'

Lockhart was furious that he had not been pre-warned and 'blew up in a storm of indignation.' He insisted that Reilly come to the embassy on the following day in order to explain himself.

Reilly agreed to meet with Lockhart but made no apologies for his actions. Indeed, he expressed his surprise that Lockhart was so angry. 'The sheer audacity of the man took my breath away . . .' fumed Lockhart, 'although he was years older than me, I dressed him down like a schoolmaster and threatened to have him sent home.'

Reilly, who was forty-five years of age, was amused to be ticked off by a man fourteen years his junior. He had already warmed to Lockhart and now used his natural charm to placate him. 'He took his wigging humbly but calmly and was so ingenious in his excuses that in the end he made me laugh.'

Lockhart was, by his own admission, captivated by the human chameleon seated opposite him. Reilly was the person he secretly wished to be. 'The man who had thrust himself so dramatically into my life was Sidney Reilly, the mystery man of the British secret service,' he would later write in his memoirs, 'and known today to the outside world as the master spy of Britain.' Reilly's methods, he said, 'were on a grand scale which compelled my imagination.'

Reilly returned to the Kremlin two days later, this time with his friend Grammatikov in tow. He was granted an audience with General Mikhail Bonch-Bruevich, Director of the Bolshevik's Supreme Military Council and 'the brain centre of the entire Bolshevik organisation.'

Reilly was at his loquacious best. He painted himself as a Bolshevik sympathiser, telling the general that he was 'very interested in Bolshevism, the triumph of which had brought me back to Russia.'

This was 'quite true', noted Reilly in his memoirs; although he had obviously not come back to celebrate the triumph.

Reilly was anxious to discover two key pieces of information from the general. First, he wanted to know the state of relations between Germany and Russia now that the two countries were no longer at war. Secondly, he wanted to know if there were any divisions in the Bolshevik leadership.

He soon discovered that the leadership was split from top to bottom on the very issue of peace with Germany. The general himself was furious with the concessions that his fellow Bolsheviks had made to the German high command. Dropping his guard, he confessed to Reilly his fears that the Foreign Commissar, Georgy Chicherin, had been 'bought by the Germans.'

Reilly had been accorded a private glimpse into the rival factions that already existed in the new regime. One of his aims was to push Russia back to war. He now knew that this was not a forlorn hope: several senior Bolshevik commissars wanted to do the same.

Over the weeks to come, Reilly went out of his way to court the general. He quickly saw the benefit of cultivating contacts within the regime, commissars who could provide access to Lenin's inner circle.

'Nobody could be more officious on our behalf than Bruevich,' wrote Reilly. He even supplied Reilly with a pass that enabled him to attend a meeting of the Soviets in the Grand Theatre.

Reilly sent a series of reports to Mansfield Cumming detailing the strengths and weaknesses of the Bolshevik leadership.

He admitted that their seizure of power was almost complete and that they were the 'only real power in Russia.' Yet he also revealed that the political opposition was growing in strength. 'If properly supported,' he wrote, '[it] will finally lead to [the] overthrow of [the] Bolsheviks.'

Reilly proposed a twin-pronged strategy for dealing with Russia. The most immediate objective was to safeguard the stockpiles of Allied weaponry in the ports in Northern Russia. This would necessitate the landing of significant numbers of British troops, something that could only be done with the co-operation of the Bolsheviks.

At the same time, Reilly recommended funding the opposition movement with the long-term aim of toppling Lenin's government. '[It] may mean an expenditure of possibly one million pounds,' he told Cumming, 'and part of this may have to be expended without any real guarantee of ultimate success.'

Reilly never received the one million pounds. It was far too much money for a country still at war. But his advice about safeguarding the Allied weaponry in the White Sea ports certainly struck a chord. There was a growing feeling in Whitehall that military intervention might be the only way of preventing the revolutionary government from playing fast and loose with the stockpile of munitions.

★

Sidney Reilly soon found that he had courted General Bonch-Bruevich rather too assiduously. '[He] intended to be obliging to the point of embarrassment,' he wrote. 'We were permitted to go nowhere unattended . . . wherever we went we were followed.'

This was deeply frustrating for Reilly, who wished to start investigating ways of toppling the Bolshevik regime from within. He could not do this while his every movement was coming under scrutiny. 'It became obvious that, if I were to carry out the mission on which I was engaged, I must disappear.'

In order to shake off the agents on his tail, he decided to pretend that he was returning to Petrograd with his friend, Grammatikov. In reality, Reilly would remain in Moscow under the assumed identity of Mr Constantine while Grammatikov would return to Petrograd with a third person pretending to be Reilly. 'Our only task was to light on someone who bore a passable resemblance to me,' wrote Reilly.

He soon found someone willing to play the game, enabling Grammatikov to leave Moscow by train with the pseudo-Reilly in tow.

The genuine Sidney Reilly watched them leave from a secret vantage point in the station. He was nervous as he saw them board the train, for he knew he had reached a point of no return. There could no longer be any pretence that he was a bona fide businessman eager to help the Bolsheviks. Now, he was embarking on an undercover life outside the law. He risked imprisonment and execution if his deception were to be unmasked.

He also felt anxious for Grammatikov and the pseudo-Reilly. 'I knew that hidden eyes were watching them, that unseen spies were dogging their footsteps.' But their deception was helped by a sudden change of weather. 'The day was squally and my representative with his nose appearing from a voluminous if ragged coat, bore a sufficiently close resemblance to me.'

Reilly spent the rest of the day perfecting his assumed identity, the Greek businessman, Mr Constantine. He decided to embark on a wholly new existence, eschewing all the acquaintances of his former life. The only exception was Grammatikov's trustworthy niece, Dagmara Karozus. A dancer at the Arts Theatre, she offered him lodgings in her apartment.

Reilly was delighted to discover that she shared her flat with a twenty-two-year-old blonde actress named Elizaveta Otten. Elizaveta had two obvious attractions: she was fluent in four languages and had the looks of a movie star. Reilly immediately marked her down as both a potential lover and potential spy.

In the first instance, however, it was Dagmara who proved invaluable. She was a good friend of a girl named Maria Friede, whose brother, Colonel Friede, was the Chief of the Bolshevik Staff.

Colonel Friede gave every appearance of being a loyal Bolshevik. He was so trusted by the regime that he had access to all of the military reports being sent to Moscow. But Colonel Friede's support for the Bolsheviks was a façade. In reality, he despised the new rulers of Russia and was prepared to betray all the secrets of the regime.

'I had one or two surreptitious meetings with Friede,' wrote Reilly, 'and when we were each assured of the others bona fides, he became my most willing collaborator.'

Reilly made the bold claim that every military communiqué of importance now passed through his hands. 'All army orders, all military plans, all confidential documents relating to the army fell within his [Friede's] province and many a copy of a highly confidential document he handled was read in England before the original was in the hands of the officer to whom it was addressed.'

Colonel Friede smuggled the documents to his sister, who then passed them on to Reilly. 'Every morning he [the colonel] would bring home copies of the Bolshevik despatches and orders,' wrote Reilly. 'The following morning, she brought them round to the Cheremeteff Pereulok, where they were duly handed over to me.'

Reilly's claim to have access to so much military information is an extraordinary one, yet it is endorsed by an unlikely source. A senior KGB general named Alexander Orlov was able to examine the Cheka's file on Reilly shortly before defecting to the West. The file bore witness to many of Reilly's claims.

'Sidney Reilly . . . formed a highly efficient network of spies,' wrote Orlov. Members of this network included Colonel Friede, Weneslav Orlovsky, the chief of the Soviet Criminal Police, Major General Zagriazhsky, Major General Politkovsky and an important clerk of the Soviet Executive Committee. All of these men handed him highly sensitive information – information that was then sent to Mansfield Cumming's headquarters in Whitehall Court.

Alexander Orlov expressed a grudging respect for Reilly. '[He] was soon able to supply London with a regular supply of fairly accurate information about the Red Army, the doings of the Soviet government and the political happenings in Russia.'

★

Sidney Reilly was not the only agent sending reports back to London. Mansfield Cumming's Russian network was steadily expanding as the nature of the threat became more apparent. Many of Cumming's agents were working in the shadows, their names unknown even to Robert Bruce Lockhart.

'I was completely in the dark regarding the work of a whole group of British officers and officials for whose presence in

Russia and for whose protection my position with the Bolsheviks was the only guarantee.'

George Hill also spoke of these officers who 'employed their energies against the Bolsheviks. They were working from a different angle; sometimes the lines on which our work ran parallel, sometimes even linked.' He was often unaware of their true identities. Like the 'inner circle' of the Russian bureau that had helped to kill Rasputin, they were moving about in total secrecy.

The growing number of reports received from Russia enabled Cumming to form a clearer picture of the situation inside the country. There was only one man who seemed capable of uniting the disparate anti-Bolshevik factions. This was Boris Savinkov, who had been Minister of War in the months that followed the first revolution.

Ernest Boyce sent a report to Cumming advising him that Savinkov was the horse to back. 'The only fighting organisation is that of Savinkov,' he wrote, 'who, thanks to his organising ability and, it is stated, to Allied support, has been able to gather around him 2,000 men.'

These troops represented the core of his Union for the Defence of Fatherland and Freedom, a private militia whose goal was the destruction of Lenin's government.

Lockhart had also been gathering intelligence on Savinkov. Although he had been sent to Russia as an unofficial representative of the British government, Lockhart's fascination with espionage and intrigue quickly got the better of him. By the spring of 1918, he was engaged in secret discussions with Savinkov's senior advisors.

Lockhart discovered some startling news, which he relayed to London in a telegram marked 'Top Secret'. Savinkov was planning a counter-revolution. Aware that the Allied governments were considering landing troops in Northern Russia, he intended 'to murder all Bolshevik leaders on [the] night of Allies' landing and to form a government which will in reality be a military dictatorship.' Lockhart believed that Savinkov had a real chance of success.

The stage was set for a dramatic power struggle, one which was witnessed by three key people: Arthur Ransome, Robert Bruce Lockhart and Sidney Reilly. All of them were present at a raucous political forum that took place at Moscow's Bolshoi Theatre on 4 July 1918.

The Fifth Congress of the Soviets was intended to provide a platform for political debate, but it presented Lenin with a serious problem. A third of the elected delegates were not Bolsheviks: rather, they were Lenin's political rivals – Socialist Revolutionaries – who stood in total opposition to peace with Germany. Now, they saw their chance to attack Lenin in public.

Robert Bruce Lockhart had been granted permission to attend the Congress as an observer. He arrived early at the theatre and was alarmed to notice that 'every entrance, every corridor, is guarded by troops of Lettish [Latvian] soldiers, armed to the teeth with rifle, pistol and hand-grenade.' These troops were mercenaries, paid by the Bolsheviks to protect them from potential troublemakers.

The initial assault on Lenin was led by the leader of the Social Revolutionary party, Maria Spiridonova. With her neatly coiffed hair and pince-nez, she looked like a prim schoolmistress. But she was a schoolmistress with a ruthless streak. She denounced Lenin in a torrent of invective, accusing him of using the peasantry for his own political ends.

She then swung her gaze around to the peasant delegates in the theatre and harangued them for allowing themselves to be used as political pawns. 'In Lenin's philosophy,' she shouted in her high, shrill voice, 'you are only dung – only manure.'

Her speech provoked wild applause from the auditorium. 'Pandemonium ensues,' wrote Lockhart. 'Brawny peasants stand up in their seats and shake their fists at the Bolsheviks. Trotsky pushes himself forward and tries to speak. He is howled down and his face blenches with impotent rage.'

Arthur Ransome had joined Lockhart in the theatre and was equally impressed by the spectacle unfolding before him. He described Spiridonova as 'looking like a nursery governess rapt into incontrollable frenzy' and he listened enraptured as she 'poured out a rhythmic, screaming denunciation of the Brest-Litovsk treaty.'

Lenin sniffed at the danger: he faced the real risk of losing the support of the crowd. If so, the entire future of his revolution stood in jeopardy. Aware that only his oratory could pacify the rabble, he rose to his feet and delivered a highly skilful response that cast a spell over Spiridonova's supporters. Not for the first time, Ransome and Lockhart were witness to Lenin's hypnotic charm. Like a magician, he was able to transfix the crowd that had been baying for his blood just moments before.

'Gradually,' wrote Lockhart, 'the sheer personality of the man and the overwhelming superiority of his dialectics conquer his audience, who listen spell-bound until the speech ends in a wild outburst of cheering.'

Lockhart knew that he was witness to an unequal political battle. He also knew that the final showdown between these political enemies was certain to have dramatic consequences.

He returned to the Bolshoi Theatre on the following afternoon and was surprised to find not a single Bolshevik in the auditorium. 'The parterre was filled with delegates, but many of the seats on the platform were vacant.' The only politicians present were Social Revolutionaries.

Lockhart remained at the theatre, unaware of the dramatic events that were taking place outside. 'At six o'clock Sidney Reilly came into our box with the news that the theatre was surrounded by troops and that all exits were barred . . . Something had gone wrong.'

The distant boom of artillery, along with close-range firing, added to the growing panic. 'Our apprehension was not diminished by a loud explosion in the corridor above us.'

Reilly conferred with a French agent who had joined them in their box. Both men feared that the Bolsheviks were about to storm the theatre, using hired mercenaries to eradicate their political enemies.

According to Lockhart, both Reilly and the Frenchman 'began to examine their pockets for compromising documents. Some they tore up into tiny pieces and shoved them down the lining of the sofa cushions. Others, doubtless more dangerous, they swallowed.'

A further hour passed before Reilly discovered more about what was taking place. Earlier that afternoon, two Social Revolutionaries had called at the German Embassy and asked for an audience with Ambassador Wilhelm von Mirbach. Invited into his office, they shot the ambassador at point-blank range. Their motive was clear: they hoped to provoke Germany into restarting its offensive against Russia.

The outcome was rather different. The assassination sparked the beginning of a desperate counter-revolution, involving all who were opposed to Lenin's regime. Two thousand armed men clashed with Bolshevik forces in the centre of Moscow and managed to capture the telegraph office. They broadcast an announcement saying that Lenin had been toppled.

Boris Savinkov had been waiting patiently in his stronghold of Yaroslavl, some 150 miles from Moscow. Now, he swung his private militia into action, undaunted by the fact that no Allied forces had landed in Northern Russia.

For the next forty-eight hours, Russia spiralled into turmoil. Lenin was so alarmed that he even considered abandoning the Kremlin. Yet the counter-revolution was abruptly stopped in its tracks. A cool-headed Trotsky called upon the services of his Latvian mercenaries. They fought with great tenacity and succeeded in driving the Social Revolutionary activists from the streets. Once the armed gangs were defeated, the Latvians made their move against the politicians.

'The Social Revolutionary delegates in the Opera House were arrested without even a protest,' wrote Lockhart who, together with Reilly, managed to slip out of the building. 'The revolution, which was conceived in a theatre, ended in the same place.' High drama had finished as farce.

The failed counter-revolution consolidated Lenin's grip on power. The Social Revolutionaries were eliminated as a political threat and Savinkov was forced to flee Russia.

It also further damaged relations between the Bolsheviks and the small group of British diplomats and officers still based in Moscow. Trotsky went so far as to accuse Lockhart of helping to finance and organise Savinkov's rebellion.

Lockhart was indignant. 'This is wholly untrue,' he wrote. 'Never at any time did I furnish Savinkov with financial aid. Still less did I encourage him in any action he took.'

But the fact remained that he had staged a number of meetings with Savinkov's advisors and Trotsky was determined to punish the Western powers. '[He] issued an order that all

French and British officers were to be refused travelling passes on account of their counter-revolutionary activities.'

The crushing of the counter-revolution taught Lockhart and Reilly an important lesson. They realised that it would take far greater guile to topple the Bolshevik regime. Espionage had revealed a great deal about the strengths and weaknesses of the regime. Now, it was time to take more direct action.

CHAPTER SIX

A DOUBLE LIFE

George Hill was alarmed by the increasing hostility of the Bolshevik regime. He had originally hoped to work alongside the new leadership, continuing to train soldiers and pilots for service on the Eastern Front. This would have provided him with the perfect cover for gathering intelligence and passing it back to London.

But now that Russia had pulled out of the war, his work as a military trainer was redundant. The time was fast approaching when the country's revolutionary government would expel all the remaining Westerners. Hill realised that he would have to create an undercover identity and go into hiding if he was to remain in Russia.

To this end, he invented a fictional persona with the name of George Bergmann, a travelling merchant of German-Baltic origin. 'It had taken me long to decide on my new name,' he wrote. 'I hated giving up the name of Hill, and finally decided to get as near to it as I could in German. That is why I chose Berg, the equivalent for Hill, and I tacked on the "mann" to make it quite certain that I was of German descent.'

He had good reason for doing this. 'While my Russian was almost word perfect, I did from time to time make mistakes and it was much better for me to claim that I was a Russian of German extraction born in the Baltic provinces.' It was a clever deceit. Neither the Cheka nor the Bolshevik authorities would be able to verify his family details, because the Baltic provinces were under occupation by the German Army.

Sidney Reilly was able to advise Hill on leading a double life, for he had already experimented with shedding his old identity and adopting a new one, not as an actor playing a part but as a wholly new personality with traits and reflexes that were distinct from those of his former existence. Adopting a fictional persona entailed far more than simply growing a beard and wearing different clothes. To avoid detection by the Cheka, Hill would need to live and breathe his new identity.

Hill and Reilly had first met shortly after the latter's arrival in Moscow. They had bonded immediately. Hill described Reilly as 'a man of action' and clearly one after his own heart. Both men had a talent for languages. Hill noted that Reilly spoke perfect English, Russian, French and German, 'though, curiously enough, with a foreign accent in each case.'

Within days of meeting they had become firm friends and would remain so for years to come.

Reilly explained to Hill that he had already created two fictional personas, Monsieur Massino and Mr Constantine. He now began working on a third, Sigmund Relinsky, with official papers to match. He managed to obtain them from a senior official who was trusted by the Bolsheviks as a staunch party loyalist. He was no such thing. He was yet another functionary who had joined the regime in order to undermine it from within.

The papers identified Rellinsky as a member of the Cheka, a singular coup for Reilly and one of which he was justifiably proud. It would enable him to get inside information from the very heart of the regime. 'It gave me opportunities which were of the greatest value to me,' he later wrote, 'and which I quickly turned to account.'

Reilly's three identities were to give him considerable freedom of movement in both Moscow and Petrograd and he proved adept at switching between them. His principal base in Moscow remained Number 3, Sheremetevsky Lane, where he lived with the two young actresses, an arrangement that would soon lead to romance. But he also made use of several other apartments in Moscow; these became places of refuge in times of danger.

Reilly and Hill met regularly and put considerable thought into how they would work together over the weeks and months to come. They also had discussions with Ernest Boyce, Mansfield Cumming's link man in Moscow, in order to discuss the practicalities of living underground.

It was decided that each of them would perform different and well-defined roles. Reilly's principal task was to oversee political intelligence. '[He] was receiving very excellent information from all possible sources,' wrote Hill. 'I considered that Lt Riley [sic] knew the situation better than any other British officer in Russia.'

He also had better connections with key officials. 'As he also had more delicate threads in his hands, I therefore agreed to . . . leave the political control and our policy in his hands.'

Hill was meanwhile put in charge of coding Reilly's reports, developing his own network of contacts and running a small destruction gang dedicated to destroying soft military targets (such as Bolshevik-controlled depots). More importantly, he was to establish a courier service that would link Moscow and Petrograd with the Stockholm bureau.

The couriers were to prove essential to the successful running of the entire intelligence-gathering operation. It was one thing to acquire secret documents, quite another to transmit the information back to Mansfield Cumming in London. Throughout the First World War, numerous spies had been caught red-handed as they attempted to smuggle documents out of the countries in which they were working. German agents had tried to lessen the risks by finding highly inventive ways of hiding information. Hill was told of one incident in which a spy had concealed documents inside his mouth. It was all to no avail.

'The searcher gently forced the mouth open, took out the top denture and from the roof of the man's mouth a tiny packet of oiled silk, not the thickness of a postage stamp, fell on his tongue. Inside the packet was information in microscopic writing.'

Reilly and Hill knew they were certain to be executed if caught with smuggled documents, especially ones containing intelligence about the Russian military. Hill's priority therefore was to establish a secure courier service that could transport information out of the country.

There were to be two routes, a northern and a southern, and both were fraught with danger. The northern route was to prove the most useful but also the most perilous. It was 500 miles from Moscow to the White Sea port of Archangel and there were numerous Red Army checkpoints on route. The risk of capture was so great that Hill decided to have information sent in duplicate, using two separate couriers travelling on different days.

The southern route was far more circuitous. It passed through areas of Russia that had become virtual battlegrounds between the Bolsheviks and their political opponents. Hill quickly realised that the northern route was the only practical one in such troubled times.

'I originally thought that it would be possible to maintain this northern service with an average of twenty-five couriers,' he wrote. But this proved a woeful miscalculation. 'It was of vital importance to get the messages through, and finally we elaborated a new plan which meant that we would have to employ over a hundred men and replace casualties as they occurred.'

Hill had conceived of one courier covering the entire route from Moscow to the White Sea – a return journey of twenty-two days. A second courier would then take delivery of the information and accompany it to Stockholm where it would be handed to John Scale.

But scarcely had the system been put into operation, in early July 1918, when it was found to have fatal flaws. The couriers repeatedly blundered into danger because they were ignorant of the system of Bolshevik checkpoints in the towns and villages to the north of Moscow.

'Six of our men in all had now been caught and executed,' wrote Hill just weeks after the service had begun. He was fortunate that none of them revealed any secret information before they were killed.

Their deaths led to a rapid change of tactic. Hill now had the idea of establishing a chain service that linked villages across Northern Russia. 'At each of them was a group commander whose duty it was to organise his men, select suitable places for living, procure documents and passports and control the funds for carrying on the work.'

Under the new system, the first courier would travel north from Moscow to the provincial town of Vyatka, where he would hand his documents to the group commander. A second courier would then travel to the next centre, where the process would be repeated. The system worked like clockwork. 'Each courier got to know his particular run, its pitfalls, dangers and dodges, and the strain was much less than would be involved in the entire journey.'

It was nevertheless a hazardous occupation for the individual couriers. 'Every time one of them set out he did so at the risk of his life and the ways in which they overcame difficulties were miraculous.'

Hill placed the courier operation under the direct command of a former Russian cavalry officer known as Agent Z. He was to prove invaluable – 'a patriot, fearless, a first-class judge of men and as good an organiser as I could have wished for.'

Agent Z's job was to prove no less hazardous than Hill's and he needed a secret base in Moscow – a place that he could use to meet with returning couriers and brief them on their next mission. He elected to rent rooms in the house of a lady whose officer husband had been killed in the war.

'For reasons best known to herself,' wrote Hill, 'she had taken to the oldest profession in the world and had been making quite a fair living on the Tverskaya Ulitza, the Bond Street of Moscow.'

Her work as a prostitute – which was known to the authorities and tolerated by them – gave Agent Z the perfect cover. 'What was more natural,' wrote Hill, 'than that unknown men should constantly be coming and going in and out of her flat.' He added that she was absolutely reliable 'and our weary couriers could rest in safety in one of our rooms there.'

This was just one of many addresses available to Hill and his couriers. He had nine other safe houses to be used in times of emergency, including a dacha in the countryside outside

Moscow. This was 'a small wooden country residence forty miles away, which was to be a final retreat and refuge if Moscow grew too hot for me or any of my agents.'

Renting so many properties was expensive but essential. Each one also had to have a cover to mask its real purpose: 'a completely plausible and natural raison d'être for its existence,' wrote Hill.

Hill's own headquarters was to be at an unassuming house on Djatnitakaia Street in one of the poorer quarters of the capital. It was here that he spent much of his time. It was here, too, that he stored his money, kept his papers and directed his espionage operations. He shared the house with three women accomplices, all of them talented and two of them beautiful. It was a happy arrangement for the womanising Hill.

The Bolshevik regime had not yet formally broken diplomatic relations with its former allies. The Western powers were also reluctant to further damage their relations with Russia. Based on the political information being received from Reilly, there was still a faint hope that Trotsky might be persuaded to rekindle the war against Germany.

Hill had no wish to commit himself to an underground existence until such time as relations between the two countries were irrevocably ruptured. He used the intervening weeks to perfect his new identity.

'By this time I was living a double life,' he wrote. 'Part of the day I would be in uniform ... and living as a British officer, the rest of the time I was dressed in mufti, visiting my agents on foot.'

A consummate spy, he knew that success lay in detailed planning. 'I was looking ahead ... beginning to organise secret quarters which would be very necessary for me once the Bolsheviks attempted to restrict my activities.'

★

At the same time as Sidney Reilly and George Hill were preparing to go permanently underground, Robert Bruce Lockhart was struggling to keep open the channels of diplomacy between the British Government and the Bolsheviks. This was proving far from easy: every decision taken by London seemed to widen still further the gulf between the two countries.

The British Government's most pressing concern remained the security of the stockpiles of Allied weaponry in the ports of Northern Russia. Ministers had been hoping that Lenin would permit them to send troops into these ports in order to ensure their safe keeping. But this was not to be: Lenin and Trotsky were vehemently opposed to such a move.

Lockhart discussed the issue with Reilly and Hill. Then, based on the information they were able to give him, he attempted to advise the British Government on matters of policy. But the only consistency to his advice was its inconsistency. One minute he proposed making friendly overtures to the Bolsheviks, the next he was advocating military intervention on a grand scale. The lack of clarity earned him a barrage of criticism from senior officials in London.

'Lockhart's advice has been in a political sense unsound and in a military sense criminally misleading,' fumed Major-General Alfred Knox, who had formerly served at the British Embassy in Petrograd.

The Foreign Office agreed with Knox's assessment, but injected a note of humour into their response. 'Although Mr Lockhart's advice may be bad,' wrote Lord Robert Cecil, 'we cannot be accused of having followed it.' It was fortunate that they were receiving a more accurate assessment of the situation from other sources, notably Arthur Ransome.

The criticism of Lockhart was not without justification, but Whitehall mandarins would have done well to turn the spotlight on themselves. In the months since the Bolshevik revolution, their dealings with Russia had been muddle-headed and inconsistent. They had vacillated, made policy U-turns and failed to inform Lockhart of their thinking. Their most important decision was whether or not to risk the Bolsheviks' wrath by landing troops in the northern ports. Yet even on this issue, there was no clarity.

'For three months London had given no indication of its policy or policies,' wrote Lockhart. It was scarcely surprising that he found it impossible to do his job.

He responded to their criticism of him with a withering assessment of their own conduct. 'There was no British policy, unless seven different policies can be called a policy.'

Even Lenin agreed with Lockhart. 'Your Lloyd George,' he said, 'is like a man playing roulette and scattering chips on every number.'

In such troubled times, Lockhart sought solace in women. He had fallen head over heels in love with the dazzlingly seductive Maria Zakrveskia, an old-style aristocrat possessed with charm, wit and unconventional good looks. Moura – that was what everyone called her – had previously been married to Count von Benckendorff, the Tsarist ambassador to London. The count's murder at the hands of the Bolsheviks had left her single. Now, she was to find herself the focus of Lockhart's most ardent devotions.

He confessed himself to be spellbound by Moura's vitality, and he lavished her with presents and praise. 'Into my life something had entered which was stronger than any other tie, stronger than life itself.'

He vowed never to be parted from his beloved Moura, who became a living obsession. 'Where she loved, there was her world,' he wrote, 'and her philosophy of life had made her mistress of all the consequences.' So fervent was his ardour that he flaunted Moura in public and did little to conceal their affair from the prying eyes of the Cheka.

Lockhart had originally been sent to Moscow as a semi-official agent of the British government. His diplomatic accreditation had given him access to Lenin, Trotsky and other senior Bolsheviks. But the rumour that he had been involved in Savinkov's counter-revolution, coupled with the increasing likelihood of Allied intervention in Northern Russia, had earned him the mistrust of the new regime.

'The sands were running out,' wrote Lockhart of the increasingly bleak political situation. 'We were drifting rapidly towards the inevitable tragedy.'

That tragedy moved one step nearer on the evening of 17 July 1918, eight months after the revolution, when Lockhart became the first Westerner to learn of the brutal execution of Tsar Nicholas II, his wife the tsarina, and all of their children. News of the killings was immediately conveyed to London, where it caused shock and outrage. The attitude of the Bolshevik government made the crime all the more heinous in the eyes of British ministers.

'There was no question of disapproval or disavowal,' wrote Lockhart. 'In its leading articles, the Bolshevik press did everything it could to justify the murder and reviled the tsar as a tyrant and a butcher.'

★

While Allied governments digested news of the tsar's execution, a game of diplomatic brinkmanship was being played out in the northern town of Vologda. It only served to reinforce Lockhart's opinion that real danger was just around the corner.

Vologda, which lay some 430 miles to the north of Moscow, was the town to which many diplomats had retreated when the threat of the advancing German Army overrunning Moscow and Petrograd had been at its height. Lockhart was one of the few who had been courageous enough to remain.

'As a connecting link with Moscow,' he wrote, 'it [Vologda] was as useless as the North Pole.'

Most diplomats had nevertheless remained there in splendid isolation, keeping themselves aloof from the dangers of Moscow. Their number included the ambassadors of America and France as well as the Italian *chargé d'affaires*. To Lockhart, their self-imposed exile was little short of preposterous. 'It was as if three foreign Ambassadors were trying to advise their governments on an English cabinet crisis from a village in the Hebrides.'

They showed no enthusiasm for meeting the Bolshevik rulers and even less interest in trying to understand the nature of the threat that the new regime posed to the world. They preferred to remain in Vologda, doing nothing except eating, drinking and playing poker.

The leader of this indolent band was David Francis, the octogenarian American ambassador. 'Knowledge of Russian politics he had none,' wrote Lockhart. 'To do him justice, he made no pretence of professing to understand the situation.'

His ignorance was matched by that of the Brazilian representative, whose attitude would have been comical had the situation not been so dangerous. 'He had reduced the art of diplomacy to a simple formula: do nothing and promotion and honours are certain.'

He slept all day, played poker all night and fulfilled a vow made several years earlier never to do a stroke of work. 'From that moment,' noted Lockhart in characteristically laconic tone, 'his diplomatic career had been one long triumph and his promotion had been as regular as clockwork.' He added that 'the formula is not so absurd as the layman may imagine. It has stood more than one British diplomat in good stead.'

Into this far-flung ambassadorial Arcadia now strutted Karl Radek, 'the Bolshevik Puck', as Lockhart described him. Employing his customary tactics of bluster and grit, he ordered all the diplomats to return to Moscow.

'He appeared before the Ambassadors with his revolver,' wrote Lockhart. 'He argued, cajoled and even threatened.' But the ambassadors refused to budge, for they mistrusted the intentions of the Bolsheviks.

In this, at least, they showed wisdom. Lenin and Trotsky were convinced that the Allies were going to land a significant number of troops in Northern Russia. 'Realising that intervention was now inevitable,' wrote Lockhart, 'they desired to hold the Ambassadors in Moscow as hostages.'

Karl Radek had not travelled alone to Vologda: he had been accompanied by Arthur Ransome. As a trusted confidant of the Bolsheviks, Ransome had been asked to act as Radek's 'interpreter and referee'.

Ransome was naïve to have agreed to this, for it put him on a collision course with the ambassadors. He told them it was ridiculous to remain in Vologda and gave the poker-loving American ambassador a curt dressing down.

He also criticised the British *chargé d'affaires*, Sir Francis Lindley, for refusing to leave the safety of Vologda and return to the capital. Lindley could hardly believe what he was hearing. 'You don't seem to realise,' he hissed to Ransome, 'that these people are our enemies.'

An ill-timed telegram from Foreign Commissar Georgy Chicherin only increased the fears of the ambassadors. The commissar warned them that their lives would be in grave danger unless they immediately returned to Moscow. His words had quite the opposite effect. On 25 July, all of the foreign diplomats in Vologda boarded a train to Archangel and left Bolshevik Russia forever.

In the aftermath of their departure, Ransome once again found himself accused of having pro-Bolshevik sympathies. Major-General Knox was the most outspoken about Ransome's intimacy with the Bolshevik leaders: on one occasion, he went so far as to say that he should be 'shot like a dog.'

But Ransome had personal reasons for fearing a rupture of relations with Moscow. It was certain to lead to his expulsion from the country, along with the other remaining Westerners, and this would have serious ramifications on his relationship with Evgenia. The two of them could not marry, for Ransome already had a wife, and Evgenia (as his mistress) was unlikely to be granted an entry visa for Britain. Yet she faced a potentially dangerous situation if she remained in Moscow. Ransome feared that the Allied powers would march on Moscow and purge Russia of its Bolshevik masters. If so, Evgenia would be caught in the maelstrom.

Ransome had spent a considerable amount of time trying to persuade Evgenia to leave Russia with him in the event of the Allies landing troops in Archangel. Evgenia had at first demurred, but Ransome eventually secured her agreement. He then went directly to Lockhart and asked for assistance in getting Evgenia the necessary papers.

Lockhart proved as obliging as ever. He sent a telegram to the Foreign Office in London asking for help. 'A very useful lady, who has worked here in an extremely confidential position in a government office desires to give up her present position,' he wrote.

He requested permission to provide her with all the necessary papers. 'She has been of the greatest service to me and is anxious to establish herself in Stockholm where she would be at the centre of information regarding underground agitation in Russia.'

This would only be possible with the assistance of the British government. 'In order to enable her to leave secretly, I wish to have authority to put her to Mr Ransome's passport as his wife and facilitate her departure via Murmansk.'

When MI5 learned of Lockhart's request they were totally against it. They feared that Evgenia and Ransome would return to England and stoke revolutionary trouble on home soil. But Arthur Balfour, the Foreign Secretary, was fully aware of the services that the two of them had performed. He overrode MI5's concerns and Lockhart was sanctioned to supply Evgenia with the necessary papers.

With international tensions at boiling point, Ransome decided to take no chances. As well as equipping himself and Evgenia with English papers, he persuaded his friends in the Bolshevik government to issue him with a Soviet passport as well. He paid a high price for this document: he was charged with delivering three million roubles in cash to the Bolshevik's International Bureau in Sweden.

Ransome kept quiet about the smuggling operation, hoping that no one would discover what he had agreed to do. But it was soon leaked to an unnamed British agent who found himself in the uncomfortable position of having to report on one of his own.

An internal telegram reported that Ransome was rumoured to be leaving Russia with 'a large amount of Russian Government money and to be travelling with Bolshevik passport.'

Evgenia was to travel separately from her English lover, leaving the country in the company of a Bolshevik mission to Berlin. From here she intended to travel to Stockholm in order to be reunited with him.

Ransome paid a final visit to Lockhart before leaving the country. '[He] told us that the show was over,' wrote Lockhart. A dangerous course was being plotted, and Soviet Russia was now on a direct collision course with the Western democracies.

Ransome's departure came in the nick of time. After a brief stop in Petrograd at the beginning of August, he made his way to the border with Finland and soon arrived in Helsingfors. By the time he was safely in the Finnish capital, all hell had broken loose in Archangel. Allied forces had landed in the port and wild stories began to circulate about the size of the invasion.

'For several days the city was prey to rumour,' wrote Lockhart. 'The Allies had landed in strong force. Some stories put the figure at 100,000.'

There were also rumours that the Japanese had landed seven divisions in the Far East and were even now marching through Siberia.

'The confusion was indescribable,' recalled Lockhart. He found it impossible to get accurate information on the landings and paid a visit on Oliver Wardrop, one of the few diplomats who had not left the country. It was while the two men were chatting that even more dramatic events unfolded.

'The Consulate General was surrounded by an armed band,' wrote Lockhart. 'It was composed of agents of the Cheka.

They sealed up everything, and everyone in the building was put under arrest except Hicks and myself.'

The Cheka foolishly neglected to search the top rooms of the consulate, much to Lockhart's relief. 'While the Cheka agents were cross-examining our Consular officials downstairs, our intelligence officers were busy engaged in burning their ciphers and other compromising documents upstairs. Clouds of smoke belched from the chimneys and penetrated even downstairs, but, although it was summer, the Cheka gentlemen noticed nothing untoward in this holocaust.'

In all, some two hundred Allied nationals were arrested by the Cheka and interned as hostages. Lockhart escaped imprisonment. Trotsky had given him a special *laissez-passer* when he first arrived in Russia and for the time being this still held good. He was free to travel around Moscow unmolested.

American nationals were also spared, as it was not yet known that their forces had taken part in the Allied landings.

There were a small number of others who had also avoided arrest. Sidney Reilly remained a free man, albeit one with an assumed name and fake papers. George Hill was also still at large. Just a few weeks earlier, he had asked Karl Radek what would happen if the Allies landed troops in Russia.

Radek was full of playful jest, but his humour was characteristically chilling. He told Hill that he would either be incarcerated or executed 'to show Bolshevik contempt for officers of a capitalist power.'

Hill was appalled. 'The joke was far too near probability for me to enter into a discussion with any feeling of enjoyment.'

For months, he had been planning the moment when he would go underground. Now, the time had come.

CHAPTER SEVEN

MISSION TO TASHKENT

wo thousand miles to the south-east of Moscow, amid the lonely peaks of the Pamir Mountains, a small party of men was winding a slow passage across high-altitude glaciers and icy scree.

They included three intrepid Englishmen, each of whom was well qualified for the task ahead. Frederick Bailey was an officer serving with the Indian Political Department, an elite band dedicated to the protection of British India. He was a distinguished explorer and recipient of the Royal Geographical Society's coveted gold explorers' medal. He had also served as a Tibetan-speaking subaltern in Sir Francis Younghusband's 1904 invasion of Tibet. Shot at Flanders and again at Gallipoli, he was deemed far too valuable to be returned to the battlefield for a third time. His exceptional linguistic skill saw him transferred to India where he was singled out for a highly unusual mission that would take him deep into Bolshevik-controlled Central Asia. 'An absolutely first class man,' was how the viceroy described Bailey.

Accompanying him across the Pamir Mountains was Percy Etherton, a tough-nosed adventurer with movie-star looks and a libido to match. His piercing eyes betrayed a hint of the Machiavellian streak that would soon be felt by the many Bolsheviks who crossed his path.

Before the war, Etherton had made a daring adventure through the heart of Central Asia, resulting in a book called *Across the Roof of the World*. His energy, dynamism and clinical ruthlessness – coupled with his experience with the Indian Army's frontier regiment – had brought him to the attention of his superiors. Now he was being posted to Kashgar where he was ostensibly going to be working as the British consul. But he was also to be engaged in espionage, gathering intelligence on the Bolsheviks.

The third member of the party was Major Stewart Blacker who had previously served with the Indian Army's elite Corps of Guides. In common with his two colleagues, he had also made voyages deep into the barren hinterland of Central Asia.

These three adventurers were being sent into the farthest flung regions of the former Russian Empire, accompanied by a group of coolies to carry their baggage.

Their mission had been organised by the government of India, which had recently received news that Bolshevism was rapidly spreading across the lands that lay to the north of India. Russian Turkestan was said to have been the most recent place to have fallen victim to Lenin's Bolshevik revolution.

Even more alarming were the rumours that the 190,000 Austrian and German prisoners of war, held in Central Asia after their capture on the Eastern Front, were being trained and drafted into the Red Army.

This set alarm bells ringing in British India. The frontier of Turkestan was separated from the Raj by a mere ten-mile wide sliver of Afghanistan which ran along the border. Lenin's

Bolshevik Army could, if it wished, be inside India within a few hours.

Prime Minister Lloyd George publicly confessed to the British Government's absolute ignorance as to the extent of Bolshevik rule in Russia's more remote regions. When he attempted to answer a parliamentary question on the subject, he could do nothing more than pose a string of rhetorical questions: 'What is the government of the Ukraine?' he asked. 'What is the government of Georgia? What is the government when you come to Baku? What is the government in the northern part of the Caucasus? What is the government in any town and city of the Don? What is the government, I will not say in Siberia, but in any city of Siberia?'

The viceroy of India was equally ignorant as to what was taking place on the other side of the Raj's northern border. A confidential memo revealed the total absence of reliable intelligence. 'We are without the means of obtaining prompt and reliable reports on what goes on in Turkestan. We do not know what party is in the ascendant.'

The despatch of a mission to Turkestan had been discussed on several occasions over the previous months. The first question was whether it should be official or unofficial: both options carried considerable risks. There was a further debate over whether or not to send a team of Indian soldiers to accompany the mission. The viceroy felt that sending troops 'would excite the liveliest suspicions in Afghanistan and might upset the whole situation.' After much discussion, the project was deemed so risky that it was quietly shelved.

But now, as the need for information became an imperative, it was decided to send Frederick Bailey and Stewart Blacker to Tashkent and Percy Etherton to Kashgar. They were to leave India immediately.

Mansfield Cumming's geographical remit did not extend to Russia's vast underbelly. Operations in Central Asia were initially orchestrated by the Department of Criminal Intelligence, which was based in Simla and answerable to the government of India. They, in turn, reported to Indian Political Intelligence in London.

But the spread of Bolshevism was clearly a concern that overlapped with Mansfield Cumming's operations and this increasingly led to the sharing of intelligence. Cumming's men in New York and Berlin had already worked in collaboration with their colleagues in India, exchanging information on the activities of Indian subversives. Now, there was to be an ever-closer liaison over the threat posed by Bolshevism.

It was most unfortunate that Cumming was not involved in planning the mission to Tashkent. He, more than anyone else, knew that a reliable support network was of vital importance if it was to have any hope of success. Yet Bailey and Blacker were being sent deep into Bolshevik Turkestan with no couriers or backup team. If things went wrong, they would be very much on their own.

The mission was also marred by the lack of a clear goal. Bailey's briefing was extremely vague and only served to highlight the woeful ignorance as to what was taking place in Turkestan. 'No one quite knew what a Bolshevik was or what were his aims and objects,' wrote Bailey. 'It seemed that it would be useful to go and see them, and find out what sort of people they were and to try to persuade them to continue the war against Germany.'

This, then, was the ostensible aim of the expedition: Bailey was being sent on a fact-finding mission as an accredited envoy of British India. But if things went wrong, or if he found himself in trouble, he was to be left to his own devices. There was no Plan B.

Bailey and his men made a gruelling crossing of the high valleys of the Hunza region and then traversed the barren peaks of the Pamir Mountains. A blizzard almost swept them away near the beginning of their hike and they encountered considerable difficulty crossing the heavily fissured Passu Glacier. But they eventually descended onto the barren Sinkiang plateau and headed for Kashgar, a sun-baked caravan city in Chinese-controlled Turkestan.

The three adventurers were given a hearty welcome by the outgoing consul, Sir George Macartney; the grand consulate dinners were particularly welcome after their six-week journey from Srinagar. The consulate's cellar of imported wines was soon consumed but there was plenty of locally distilled fire-water to enliven the evenings.

'After dinner,' wrote Bailey, 'we would play the gramophone and dance Russian dances or gamble mildly at *Deviatka* in depreciated Russian currency.'

Kashgar marked the end of the journey for Percy Etherton. He was to remain in the city, sending intelligence back to Delhi and thence to London. But he would also find himself engaged in a lonely and highly personal war against the Bolsheviks, or 'Red Scum' as he called them. He would become so reviled inside Soviet Russia that he would end up with a price on his head.

Bailey and Blacker remained in Kashgar for six weeks. Then, in the third week of July, they set off on an arduous overland journey to Tashkent. They were accompanied by a Russian couple named Mr and Mrs Stephanovich who were returning to Turkestan after a tour of duty in Kashgar's Russian consulate.

It took a week to reach the frontier of Russian-controlled Turkestan, their journey fortified by fermented mare's milk. They had been expecting difficulties at the border and were surprised to receive a warm welcome from the Russian guards.

'They were certainly not in sympathy with the Bolsheviks,' wrote Bailey, 'and were living in a state of great uncertainty.'

It was another fortnight's journey to Tashkent, during which time their mission became public knowledge. 'The most fantastic rumours about our party had preceded us,' wrote Bailey. 'We were the vanguard of a force of twelve thousand men sent from India to capture Ferghana and Turkestan [and] our servants were all sepoys in disguise.'

The journey proved tough going: there was a biting chill at night and the ground was frozen to iron, even though it was midsummer. Amid the patches of wind-dried snow, Bailey noticed 'the bones of countless animals and even of some men who had lost their lives on this dangerous road.'

They made frequent stops en route, for Bailey had brought his butterfly net and he now took the opportunity to pursue his passion for collecting rare specimens. Clouds of them rose from the grassland as they passed and he managed to capture more than a hundred different types, including a magnificent Himalayan Parnassus.

At one point the men met their first Bolshevik commissars, 'picturesque fellows in Russian blouses and top boots, with a revolver conspicuously worn in the belt. They were evidently out to impress us but failed entirely to do so.'

After two weeks on the road, Bailey and Blacker finally arrived in Tashkent. They checked into the Regina Hotel (the best in town) and began preparing their visit to the Tashkent Foreign Office. Their coolies meanwhile set off on the long route back to India.

Bailey was hoping to open a dialogue with the new regime but was soon disabused of this notion. The revolutionary apparatchiks who had seized control of the city were ill educated and entirely lacking in government experience. Just a few months earlier, they had been mechanics and oilers on the railways. Now, they held the reins of power.

Not everything had fallen prey to the revolution. The city's bars and outdoor brasseries were still open for business and would spring into life in the late afternoon sunshine. Each had its own *thé dansant* orchestra comprised of Austrian prisoners of war who were being held in semi-freedom in this remote corner of the former Russian Empire. They played their violins in the cool shade of the mulberry trees.

Bailey and Blacker frequented the Chashka Chai (Cup of Tea) and soon became known to the band. 'They used to break off their tune and play "Tipperary" as we entered,' wrote Bailey. The local cinema provided another distraction. When the two Englishmen arrived in town, it was showing *The Prisoner of Zenda*.

Bailey learned that Tashkent's road and rail links with Moscow had been cut by fighting, leaving the city all but isolated from the outside world. He also discovered that a few European residents had been left adrift by the unrest that had followed the revolution.

Among those trapped in the city were an English couple, Mr and Mrs Edward, and an elderly English widow known as Madame Quatts. She had once been governess to the children of General Konstantin von Kaufman, the first governor-general of Russian Turkestan, but had almost forgotten her English. '[She] spoke with hesitation and made mistakes in words and grammar but with this had no trace of a foreign accent,' wrote Bailey.

Tashkent was also home to Roger Tredwell, the beleaguered American consul-general. Tredwell shared lodgings with a local family who employed an eccentric Irish governess, Miss Houston. From her, Bailey heard colourful stories of various wandering travellers and oddballs. He also had his own encounters with local eccentrics, including an Englishman passing through Turkestan with a troupe of performing elephants. Who he was, and what happened to him, Bailey was unable to discover.

It was clear that the revolution was causing severe hardship to the inhabitants of Tashkent. The markets were devoid of fruit and vegetables and the number of unemployed was rising by the week. More serious was the fact that the city's professional class had been eliminated in the economic catastrophe that had followed the revolution.

'The workmen were running things badly and dishonestly,' wrote Bailey. They stuck rigidly to the new ideology 'and had no hesitation in forbidding many of the things they professed to be fighting for, especially for example freedom of the press and freedom of public meeting.'

Bailey had been charged with sending information about the political situation back to Simla. But communication was to prove far from easy, for the Bolshevik authorities controlled the only telegraph office in Tashkent. The lack of a courier system, like the one developed by Reilly and Hill, was to cause serious difficulties.

Bailey had intended to use Blacker's motorcycle to relay messages across the plains of Turkestan and then forward the information over the Pamirs using carrier pigeons. Blacker overcame the shortage of petrol by running his bike on vodka, but the supply of pigeons had been exhausted before they had even reached Tashkent. '[They] mostly served to fatten the beautiful falcons of the Hunza Valley,' wrote Bailey.

Undaunted, he endeavoured to discover more about the intentions of Tashkent's Bolshevik regime by paying a visit to Commissar Damagatsky, one of the most senior functionaries in the city. The meeting got off to a bad start. Unbeknown to Bailey, a battalion of British troops based in North-East Persia had recently clashed with Bolshevik forces on the other side of the border. The British had inflicted considerable loss of life. Commissar Damagatsky was fuming with anger and demanded an explanation.

Bailey was entirely ignorant of the attack: he suggested that the commissar's information was faulty and asked him how he could be so sure that the troops were British.

'The answer was simple and flattering,' wrote Bailey. 'The artillery was good, far better than anything in Russia.' The commissar added that there was English writing on the shells and said that if Bailey refused to believe him, he would 'get a prisoner to convince me.'

Damagatsky was deeply suspicious of these two uninvited Englishmen and remained unconvinced that they were official representatives of British India. It didn't help matters that when he asked to see their credentials, he was told that they weren't carrying any. 'When we were unable to produce the much desired papers, we were accused of being spies.'

Bailey acted with studied indifference. He repeatedly insisted that he was on an official mission and he also asked Damagatsky for assurances the 190,000 Austrian and German prisoners of war in Turkestan would be properly controlled. This was not forthcoming. Indeed, Bailey soon discovered that at least one contingent of soldiers was being prepared for enrolment in the Red Army.

'Under the command of an ex-sergeant-major with a fierce moustache, a detachment of about sixty Germans could be seen at the big parades in Tashkent, smartly dressed in black leather.' Bailey watched them saluting and drilling and singing 'The Internationale' as they marched.

He was disquieted by the sight. These troops could easily have marched across the sliver of Northern Afghanistan and into India, 'with possibly grave effects for us on the course of the war.'

Bailey was even more alarmed when Commissar Damagatsky openly admitted that this small contingent was merely the precursor to a much larger force. 'It was the hope of the government,' he told Bailey, 'to revolutionise them and enrol them in the Red Army.'

Bailey next tackled the issue of Turkestan's stockpile of cotton, an essential component in the production of war munitions. He asked that the supplies be adequately guarded to prevent their export to Germany.

Damagatsky gave a dismissive wave of his hand and said 'that the war among the imperialist powers was of no great concern to Soviet Russia and anyone could have the cotton who would pay for it and take it away.'

Bailey's final demand was that Tashkent should stop all attempts to encourage Islamic rebellion against British India. Lenin's call for the Indians to rise up against the British had been a cause of serious alarm, particularly given the unrest in the overwhelmingly Islamic North-West Frontier province.

'This danger seemed to us, at the time, not only to be very real and of immediate urgency, but also we envisaged the danger of awkward complications after the war,' wrote Bailey.

On this issue, at least, Damagatsky offered some crumbs of comfort. Religious propaganda, he said, was contrary to the policy of the Soviet Government. He professed no interest in fomenting Islamic rebellion.

As the inconclusive meeting drew to a close, Bailey feared that he and Blacker would be arrested as spies. 'Internment for any length of time would, as I realised later, have meant almost certain death,' he wrote.

The only place they could be held was the city prison where survival was a matter of chance. 'A party of drunken soldiers would go to the gaol, take people out and shoot them. Once we were walking down the street, we heard cries and shots from a house. One of these murders was being perpetrated.'

Bailey added that 'slightly more justifiable executions took place when the gaol was full and it was necessary to make room.'

In the event, Damagatsky chose to bide his time. He allowed Bailey and Blacker to walk free from the Commissariat of Foreign Affairs. But they knew they were marked men. 'We were followed everywhere by spies and when we returned home at night after going to a concert or cinema, electric torches flashed mysterious signals and bells were rung to report our safe arrival. The police made frequent searches by day and night and once came to us at two o'clock in the morning.'

It was clear that their lives would be in continued danger if they remained in Tashkent. Sooner or later they would be arrested and quite possibly be killed. Yet flight from the city was also fraught with difficulty. The Cheka was already viewing them as valuable hostages and Bailey knew that Cheka agents would be certain to swoop the moment they attempted to flee.

With so many factors weighing against them, Bailey and Blacker could do little but sit tight. But they had already realised that the time would soon come when they would have to disappear from view.

Then, like Mansfield Cumming's agents in Moscow and Petrograd, they could re-emerge as completely different people.

CHAPTER EIGHT

GOING UNDERGROUND

Sidney Reilly and George Hill found Moscow increasingly dangerous in the days that followed the landing of Allied forces in Northern Russia.

The Bolshevik leadership was incensed by what had taken place and was already calling it an invasion. In reality, it was not an invasion at all. A mere 1,500 men had been put ashore and their goal was to secure the stockpiles of unused weaponry, not to attack the Bolsheviks. Yet it had led to a swift reaction from Lenin and Trotsky. The raid on the Western consulates on the day of the landings was a clear sign that Bolshevik Russia was now a hostile power.

George Hill had been preparing to go underground for many months. Yet when the time finally came, he felt a sudden panic. 'I had a momentary but first-class attack of nerves,' he wrote. 'In half an hour, I should be a spy outside the law with no redress if caught, just a summary trial and then up against a wall.'

He took a few deep breaths to calm himself down. Then, after convincing himself that he was doing the right thing, he prepared to leave his flat and begin a wholly new life, taking a last glance at the treasured possessions he was leaving behind: 'My hat and sword, my photographs and favourite books, one or two prized decorations, various small things I had bought to take back to England . . .'

He abandoned his Mauser and his Webley-Scott revolvers, reasoning that they would serve him no purpose. 'Nine times out of ten, a revolver is of no earthly use and will seldom get a man out of the tight corner.' He much preferred his trusty swordstick, which he had wielded to deadly effect several months earlier.

The process of adopting his new identity was done in two stages. First, he left his apartment and went to a secure house that he had rented several months previously. 'I went out by a different entrance from the one I had used in entering, casually glanced round to see that I was not being followed, stepped into a cab and drove to the other end of Moscow.'

Once arrived, he changed into a new set of clothes. These had been made to measure and delivered to the safe house some days earlier. 'There were three or four dark blue hessian shirts which buttoned at the neck, some linen underclothing, a pair of cheap ready made black trousers, peasant-made socks such as were on sale on the stalls in the market, a second-hand pair of top-boots and a peak cap which had already been well used.'

Hill dressed hastily and then prepared to send his former identity up in smoke. 'I put my English suit, underclothing, tie, socks and boots into the stove; I laid a match to the kindling wood and shut the stove door. Ten minutes later, my London clothes were burnt.'

His chief courier, Agent Z, arrived shortly afterwards with a new set of identity papers complete with stamps and visas for added authenticity. He also brought a cheap mackintosh, a hundred Russian cigarettes and the latest reports from various agents, 'which I put into the bag and then left the flat as George Bergmann.' The switch of identities was complete: George Hill had ceased to exist.

He made his way to one of the poorer quarters of town, south of the Moscow River, to another of the flats he had rented. Here, he met up with his secretary, Evelyn, 'who was *au courant* with all the work I had been doing.' Evelyn was partly English, but she had been educated in Russia and spoke both languages fluently, as well as German, French and Italian.

'We had decided that our best chance of success was to become people of the lower middle class and to live an entirely double life.' Evelyn had managed to get a job as a teacher in one of the new Bolshevik-run schools. 'This gave her the necessary papers and also the very coveted ration cards from the Bolshevik organisation; coveted because without cards or enormous sums of money, it was impossible to get food.'

Hill also managed to get employment, working as a film developer in a cinematograph studio. This entitled him to ration cards as well, and it brought another unexpected advantage. He got to see the day's newsreels before the general public, allowing him to stay one step ahead of the game.

Hill hired the services of two girls of English birth but Russian upbringing named Sally and Annie. They were to help in the running of his underground cell. Hill immediately took a shine to Sally. 'One of the most beautiful girls I have ever seen,' he wrote. 'She had raven-black hair, a peach-like complexion and the most sensitive, pale, transparent hands.' Annie, by contrast, had no share in her sister's good looks. She was dumpy but merry – 'a good-natured soul.'

Annie was to prove a key member of the team. Her cover was to be that of a dressmaker, in which guise she was able to provide Hill and his couriers with costumes. But she also took orders from the wider public. It was a clever ruse. 'At a dressmaking establishment it was only natural that there would be people coming and going.' Secret information could be brought to the apartment and forwarded to couriers with very little suspicion.

They soon needed another person to help with the running of messages. After much consideration, they invited a trusted young Russian orphan girl named Vi to join the team. Hill found her no less alluring than Sally. '[She] was a tall blonde with blue eyes and the most appealing ways and time proved that she was also full of pluck.'

Faced with the choice of flirting with Sally or Vi, he was initially tempted by the latter, even though she had just turned seventeen. 'Dear Vi . . .' he wrote, 'she made many a long hour pass quickly for me and at one time we gravely discussed having an affair.' But Hill was concerned by her extreme youth and decided to desist. Besides, he first needed to get his espionage operations up and running.

Hill and the four girls soon slipped into a routine, always taking extreme care not to arouse suspicions. The flat where they lived had been carefully chosen: it was a low, single-storey block that contained many other apartments. 'It had two great advantages,' wrote Hill, 'a front door opened on the street and a back door led out into a large yard shared by the other houses around it.'

The only problem – common to all shared blocks – was the presence of a *dvornik* or porter. These *dvorniks* were on the payroll of the Cheka and 'pried into the doings and sayings of the people living in every block.'

The girls had already hatched a story about taking in a lodger who was suffering from malaria. '[This] was framed with the purpose of giving me time to grow a beard,' wrote Hill. His face was well known in Moscow and it was important for him to radically alter his appearance.

The beard growing proved a torture. 'First of all, the beastly thing was of a brilliant red colour . . . then, as the hair sprouted they turned round and bit my face and covered my skin with a sore and irritable rash.' It took a bottle of fine old brandy to restore his humour.

Hill soon found himself with a great deal of work. He had made many contacts during his months in Russia and now had reliable anti-Bolshevik agents working for him on many fronts, particularly in towns and villages where White Russian soldiers were attacking troops of the Red Army. Hill knew that the Western Allies were considering taking a more offensive role against the Bolshevik government. But before they could land more troops, accurate military information was an imperative. This is where Hill's men proved their worth.

'[They] had to find out the best roads, know all of the traps, take stock of the disposition of the Soviet troops, guns, food stores, dumps and morale of the army . . . [and] if necessary, they were also to occupy themselves with gentle sabotage.'

Some of these sabotage operations were directed against the German Army in the Ukraine; others targeted the Red Army. They were never as 'gentle' as Hill suggested. He personally took part in one of these operations, blowing up an industrial gasworks with homemade explosives.

'There was a blinding flash followed by a terrific explosion and then a deadly silence. We staggered away. For hours afterwards, my nose bled most violently and nothing I did would stop it.'

His attacks on German targets were so successful that they prompted an attempt on his life. He was parking his car next to a hangar at the Moscow Aviation Park when a German hit-man stepped from the shadows and tossed a grenade at his feet.

It failed to explode and Hill was quick to respond. He caught his would-be assassin and dashed a brick into his face, leaving him severely wounded. 'I never knew whether I had killed him or not,' wrote Hill, 'but at the time I sincerely hoped I had.'

Hill gathered a great deal of information on the fighting abilities of the White Armies that were organising resistance to the Bolsheviks. His reports made for alarming reading, for he found them to be disunited and poorly led.

'Lack of order, supplies, ammunition, material were constantly being reported and internal strife was rumoured,' he warned in a coded memo to London.

Forwarding military intelligence was a risky business and Hill had to act with prudence. Every document had to be coded and then typed up by one of the girls using a typewriter that had been smuggled into the apartment. 'Two short floorboards had been taken up along the inner wall of the living room and there the typewriter and codes were housed.'

Whenever Hill was coding the military documents, he kept a little bottle of petrol to hand. 'If the house was suddenly raided, messages and codes were to be pitched into the typewriter cover, the petrol poured over them and set alight.'

The capture of three of his couriers and the discovery of their coded messages led Hill to change the system of transmitting information to John Scale in Stockholm. 'The men had been caught because the messages, sewn into the lining of their coats, had rustled when they were frisked.'

Henceforth, messages were typed onto strips of linen and then sewn into the collars of coats. 'Tedious work,' commented Hill, 'and took infinitely longer than typing on paper.'

The pressures of work were such that Hill had little time for pursuing Sally. Besides, she had proved rather too successful in perfecting her disguise as a downtrodden Moscow girl. On one occasion, Hill returned to the flat and was surprised to see a ragged figure tipping dirty water into a drain. 'It was Sally, the beautiful Sally, transformed into a barefooted slut who wore a begrimed white blouse.' As he passed, she blew her snotty nose into the gutter in a most undignified manner.

After a few weeks living as George Bergmann, Hill found that he had learned to live and breathe his new identity. When he sauntered down the street with his ginger beard and fingers stained yellow-brown from the chemicals in the film laboratory, he cut a very different figure from the old George Hill, with his military uniform, spats and Royal Flying Corps insignia. He was confident that no one would see through the disguise.

Yet he still made mistakes that could all too easily have cost him his life. On one occasion, Evelyn had glanced out of the window and noticed that he was striding down the street like a British officer on parade. 'Your walk gives you away completely,' she told him when he arrived back at the apartment. 'No Russian of your class would ever walk like that.'

On another occasion, he entered a grocery store and, momentarily forgetting his adopted persona, ordered his goods in a tone of voice that no shabbily dressed Russian would ever have used. 'I was behaving like the customer who was in the habit of giving such an order,' he wrote. 'The attendant gave me a searching look which brought me back to realities and, with a sick feeling, I, who should not have had a penny in the world, paid for my purchase and walked out of the shop.'

It was a dramatic reminder of the dangers of life as a spy and, Hill vowed, the last time he would make such a mistake. 'I was constantly haunted by the fear of being caught, and always before my mind I had a vivid picture of the spies I had seen executed in Macedonia.'

Hill had not been in contact with Sidney Reilly for some days. Now, with Vi's help, he managed to arrange a rendezvous in one of the Moscow parks.

'I shall never forget my first glimpse of him,' wrote Hill. 'He, too, had grown a beard and he did look an ugly devil. I told him so and he returned the compliment.'

Reilly had obtained a great deal of sensitive military information from Colonel Friede and even more secretive documents from one of his high-level contacts serving in the Criminal Department of the Cheka. He had also obtained intelligence about the state of the Russian fleet at Krondstadt. All of this now needed to be forwarded to Whitehall Court, along with a sheaf of other documents.

What's more, Reilly had a plan – one so bold that even his fellow spy was taken aback.

★

Mansfield Cumming had confessed to having a number of reservations about Sidney Reilly when he first offered him employment as a spy. Reilly's reputation for being unscrupulous, together with his sharp business practices, had rung warning bells from the outset.

Yet ever since he had arrived in Russia, Reilly had proved himself of great value. He had managed to lay his hands on an impressive amount of classified information that shed light on the precarious state of the new regime. He had vindicated Cumming's belief in human intelligence: only by having men on the ground could he form an accurate assessment of what was taking place inside Russia.

Hitherto, Reilly had confined his activities to acquiring secret documents and forwarding them to London. But in the third week of August, he allowed his vanity to get the better of him. At his meeting with George Hill, he confided some truly sensational news. There was a plot to assassinate the entire Bolshevik leadership and he, Reilly, stood at its epicentre.

The extraordinary events that followed were to involve spies, disgruntled army officers and at least one traitor, all of whom conducted themselves with maximum duplicity. 'Bold and masterfully conceived,' was how Hill described Reilly's plot. He was kept informed of developments 'so that should Lt Riley [sic] for any cause be prevented from bringing the work to a finish, I should at once be able to pick up the threads and carry on.'

The plot was initially conceived in Lockhart's private apartment on the Khlebny Pereulok, an address to which he had moved shortly after the Allied landings. At lunchtime on 15 August 1918, he was surprised by a knock on his front door. When he opened it, he found himself face to face with two Latvian soldiers who said they needed to speak with him in private.

'One was a short, sallow-faced youth called Smidchen,' wrote Lockhart. 'The other, Berzin, a tall powerfully-built man with clear-cut features and hard steely eyes, called himself a colonel.'

Colonel Berzin did most of the talking. He told Lockhart that he was a senior commander of the Lettish (Latvian) regiments that had been protecting the Bolshevik Government ever since the revolution. These regiments had proved indispensable to Lenin, saving his regime from several attempted *coups d'état*. Without them, the Bolsheviks would almost certainly have been swept from power.

Lockhart was initially suspicious of his unexpected visitors. But when they produced a letter from Captain Cromie, Britain's naval attaché in Petrograd, he was prepared to give them the benefit of the doubt.

'Always on my guard against agents provocateurs, I scrutinised the letter carefully,' he wrote. 'It was unmistakably from Cromie. The handwriting was his . . . The letter closed with a recommendation of Smidchen as a man who might be able to render us some service.'

Lockhart invited the men into his apartment and asked them a string of questions. They told him that the Latvian regiments had lost all enthusiasm for protecting the Revolutionary Government. They had only served Lenin because he paid them. But they were deeply concerned by the possibility of being sent into battle against the Allied forces in Northern Russia. To avoid this prospect, they wanted to return to their native Latvia.

This was impossible while it was under German occupation. But if the Allies were to win the war, as seemed increasingly likely, it would become a real possibility. In short, they asked Lockhart if he could send a message to the leader of the Allied forces in Northern Russia, General Poole, requesting him to facilitate their surrender.

Lockhart listened to the Latvians with interest but told them that he was unable to give them an answer straight away: he suggested that they return on the following day. As soon as they had gone, he made his way across town in order to discuss the matter with two of his French colleagues, General Lavergne and Consul Grenard.

The three of them agreed that it would do no harm to forward Colonel Berzin's request to General Poole. After all, it was very much in the Allied interest for the Latvian troops to surrender. But it was extremely important that the matter should remain secret. Lockhart could not afford to be discovered assisting them.

The two Latvians returned to Lockhart's apartment the next day as agreed. They were introduced to Consul Grenard, who had expressed a wish to meet them, and spoke of their willingness in helping the Allies to liberate Latvia from German rule.

Consul Grenard listened with care before making a wholly unexpected suggestion. He said that Colonel Berzin's forces could be assured of a vigorous Allied campaign to defeat the German Army in Latvia if they would first help to overthrow the Bolshevik government.

This took the two Latvians by surprise. Consul Grenard was suggesting something far more dramatic and dangerous than their own proposition.

There was one other visitor in Lockhart's apartment on that day. A heavily disguised Sidney Reilly was also in attendance and he was extremely interested in what Consul Grenard had to say. He had long dreamed of toppling the Bolshevik Government. Now, suddenly, he saw his chance.

'The Letts were not Bolsheviks,' he would later write, 'they were Bolshevik servants because they had no other resort. They were foreign hirelings. Foreign hirelings serve for money. They are at the disposal of the highest bidder. If I could buy the Letts, my task would be easy.'

Reilly paid a visit to George Hill shortly after the meeting at Lockhart's apartment and told him of the discussions that had taken place. Both men agreed that Lenin's government would be doomed if the Letts abandoned the Bolsheviks.

'The Letts were the corner stone and foundation of the Soviet government,' wrote Hill. 'They guarded the Kremlin, gold stock and the munitions.' They also occupied many other positions of consequence. 'At the head of the Extraordinary Commissions [Cheka], the prisons, the banks and the rail-roads were Letts.'

Essentially, though, Reilly was allowing his enthusiasm to cloud his judgement. It was one thing for the Latvians to talk of withdrawing their support for the Bolshevik regime – quite another for them to take up arms and overthrow it. Still, the conversation with Smidchen and Berzin had rekindled Reilly's dream of being a second Napoleon.

'A Corsican lieutenant of artillery trod out the embers of the French Revolution,' he wrote. 'Surely a British espionage agent with so many factors on his side could make himself master of Moscow?' After discussing matters with Hill, he returned to Lockhart's apartment in order to talk about the practicalities of organising a coup d'état.

Lockhart would later seek to distance himself from the entire plot. He would also claim that he and Consul Grenard both tried to discourage Reilly. '[He] was warned specifically to have nothing to do with so dangerous and doubtful a move.'

But Lockhart's back-pedalling is at variance with a top-secret memorandum that he submitted to the British Government at the time. This revealed that he was implicated in the early stages of the coup, along with Reilly, and that he was also personally involved in raising finances.

On 17 August, Reilly met with Colonel Berzin at the Tramble Café on Tverskoy Boulevard. It was always busy, making it a perfect place to discuss the proposed coup without risk of being overheard. Once Reilly was satisfied that Berzin could be trusted, he set out his plans for destroying the Bolshevik regime.

This time Colonel Berzin raised no questions as Reilly unveiled his plot. Indeed, he assured him that Latvian support would be forthcoming. 'The Letts were full of disgusted loathing for their masters,' he told Reilly, 'whom they served only as a *pis aller* (last resort).'

Reilly could scarcely have wished for more. To show that he meant business, he handed Colonel Berzin the huge sum of 700,000 roubles and promised that there would be plenty more to come. Much of the money had been collected by Lockhart, who had received 200,000 roubles from the Americans and the rest from the French.

By the third week of August, Reilly was having regular meetings with Colonel Berzin, George Hill and Ernest Boyce, who remained Mansfield Cumming's most senior operative in Moscow. Boyce was of a far more cautious nature than Reilly and remained unconvinced by the proposed coup. His agents had been sent to Moscow to gather secret intelligence, not to overthrow the regime. He told Reilly that he considered 'the whole thing was extremely risky'.

Reilly refused to backtrack. After much persistence, he wrung a lukewarm endorsement from Boyce. He told Reilly 'it was worth trying', but stressed that it was a matter of such extreme sensitivity that it must remain a private undertaking. It was to be Reilly's coup and the British Secret Service was not to be involved in any way.

'The failure of the plan,' he said, 'would drop entirely on Reilly's neck.' With these words, he handed over to Reilly full operational responsibility for everything that was to follow.

★

Sidney Reilly now set to work on the detailed planning of the coup. It was to depend almost entirely on the Latvian soldiers based in Moscow. They were to arrest Lenin and Trotsky during a meeting of the Congress of Soviets, when all of the Bolshevik leadership would be gathered under one roof.

Once their downfall had been broadcast to the country, Reilly wanted 'to parade them publicly through the streets, so that everybody should be aware that the tyrants of Russia were prisoners.'

Reilly also intended to convene a new government within hours of Lenin and Trotsky being seized. This would lessen the risk of a dangerous vacuum with no one in control.

One of his friends, General Judenitch, was to step in initially and hold the reins of power. There were to be senior positions for other close acquaintances: Grammatikov was to become Minister of the Interior and a former business associate by the name of Tchubersky was to be Minister of Communications. These three men would be given the authority 'to suppress the anarchy which would almost inevitably follow such a revolution.'

Reilly met with Colonel Berzin on several more occasions, handing over two further payments totalling 500,000 roubles. The two men agreed on most elements of the *coup d'état*, although Berzin was strongly against Reilly's idea of parading Lenin and Trotsky through the streets. This, he said, was theatrical nonsense. He insisted that the two men should be executed, arguing that 'their marvellous oratorical powers would so act on the psychology of the men who went to arrest them that it was advisable not to risk it.'

Reilly discussed the matter further with George Hill and the two of them decided to stick to the plan of putting Lenin and Trotsky on public display. 'The policy should be not to make martyrs of the leaders,' said Reilly, 'but to hold them up to ridicule before the world.' It was a rare moment of weakness in one who was usually so decisive.

On 25 August, Reilly attended an important meeting at the American Consulate in Moscow. It was convened in order that the intelligence agents of America and France could be informed of what was due to take place. The head of American operations in Russia was Xenophon Kalamatiano, a flamboyant businessman-turned-adventurer with a reputation for intrigue. France's principal agent was Colonel Henri de Vertement.

'I had an uneasy feeling,' wrote Reilly, 'such as one frequently gets in dangerous situations, when one's nerves are constantly on the "qui vive", that I should keep myself to myself and not go to the meeting which had already been arranged for me. But in the end, I allowed myself to be persuaded.'

There were two items on the agenda: Reilly's planned coup d'état and a possible campaign of mass sabotage. The meeting also provided an opportunity for the three agents – Reilly, Kalamatiano and Colonel de Vertement – to discuss future joint projects.

Reilly chatted with his American and French counterparts. Then, to his surprise, another invitee arrived at the consulate. It was René Marchand, the Moscow correspondent of *Le Figaro*, and a man whom Consul Grenard described as a secret agent of the French government.

'And here it was, that the uneasy feeling, which had been haunting me all along, became acute,' wrote Reilly. A sixth sense was warning him that Marchand could not be trusted.

His suspicions increased still further during the course of the discussions. At one point, Reilly discreetly drew Colonel de Vertement into an adjoining room in order to discuss some important details of the coup d'état. 'The room in which we were [standing] was long and badly lighted. In the midst of an animated discussion, I suddenly became aware that Marchand had crept into the room and no doubt had already overheard a large part of our conversation.'

In spite of Reilly's concerns about Marchand, the planning of the coup continued in the days that followed the meeting at the consulate. Colonel Berzin assured Reilly that his most loyal Latvian troops would be guarding the theatre on the day of the Congress of Soviets.

'At a given signal, the soldiers were to close the doors and cover all the people in the Theatre with their rifles, while a selected detachment was to secure the persons of Lenin and Trotsky,' wrote Reilly.

He, meanwhile, would be hiding behind the theatre curtains in order to monitor the unfolding coup. 'In case there was any hitch in the proceedings,' he wrote, 'in case the Soviets showed fight or the Letts proved nervous ... the other conspirators and myself would carry grenades in our place of concealment behind the curtains.'

There was one last-minute change of plan: Reilly learned that the meeting of the Congress of Soviets had been unexpectedly postponed until 6 September. This meant that the date of the coup also had to be shifted.

Neither Reilly nor Colonel Berzin was unduly concerned by the postponement. Indeed, it provided Reilly with more time to plan the interim government that was to take control after the overthrow of the Bolsheviks. On 28 August, he left Moscow for Petrograd in order that he might confer with one of his fellow conspirators, Alexander Grammatikov.

It was while Reilly was away from the capital that two unforeseen incidents occurred. The first unwelcome surprise came on 30 August when a young military cadet assassinated Moisei Uritsky, the head of the Petrograd Cheka. He claimed to have been motivated by his disgust at the mass executions ordered by Uritsky. On the same day, a Socialist Revolutionary named Fanya Kaplan shot Lenin as he left a meeting at a Moscow factory. She fired two bullets at point-blank range: one missed Lenin's heart by less than an inch and the other just failed to penetrate his jugular vein. Although he was not dead, he was severely injured and there was every chance that he would not survive.

It was Grammatikov who broke the news of the shootings to Reilly. After recovering from the initial shock, Reilly realised that the two incidents had changed everything. There was certain to be an unleashing of terror on the part of the Bolsheviks in revenge for what had taken place. There would be mass arrests, interrogations and summary executions.

It was obvious that the planned coup would have to be postponed, perhaps indefinitely. This was a great disappointment to Reilly, who had felt tantalisingly close to success. More worrying was the possibility that his fellow plotters would get caught up in the inevitable wave of arrests. If so, they might break down under interrogation and betray the planned coup in order to gain their release. Reilly feared that 'the danger to ourselves and our friends was imminent.'

He was entirely correct in this assessment. The first person to feel the danger was Robert Bruce Lockhart, 400 miles away in Moscow. At 3.30 a.m. on Saturday 31 August, he was woken by a rough voice ordering him out of bed. 'As I opened my eyes, I looked up into the steely barrel of a revolver. Some ten men were in my room.'

An indignant Lockhart asked what the hell they were doing. 'No questions,' answered one of the men. 'Get dressed at once.

You are to go to Loubianka No 11.' As Lockhart well knew, this was the infamous headquarters of the Moscow Cheka.

Lockhart realised that something had gone seriously awry with Reilly's planned coup. As he threw on some clothes, 'the main body of the invaders began to ransack the flat for compromising documents.'

He and Captain Hicks, with whom he shared his apartment, were then bundled into a car and driven at high speed to the Cheka headquarters. They were led to a small unfurnished cell and locked inside.

After an agonisingly long wait, the door crashed open and two gunmen barged into the room. They pointed at Lockhart, ordered him to stand to his feet and then led him down a long unlit corridor. Eventually they stopped at a door and knocked. A ghostly voice told them to enter. Lockhart found himself in a large room lit by a single desk lamp on a writing table.

'At the table, with a revolver lying beside the writing pad, was a man, dressed in black trousers and a white Russian shirt.' His face was sallow and sickly, as if he never saw the light of day. 'His lips were tightly compressed,' wrote Lockhart, 'and, as I entered the room, his eyes fixed me with a steely stare'. It was Yakov Peters, Dzerzhinsky's deputy at the Cheka.

Lockhart, struggling to keep up a show of bravado, formally protested against his arrest. He remained an accredited diplomat and he expressed his outrage at being treated in such a fashion. Peters did not care to listen. After informing Lockhart of the gravity of the situation in which he found himself, he fired two questions in quick succession. The first was, 'Do you know the Kaplan woman?' The second was, 'Where is Reilly?'

He then added a third question that was even more alarming. He produced the letter that Lockhart had personally written for Colonel Berzin. It provided him with an introduction to General Poole, head of the Allied forces in Northern Russia. 'Is that your writing?' snapped Peters.

Lockhart refused to answer and Peters did not press the issue. But he took the opportunity to inform Lockhart that it was 'a very grave matter' and one that was certain to have serious ramifications.

After a few more minutes of unpleasantness, Peters rang a bell and ordered the gunmen to escort Lockhart back to his cell, where Captain Hicks had been waiting anxiously. The two men dared not speak with each other, for they knew that the room was certain to be bugged, but it was obvious to Lockhart that the Bolsheviks were trying to implicate him in the attempt on Lenin's life.

No less alarming was the mention of Reilly. 'I guessed,' wrote Lockhart, 'that there had been a hitch somewhere and that my two Lettish visitors' – the two Latvian soldiers – 'were agents provocateurs.'

Lockhart and Hicks spent the night locked inside their cell. At six in the morning, the door was unlocked and a woman was pushed inside. 'Her hair was black and her eyes, set in a fixed stare, had great rings under them.' Lockhart guessed it was Fanya Kaplan. She was executed a few hours later.

At 9 a.m., Yakov Peters entered the room in which the two men were being held. He breezily informed them that they were free to go, offering no explanation as to why they were being released. Lockhart was as perplexed as he was relieved. He could not fathom Peters' change of heart and would not learn the reason for several hours. In the meantime, he returned home in order to shave and take a bath. He then paid a visit on Herr Oudendyke, a friend who worked at the Dutch Legation, in order to discuss the alarming turn of events.

'I found him in great agitation,' wrote Lockhart. 'There had been a terrible tragedy in St Petersburg.'

It was a tragedy in which Sidney Reilly was dangerously entangled.

CHAPTER NINE

VANISHING TRICK

TOP SECRET

Two thousand miles from Moscow, in distant Tashkent, Frederick Bailey was finding life increasingly perilous.

The local government faced anti-Bolshevik armies on no fewer than four fronts and it was making the commissars understandably jumpy. The attempted assassination of Lenin had only increased their nervousness. The local press was filled with vitriolic articles about the British.

'Red Terror and wholesale executions were advocated in revenge for the attempt on Lenin's life,' wrote Bailey. 'Every day, the papers contained bulletins of the temperature, pulse and respiration of Comrade Lenin.'

Bailey's comrade, Major Blacker, had fallen sick and been permitted to leave the country – a rare act of clemency on the part of Tashkent's revolutionary leaders. Bailey himself was strictly forbidden from returning to India. This was typical of the unpredictability of the authorities. Commissars and ministers changed positions on a weekly basis and everyone seemed to be making policy on a whim.

In Major Blacker's absence, Bailey's principal companion became the American consul, Roger Tredwell. He had valiantly remained at his post, even though he was suspected of espionage by the local authorities. Like Bailey, his movements were carefully monitored.

'The whole of this time we were watched by spies,' wrote Bailey. 'Tredwell and I were each honoured with the company of three of these gentlemen. They took rooms opposite the houses we were occupying and spent many hours looking out of the windows in a bored way.'

Bailey found it almost impossible to send information back to British India. Yet he was not entirely without news from the outside world. One morning, he was surprised to be woken by a heavily disguised former soldier of the 11th Bengal Lancers who had been sent from Kashgar in order to make contact. The soldier's overland journey had been one of such extreme danger that it would not be repeated. He had spent two days in jail and a third in detention, at great risk of being executed. But he had eventually been released and then used considerable guile to smuggle himself into Tashkent without the knowledge of the local authorities.

His return to Kashgar is not recorded by Bailey, but it is almost certain he took with him the dossier of secret intelligence that Bailey had managed to gather. This contained the very first hint of a plot that threatened to engulf the entire region in bloodshed and anarchy. According to Bailey, Moscow's Assistant Commissar for Foreign Affairs, Lev Karakhan, had ordered the Soviet minister in Kabul to start supplying arms to the Islamic tribes on the North-West Frontier.

This was exactly what was most feared by the government of British India. A Soviet-backed armed rebellion in the volatile region of the Hindu Kush was indeed a serious threat.

Unrest would rapidly spread to other areas and the meagre forces of British India would be unable to cope.

Bailey's most urgent task was to find out how, and where, any rebellion would occur. But this was far from easy. He was daily expecting to be arrested and accused of some trumped-up charge, especially in the days and weeks after the attempt on Lenin's life. Bailey felt as if he was a pawn in a very danger-ous game; a game for which he no longer knew the rules.

All he could do was prepare himself for the inevitable search of his lodgings. 'I destroyed certain papers [and] put my private correspondence into a safe place, leaving a few letters from tradesmen to be found.'

He also concealed an Austrian army uniform that he had only recently acquired: it was to form a part of his disguise if and when he went underground.

Bailey had learned the importance of staying one step ahead of the game. He now planned an elaborate ruse that would help him out of difficulty if ever he came to be arrested by the Cheka. He wrote a letter addressed to the British Government in which he described a huge anti-Bolshevik uprising that he knew was being planned in the mountains to the east of Tashkent.

He revealed that the uprising was intended to destabilise Turkestan's revolutionary government and added that it was being heavily financed by Germany. 'This sentence in my letter was to make all the difference to me,' he confessed when he later wrote about the incident, 'and probably saved my life.'

The reason why the sentence was so important only became apparent when Bailey was indeed arrested by the Cheka. Accused of involvement in the uprising, he feigned indigna-tion and warned that the British Government would be furi-ous when news of his arrest reached the House of Commons.

The corpse of Grigori Rasputin. Recently discovered evidence points to the role of British spy Oswald Rayner in his gruesome murder.

Lenin addresses the crowds in Moscow in 1918. His goal was to bring down British India and destroy the Western democracies.

Trotsky directs his Red Army soldiers. He was unaware that his secret telegrams were being intercepted by British Intelligence.

Mansfield Cumming, or 'C', the eccentric founder of the Secret Intelligence Service (MI6). He led the undercover operations inside Russia for seven years.

Felix Dzerzhinsky, or 'Iron Felix', the ruthless head of the Cheka, Russia's secret police. He was tasked with tracking down and catching Cumming's undercover agents.

Evgenia Shelepina - 'the big girl' - was Trotsky's personal secretary. She was also Arthur Ransome's lover, providing him with unique access to the regime.

Arthur Ransome. Best known for his children's book, *Swallows and Amazons*, he was also a British spy working at the very heart of the Russian revolutionary regime.

Karl Radek, the irascible Vice-Commissar for Foreign Affairs. He was on close terms with Arthur Ransome, who described him as 'a spectacled revolutionary goblin.'

Robert Bruce Lockhart, unofficial British representative to the revolutionary Bolshevik government. He was imprisoned for his involvement in a plot against Lenin's life.

George Hill was the 'perfect spy'. He proved remarkably adept at living underground and in disguise in Moscow under the assumed name, George Bergmann.

Sidney Reilly, the so-called 'Ace of Spies', lived under three different identities. Resourceful, egocentric and vain, he was one of the only British spies to be captured and killed.

Frederick Bailey lived undercover in Tashkent, disguised as an Albanian mercenary named Joseph Kastamuni. The badge on his *kepi* (cap) was stuck on with apricot preserve.

Bailey's forged identity papers, complete with fake stamps. They were convincing enough to fool Bolshevik guards and commissars.

A rare photograph of Red Army soldiers drilling in Tashkent. Troops such as these were to spearhead the assault on British India.

Paul Dukes, the only spy to be knighted for services to espionage, in his various disguises. Clockwise from top left: as Joseph Afirenko (note the missing tooth), Sergei Ilitch, Alexander Bankau and Alexander Markovitch. Paul Dukes, as himself, is in the centre.

Augustus Agar, sent to rescue Paul Dukes from Petrograd. He was awarded the Victoria Cross for attacking the Russian fleet, even though it was contrary to orders.

A Coastal Motor Boat, or skimmer, sent to rescue Paul Dukes. Propelled by two massive petrol engines, it skimmed safely over the surface of the minefields that ringed Petrograd.

The lethal M-Device, Winston Churchill's favoured weapon for use against the Bolsheviks. 'The most effective chemical weapon ever devised,' wrote one British general.

An M-Device explodes in daylight in Northern Russia, spreading a cloud of toxic gas. Victims coughed up blood before collapsing unconscious. The British shipped 50,000 shells to Russia for use against the Bolsheviks.

The vanguard of the Great Game: Bolshevik mounted troops on frontier patrol in Soviet-controlled Central Asia.

Wilfrid Malleson ran a vast network of spies in Central Asia and fought a dirty but highly effective war against the Bolsheviks.

Grigori Zinoviev, the fiery head of the Comintern, whose goal was global revolution. 'We summon you to a holy war against British imperialism,' he told Islamic delegates at the Baku Congress.

Manabendra Nath Roy was chosen to spearhead the attack on British India. Here he is disguised as Father Martin, a Catholic priest.

Roy in Moscow. 'You are so young,' said Lenin. 'I expected a bearded wise man from the East.' He nevertheless hired Roy's services as Indian revolutionary.

The first International Brigade of the Red Army, formed from German and Austrian prisoners of war. Their role was to lead the advance into British India.

It was a throwaway line but a clever one. Many of Tashkent's commissars were under the impression that Britain was locked in its own revolutionary struggle between the House of Commons and House of Lords. The last thing they wanted to do was offend the House of Commons, the very body they hoped would soon recognise the Bolshevik Government.

'I had learnt that in the eyes of the type of man in the employ of the Bolsheviks, the House of Commons was an assembly of riff-raff who were almost Bolsheviks themselves.'

Bailey informed his captors that he had in his possession a sealed letter that he had written to the House of Commons. He said that it contained important information about German support for the anti-Bolshevik uprising. But he refused to open the document on account of the many secret revelations within.

'I certainly cannot prevent you from breaking the seal,' he said, 'but I would not care to be the man who had done it when the news reaches the House of Commons and they protest to Moscow.'

After an animated discussion, Bailey eventually agreed to open the envelope on the condition that he would be set free if the promised information about Germany was contained within. His captors agreed to this and watched intently as Bailey prised off the impressive lump of red sealing wax. 'I rather feared I had overdone the seal,' he later wrote.

He read the relevant sentences about German backing for the anti-Bolshevik uprising and then gave his captors time to consider the information. They were astonished by the contents and not a little perplexed. Unaware that Bailey had written the letter with the express purpose of tricking them, they confessed their shock at Germany's involvement in the anti-Bolshevik movement. After discussing the contents of

Bailey's letter among themselves, they withdrew all their accusations. '*Voi svobodni!*' they shouted. 'You are free.'

Bailey had had a lucky escape. The incident had been an unpleasant one and he had come within a whisker of being imprisoned. But he remained under suspicion and now had six spies appointed to monitor his every move.

His position was rendered more precarious by the fact that the rule of law in Tashkent had almost completely broken down. 'Even if I were not executed by the government,' wrote Bailey, 'there was always the possibility of soldiers (drunk or sober) taking the matter into their own hands.'

He had long been toying with the idea of going underground. Now, he felt the moment was fast approaching. He was lunching with Roger Tredwell when he was handed a secret message informing him that he was to be arrested once again, along with a number of suspected agitators. The message ended with the sentence: 'For Bailey, the position is especially dangerous and shooting is not out of the question.'

'This was not a nice dish to be served up at lunch,' wrote Bailey.

He had already made preparations for safe accommodation in the event of having to disappear. Now, he burned all his private papers and concealed his field glasses, telescope and camera. He then prepared his new clothes, an Austrian jacket and kepi, before taking them to a house that he knew to be safe. It was a terraced building with a long row of adjoining gardens at the back.

'My plan was to enter the house in the usual unsuspicious way, to change with great rapidity, to run through the gardens behind, and to come out into the street further down in such a short time that, even if the six spies were sufficiently wide awake, they could not suspect that an Austrian walking out of a house some way down the street was the man they were watching, whom they had just seen walk into another house, dressed entirely differently.'

The success of his plan was to be entirely dependent on speed. As he entered the first property, he slammed the door behind him, aware that there was not a moment to be lost. 'I tore off my overcoat, pulled on the Austrian tunic and kepi . . . wrapped my overcoat round the civilian hat . . . [and] dashed out into the garden.' Less than a minute later, he emerged from a house at the far end of the terrace.

In the time that he took to change his costume, Frederick Bailey had ceased to exist. He now had a completely new identity and would henceforth answer to the name of Andre Kekeshi, an Austrian prisoner of war and a cook by profession.

'I now had to adopt in every way I could think of the habits and manners of an Austrian prisoner,' wrote Bailey. He remembered the advice that Richard Hanney had been given in *The Thirty-Nine Steps*: to melt into the background and become nothing more than a face in the crowd.

Yet he found it a disquieting experience to live as an underground fugitive. 'On my disappearance, the town was searched for me. Notices were placarded in the streets of the town and in every country village and railway station, not only offering a reward for my arrest . . . but also threatening with death and confiscation of property . . . anyone who helped or harboured me in any way.'

Bailey knew that he was now on his own. Like Sidney Reilly and George Hill, he would henceforth be entirely reliant on his own wits.

CHAPTER TEN

THE PLOT THICKENS

S idney Reilly was still in Petrograd when events turned sour. His plan to overthrow the Bolshevik Government had spun wildly out of control and he knew he would need his wits about him if he was to keep one step ahead of the Cheka.

He first realised that something was seriously awry when Captain Cromie, naval attaché at the British Embassy, failed to turn up to a secret rendezvous on the afternoon of 31 August. 'Not like Cromie to be unpunctual,' observed Reilly.

After waiting for another fifteen minutes at the pre-agreed location, he decided to make his way towards the embassy. It was 'a dangerous move' – for he risked being searched – 'but I had brought it off successfully before.'

He turned into Vlademirovsky Prospect, only to be confronted by a group of men and women running towards him in panic. 'They dived into doorways, into side-streets everywhere.'

Reilly was perplexed as to what was happening. A military car sped past, filled with Red Army soldiers. It was heading in the opposite direction to the crowd, racing towards the embassy. Reilly quickened his pace as he reached the end of Vlademirovsky Prospect. As he turned the corner, he immediately realised that something was seriously wrong.

'The Embassy door had been battered off its hinges. The Embassy flag had been torn down. The Embassy had been carried by storm.'

On the pavement outside there were several bloodstained corpses. Reilly glanced at them and noticed that they were not English. They were Russians, Bolsheviks, who he presumed to have been killed while storming the building.

It was to be some hours before Reilly discovered the grim details of what had taken place. Others had been rather closer to the action. Nathalie Bucknell, wife of one of the few remaining staff at the embassy, was in the passport office on the ground floor when she heard the crack of gunshots coming from upstairs. It was exactly 4.50 p.m. She poked her head into the entrance hall, only to hear more intense shooting and 'terrible screams'. She was as frightened as she was puzzled; she had not heard any soldiers entering the building.

The embassy porter crept into the hall and peered nervously up the stairwell. He motioned for her to take cover. She did so just in time. As she crouched in the small lobby adjoining the hall, a group of men could be heard careering down the grandiose staircase. At its head was Captain Cromie, wildly firing his revolver. Behind him, and in hot pursuit, were Red Guards. They too were firing their guns.

Nathalie sank to her knees in fear. There was a constant crackle of gunfire as the shoot-out intensified and bullets began to ricochet off the marble walls and columns. She peeked through the keyhole just as one of the bullets hit its target. 'Captain Cromie fell backwards on the last step.'

He was seriously wounded and clearly in need of urgent medical attention.

The Red Guards dashed into the street, seemingly confused by the lack of other gunmen. As they did so, a second group of soldiers came clattering down the stairs, equally dazed by the shoot-out. One of them paused for a moment to kick Cromie's half-conscious body.

Nathalie could hear the sound of yet more soldiers on the first floor of the building; they were bawling to the embassy staff who had hid themselves away in fear of their lives. 'Come out of the room, come out of the room, or we will open machine-gun fire on you.'

Nathalie was joined by her friend Miss Blumberg, who had taken refuge in one of the downstairs rooms. Together, the two women gingerly stepped into the hall in order to see what they could do for Captain Cromie. He was smeared with blood. 'Bending over him, [we] saw his eyelids and lips move very faintly.'

As Miss Blumberg attempted to speak to him, a group of Red Guards reappeared and started shouting insults. 'Pointing their revolvers at her, [they] called very rudely: "Come upstairs immediately or we will fire at you." '

The two women did not dare to argue; they were led up to the first floor with revolvers poking into their bodies. Nathalie saw graphic evidence of the shoot-out that had taken place. On the floor, lying in a pool of rapidly congealing blood, was the corpse of a Red Guard.

The two ladies were jostled into the Chancery room where Ernest Boyce, head of Mansfield Cumming's operations inside Russia, was being held at gunpoint. 'At that moment, the Red Commissary entered and told everyone that they must keep quiet with their hands up and that the Consulate was taken by the Red Guards.'

Miss Blumberg bravely asked if she could give the dying Cromie a glass of water. Her request was brusquely denied by the soldiers. The chaplain was treated with equal contempt when he asked to attend to the semi-conscious English captain.

The rest of the British staff were now brought into the Chancery and told that they were being held as prisoners. Most were still reeling from what had taken place. They knew of the assassination of Uritsky and of the attempt on Lenin's life, but only Ernest Boyce was aware of Reilly's planned coup and even he did not know that it had been exposed by the Cheka.

'The room was now full of soldiers and sailors who were most brutal in their behaviour,' wrote Nathalie. The porter was led through each room with a revolver pressed to his head. The guards said they would shoot him if he did not unlock every door and cupboard.

The hostages were held for several hours while the embassy was stripped of everything of value, including all its archives and secret documents. The staff were then marched down the stairs, passing the now-dead Captain Cromie, and taken to a nearby building. For the next fifteen hours, they were held prisoner and interrogated, one by one.

Nathalie overheard a soldier saying that five of them, including Boyce, were going to be shot. But the executions were inexplicably annuled before they could be carried out. At 11 a.m. on 1 September, all of the prisoners were informed that they were free to go. Bewildered as to why they were being released, but not daring to ask any questions, they gratefully made their way into the street.

★

Sidney Reilly's arrival at the embassy had coincided with the end of the shoot-out and he was unaware of what had taken place. As he stood in Vlademirovsky Prospect he could only guess at what had happened.

He reached inside his pocket and felt for the forged Cheka papers of Sigmund Relinsky, the person he was pretending to be. Then, with characteristic brazenness, he approached one of the Cheka agents who was standing guard at the embassy gates. After showing his card, he asked for information. He was told that the Cheka 'were endeavouring to find one Sidney Reilly and had actually raided the British Embassy in the hope that he would be there.'

Most men would have fled the country on hearing this news. But not Reilly. Instead of crossing the border into nearby Finland or Sweden, he decided to return to Moscow in order to place himself in the eye of the storm.

Tumultuous events were under way in the Bolshevik capital and he wanted to be there in order to influence their outcome.

★

Mansfield Cumming knew nothing of what had taken place in Petrograd. He was as yet unaware of the temporary arrest of Ernest Boyce and nor did he know that his Russian operations were hanging by a thread. It was to be some days before he learned that all of his senior agents had been compromised by Reilly's attempted coup d'état.

In Moscow, there was an unnatural calm for almost twenty-four hours. As in Petrograd, all of the English prisoners had been released without explanation. For the time being, Lockhart was still a free man. But on 2 September, the Bolshevik newspapers splashed their front pages with news of a most dramatic nature. The government had uncovered an

Anglo-French conspiracy that involved undercover agents and diplomats: its goal was nothing short of the overthrow of the Bolshevik regime. Reilly and a number of others were named as organisers of the conspiracy.

There was worse to come. A second bulletin revealed a number of key details about the plot. 'Ten million roubles assigned for this purpose,' it read. 'Lockhart entered into personal contact with the commander of a large Lettish unit ... should the plot succeed, Lockhart promised in the name of the Allies immediate restoration of a free Latvia.'

Each new bulletin contained new and more damning revelations. 'Anglo-French capitalists, through hired assassins, organised terrorist attempts on representatives of the Soviet.' The plotters now stood accused of the murder of Uritsky and the attempted assassination of Lenin.

Most alarming, for Lockhart at least, was the fact that he was being named as the organiser of the plot. The Bolshevik-controlled newspaper, *Pravda*, labelled him 'a murderer and conspirator against the Russian Soviet government'. They then gave a detailed description of his alleged crimes.

'A fine diplomatic representative organising murder and rebellion on the territory of the country where he is representative. This bandit in dinner jacket and gloves tries to hide like a cat at large, under the shelter of international law and ethics. No, Mr Lockhart, this will not save you. The workmen and the poorer peasants of Russia are not idiots enough to defend murderers, robbers and highwaymen.'

Lockhart remained in his post, even though the accusations against him grew ever more damning. He spent his daytime hours studying the newspaper stories being published about him.

'We read the full tale of our iniquities in the Bolshevik Press,' he later wrote, 'which excelled itself in a fantastic account of a so-called "Lockhart plot".' He said that the entire story 'read like a fairy tale', but he must already have guessed that the ending would not be a happy one.

Lockhart's situation was rendered more complicated by the fact that his love affair with Moura was public knowledge. He had flaunted her at dinners, balls and gypsy dances in the countryside. When news of the so-called Lockhart plot reached the Cheka, the first thing they did was arrest Moura.

Lockhart was distraught at the thought that he had been the cause of her incarceration. On 4 September, after another day of sensational stories in the press, he could bear it no longer. He decided to appeal to the Assistant Commissar for Foreign Affairs, Lev Karakhan, and beg for Moura's release.

Karakhan listened patiently to Lockhart's pleas, as well as to his vigorous denials of the stories printed in the Bolshevik press. 'Now you know what we have to put up with from your newspapers,' he said.

He made it abundantly clear that he would not be able to secure Moura's freedom, whereupon Lockhart decided to take his complaint to Yakov Peters, Deputy Chairman of the Cheka. In doing so, he was placing himself in the lion's den: it was Peters who had interrogated him just four days earlier.

Lockhart strode boldly up to the front entrance of the Loubianka and knocked at the door. When the guards asked the reason for his visit, he demanded an immediate meeting with Peters. This caused 'some excitement and much whispering among the guards in the entrance hall.'

Peters allowed himself a private chuckle when he learned that Lockhart had come to see him and immediately invited him to step into his office. 'I tackled him at once about Moura,' wrote Lockhart. 'I told him that the conspiracy story was a fake and that he knew it. Even if there were a grain of truth in it, Moura knew nothing about it.'

Peters listened with great patience and promised to do whatever he could. He then stared Lockhart in the eye and delivered his bombshell. ' "You have saved me some trouble," he said. "My men have been looking for you for the last hour. I have a warrant for your arrest. Your French and English colleagues are already under lock and key." '

Peters called for his guards and Lockhart was led away to the cells. It was not long before he learned that he stood accused of assassination, attempted murder and planning a coup d'état. All three crimes carried the death sentence.

★

The Cheka had been extremely busy in the days that preceded Lockhart's arrest. Within hours of the attempt on Lenin's life, their operatives instigated mass arrests right across the capital.

Among those arrested was Elizaveta Otten, with whom Reilly had only recently started a love affair. She also happened to be one of his chief couriers. News of her arrest alarmed Reilly, for she was privy to countless secrets.

The Cheka officers immediately began interrogating her, bombarding her with questions. She played innocent, professing ignorance as to Reilly's real identity. When the officers told her that her lover was an English spy, and a most dangerous one at that, she feigned indignation and shock.

In a petition she later wrote to the Red Cross Committee for the Aid of Political Prisoners, she said that she had been horrified to discover that Reilly was not who he claimed to be.

'I discovered that Reilly had been foully deceiving me for his own political purposes,' she wrote, '[and] taking advantage of my exclusively good attitude to him.'

Given that she had been working as his chief courier, her words must be read with a large dose of salt.

The Cheka officers were still interrogating Elizaveta when young Vi, one of George Hill's agents, happened to arrive at her apartment. 'The door was opened and Vi found herself covered with the revolver of a Cheka agent.' So wrote Hill, who learned of the incident later that day.

Despite her youth, Vi remained remarkably cool under pressure. She pretended not to know Elizaveta and gained herself time to think by bursting into floods of tears. She told the officers 'that she had simply brought a blouse for the lady which she had made herself.'

She was nevertheless interrogated and asked scores of questions as to whom she knew and why she knew them. 'The Chekists failed to break down her story, though one of them, holding a revolver to her head, said she was lying.'

Unable to uncover anything incriminating, the officers eventually told her that she was free to go.

It was as she turned to leave that disaster struck. Sidney Reilly's most important agent, Maria Friede, now arrived unexpectedly at the flat. It was most unfortunate that her visit coincided with the Cheka raid. She, after all, had supplied Reilly with a large number of military secrets obtained from her brother, Colonel Friede. Indeed, she had come to the apartment in order to drop off yet another batch of compromising documents.

'On seeing the Chekists, she completely lost her head and begun to scream,' recounted Hill. 'The officials seized her and after a moment's search had the documents in their possession.'

They were so pleased with what they had found that they failed to notice Vi slip quietly out of the front door and hurry off down the street. She dived into a shop, hoping that she had not been seen or followed. Then, after waiting a while, she took herself to one of Moscow's public baths and spent two hours in the steam room. Only then did she consider it safe to return to the secret address that George Hill was still using as his headquarters.

Another of Reilly's agents, Dagmara Karozus, had also been visiting Elizaveta's flat at the time of the raid. She, too, managed to get away. The Cheka officers repeatedly interrogated her but failed to find anything incriminating. She was told that she was free to go and she immediately made her way to a safe house on the other side of town. It was an extremely lucky escape.

Maria Friede was not so fortunate. She was terrified by the Cheka agents and broke down in tears. She confessed that her brother had been working for Reilly ever since his arrival in Russia. This news was swiftly transmitted to the Cheka's headquarters and the colonel was arrested shortly afterwards. He was then put through an intense and gruelling interrogation.

Friede knew the game was up. According to the KGB defector, Vladimir Orlov, he 'admitted that he regularly supplied Sidney Reilly with data regarding the strength and movements of Red Army units.'

He also revealed that he had worked for the American Secret Service, supplying their chief agent, Xenophon Kalamatiano, with false identity papers. He almost certainly hoped that his confession would entitle him to clemency. It did not. He was summarily executed by firing squad.

Each new search undertaken by the Cheka turned up ever more damning revelations. They were soon on the trail of

Colonel de Vertemont, the French spy, and raided his apartment without warning. The colonel was caught red-handed with 18 pounds of pyroxylin, detonation capsules, a secret spy code and 28,000 roubles in cash.

The Cheka also arrested Kalamatiano and interrogated him. Although he revealed nothing, one of the Cheka officers noticed that he never parted with the cane that he held in his hands. The officer asked to see the cane and began to examine it closely.

'Kalamatiano turned pale and lost his composure,' wrote Vladimir Orlov in his account of the incident. 'The investigator soon discovered that the cane contained an inner tube and he extracted it. In it were hidden a secret cipher, spy reports, a coded list of thirty-two spies and money receipts from some of them.'

Kalamatiano was in serious trouble.

★

The Cheka had proved ruthlessly efficient in times of crisis. It had been founded less than nine months earlier, yet it had been highly professional in crushing internal dissent.

Its efficiency was due in part to Dzerzhinsky's uncompromising leadership. He had been given a free hand in the running of his agency and had been offered every possible support from the regime. Unlike Mansfield Cumming, he did not have constant interference from other government departments. Nor were his agents working in dangerous and hostile foreign countries. Almost all of Dzerzhinsky's men were operating on home soil and this gave them a significant advantage over Cumming's spies.

The Cheka had proved particularly adept at penetrating the networks of foreign agents working in Moscow and

Petrograd. Although Sidney Reilly had escaped capture, his presence in Russia was now known. His couriers, too, had been compromised by the planned coup d'état. If caught, they were certain to be shot.

Reilly was en route to Moscow at the very time when the Cheka officers were rounding up suspects. He was acutely aware that Dzerzhinsky's agents would soon be on his trail and he decided to avoid all of his old haunts. Instead, he made his way to the home of an anti-Bolshevik friend where he found Dagmara Karozus hiding in fear of her life. She had scarcely stepped outside since the Cheka had let her walk free from Elizaveta Otten's apartment.

Dagmara warned Reilly that he was in extreme danger. She also gave him her own account of the raid on Elizaveta's flat – a story that would eventually find its way into Reilly's memoirs. 'In a drawer of the bureau were over two million roubles in 1000 rouble notes,' wrote Reilly. 'When the agents of the Cheka thundered on the door demanding admission, Dagmara had picked up a bundle of notes and thrust them between her legs and there had kept them during the whole period of the search.'

Reilly's meeting with Dagmara was to prove crucial to his survival. She was able to inform him of all the arrests that had taken place and provide him with several new addresses that she knew to be safe. Reilly himself was acutely aware of the perilous situation in which he now found himself.

'A price was on my head. I was an outlaw. I was to be shot at sight by anyone who identified me. My identity was known. My *noms de guerre*, Constantine and Massino were known. Everything was uncovered.'

He had only himself to blame. His vainglorious plan to topple the Bolsheviks had led to this sorry situation.

Reilly spent several days at the apartment of Olga Starzhevskaya, one of his several lovers. It gave him the opportunity to meet George Hill and work out a strategy for future operations. He told Hill of his urgent need for a new passport and a change of clothes. Yet he remained sanguine in the face of adversity.

'Reilly's bearing when I met him was splendid,' wrote Hill. 'He was a hunted man, his photograph with a full description and a reward was placarded throughout the town . . . yet he was absolutely cool, calm and collected, not in the least down-hearted and only concerned in gathering together the broken threads and starting afresh.'

Reilly left Olga's flat on 4 September, just in the nick of time. It was raided by the Cheka on the following day and Olga herself was subjected to a lengthy interrogation. When she was told that her lover, Konstantin Markovich Massino, was actually Sidney Reilly, she feigned disbelief. She told the Cheka officers that she had always understood him to be Massino, 'who I deeply loved and intended to share my life with.'

She also said that she had never doubted him to be anything other than Russian. 'I believed him and loved him, regarding him as an honest, noble, interesting and exclusively clever man.'

With Hill's help, Reilly was able to move temporarily into the offices of a Soviet business. But fearing capture, he constantly switched addresses, never spending more than one night in the same apartment. He also changed his identity on a daily basis. 'Now I was a Greek merchant . . . now I was a Tsarist officer . . . now a Russian merchant.'

He was unwittingly aided in his underground life by the Bolshevik press. 'They were so conceited over the discovery of the conspiracy that, from day to day, they published the fullest reports of the progress they were making.' As a consequence, Reilly was able to keep himself informed as to who had been arrested and who was under suspicion.

The Cheka used the conspiracy as a means to liquidate all the most prominent opponents of the Bolshevik regime. In revenge for the attempt on Lenin's life, they summarily executed five hundred well-known figures from the old regime, including politicians, businessmen, publishers and writers.

'Next morning,' wrote Hill, 'they published a list of all the people whom they had executed. I do not think that I have ever read anything quite so terrible. The people they had seized were entirely innocent.'

This was the beginning of the Red Terror, a wave of bloodshed that swept through the capital. It was enthusiastically endorsed by the regime, which encouraged people to strike at anyone who was not a committed Bolshevik.

'For every head of ours, we shall cut off a hundred stupid bourgeois heads . . .' declared Karl Radek. 'But it is you, comrades, who must take part in this terror. The Red Terror is the terror of the workmen, the terror of class against class. The last rouble, the last fur coat must be taken from the bourgeois.'

★

One central question remained unanswered: who had betrayed Reilly's coup d'état to the Cheka? Reilly began investigating as soon as he arrived in Moscow and it did not take him long to discover what had happened. The finger of accusation pointed directly at René Marchand, the correspondent for *Le Figaro* who had first aroused Reilly's suspicions at the meeting at the American Consulate.

Shortly after this meeting, in which Marchand overheard many details of the plot, he had called Felix Dzerzhinsky and asked for an urgent meeting.

Dzerzhinsky immediately summoned Marchand to his private apartment, which was just a stone's throw from the Kremlin. At their meeting, Marchand betrayed everything he knew of Reilly's planned coup. He told Dzerzhinsky that Reilly was intending to seal off the Congress of Soviets at the Bolshoi Theatre and have Lenin and Trotsky seized at gunpoint.

'At a signal given by Reilly,' said Marchand, 'the Lettish soldiers would close all exits and cover the audience with their rifles, while Reilly, at the head of his band, would leap on to the stage and seize Lenin, Trotsky and the other leaders. All of them would be shot on the spot.'

Reilly had been right to suspect Marchand. The Frenchman had long been a secret Bolshevik sympathiser who was prepared to betray everyone involved in the coup.

The near success of the plot stunned Dzerzhinsky and he immediately informed Lenin, who was still in a critical state from his gunshot wounds. Lenin's first question was whether or not Marchand would allow his revelations to be published in the Soviet newspapers. This, after all, was an unprecedented scoop. It laid bare the network of Allied agents working against the Bolshevik Government.

Marchand had already told Dzerzhinsky that public exposure was impossible. '[It] would mean the ruination of his journalistic career and he would be ostracised by all the Western countries.'

Lenin came up with another idea, one that would expose the planned coup but without directly implicating Marchand. 'Ask him to describe what he had been a witness to in a letter to President Poincaré,' he said. This letter would then be 'discovered' by Cheka officers during a routine raid on his apartment.

Marchand agreed to this proposal. He was a personal friend of the French president and might reasonably be expected to inform him of what was taking place. It was equally plausible that the Cheka would find the letter during an inspection of his apartment.

This was exactly what now took place. The letter was 'discovered' and then published in order that the Bolshevik regime could instigate a brutal retribution against all Allied nationals in both Moscow and Petrograd.

★

Sidney Reilly and George Hill were still on the run and had yet to be arrested by the Cheka. Lockhart was not so fortunate. He was now being held in solitary confinement in a small room at the heart of the Loubianka. Guarded by two sentries who rarely spoke, he was terrified about his fate. He knew that if Lenin died from his gunshot wounds, he was certain to be executed.

Each night at around midnight, he was taken to be interrogated by Yakov Peters. From Peters he learned that almost all the remaining English and French nationals in Russia were now under arrest. He also witnessed Yakov Peters' personal involvement in the Red Terror. One day, while he was standing in Peters' office, he saw an empty van drive into the Loubianka's central courtyard. Three former Tsarist ministers were led outside and pushed into the van, followed by a grotesquely overweight priest. Lockhart asked where they were going.

'They are going to another world,' said Peters dryly. 'And that man,' he said, pointing to the priest, 'richly deserves it.'

Lockhart found Peters a curious figure, half bandit and half gentleman. He brought books for Lockhart and made a great show of his generosity. Yet he had a ruthless streak that chilled the blood. He had lived for some years in England as an anarchist exile and had even been tried at the Old Bailey for the murder of three policemen. To the surprise of many, he had been acquitted. In conversations with Lockhart he recalled the happy years he had spent living in London as a gangster.

After five days of imprisonment in the Loubianka, Lockhart was transferred to the Kremlin. Accusations continued to be levelled against him in the press and he was told that he was to be put on trial for his life. Yet the trial was continually delayed and he eventually heard that it was unlikely to go ahead. The explanation for this was straightforward: the British Government had arrested the Soviet envoy, Maxim Litvinov, along with a number of other Russians living in England. It was to prove a classic tit-for-tat manoeuvre: Litvinov would only be released once the British hostages had been freed.

Reilly and Hill kept themselves out of danger, but they soon came to the conclusion that there was little to be gained by remaining in Moscow. Their network was in tatters and six or seven of Hill's couriers had recently been caught and executed by the Cheka. It was only a matter of time before they themselves would be ensnared.

'Never in my life had I been so talked about,' recalled Reilly of this difficult time. 'My name was in everybody's mouth. My description was posted up all over Moscow.'

According to Hill, Reilly was sharing lodgings with a broken-down prostitute who 'was in the last stages of the disease which so often curses members of her profession.' He added that Reilly had always been 'the most fastidious of men, and while being caught by the Bolsheviks had little terror for him, he could hardly bring himself to spend the night on the couch in her room.'

The net steadily closed in on both men as more and more of their accomplices were arrested. 'I was quite without cover,' wrote Reilly. 'I dared reveal myself to no one.' He felt as if there were eyes in every wall.

The endgame came soon enough. Reilly was woken in the early hours of the morning by the noise of a car outside his lodgings. It was the clearest possible signal that the Cheka had arrived, since they were the only people in Moscow with access to vehicles.

'Our house was being raided,' wrote Reilly. 'Nearer and nearer came the secret police. Doors were flung open. Muffled screams could be heard. The tramp of feet sounded in the next room. It was now or never.'

With supreme calmness, Reilly put on his overcoat and slipped out of his apartment unseen by the Cheka. At the gate a lone Red Guard was smoking a cigarette. 'I strolled slowly over towards him, pulling out a cigarette of my own. "Give me a fire, comrade," ' said Reilly.

He knew there was no sense in remaining in Moscow. He had already consulted with George Hill and the two of them agreed that he should assume Hill's alias (that of the Baltic merchant George Bergmann) and head to Petrograd on the fake Bergmann passport.

This is what Reilly now did. The journey, though dangerous, went entirely to plan. Reilly made it to Petrograd and thence to Kronstadt. From here, he took a motor launch to Reval and checked himself into the luxurious Hotel Petrograd. 'After ten days I departed secretly on the launch for Helsingfors and from there to Stockholm and London.' He finally arrived back in England in the second week of November.

Lockhart had remained in prison during this time. He grew increasingly hopeful that he would be released, especially now that the British Government had arrested Maxim Litvinov. But he had no idea how long the process might take.

On 22 September, to Lockhart's surprise and joy, Yakov Peters arrived at his cell with Moura in tow. 'It was his birthday,' wrote Lockhart of Peters, 'and, as he preferred giving presents to receiving them, he had brought Moura as his birthday treat.'

He did not allow Moura to speak privately with Lockhart lest she pass any messages to him. But he proved less attentive when it came to watching her as she paced up and down Lockhart's room. Unseen, she managed to slip a note into his copy of Thomas Carlyle's *French Revolution*.

Lockhart had to wait until his guests had left before pulling out the note and reading it. 'Say nothing,' it read. 'All will be well.'

This proved to be correct. On 2 October, Lockhart was told that he was being released. Soon afterwards, he was taken under escort to his apartment. He learned that all the other English nationals were also due to be set free in order that they might be expelled from the country aboard a special train bound for Finland.

There was to be a surprise addition to the party of people aboard this train. George Hill had decided to leave Russia and he intended to do so with customary panache. He had already given his Bergmann passport to Reilly. Now, he decided to re-emerge as his real identity: he was to step back into the world as George Hill, accredited military attaché of the British government who had not been seen in public for some months.

'The first thing I did therefore was to get rid of my hateful beard,' he wrote. 'Then I went to the best Moscow tailor where I picked up one of the few remaining pieces of English cloth and had a new suit made. I bought boots, a hat and a pair of white spats and reappeared dressed again as an Englishman.'

Consul Wardrop refused to put Hill's name on the official list of Englishmen leaving the country for fear of putting everyone's lives at risk. After all, there was every chance that the Cheka would investigate Hill's movements over the previous months and realise that he had been living under an alias. But Lockhart overrode Wardrop's decision, as he had done so often in the past. He knew that Hill was certain to be caught and executed if he remained behind.

All that was now left for Lockhart to do was to say his farewells to his beloved Moura, who was to remain behind in Russia. Their final scene together took place at the train station.

'In the cool, starlit night, Moura and I discussed trivialities. We talked of everything except ourselves. And then I made her go home . . . I watched her go until she had disappeared into the night. Then I turned into my dimly lit carriage to wait and to be alone with my thoughts.'

After a painfully slow three-day journey, Lockhart and his fellow nationals reached the Russo-Finnish border. There was a last-minute hitch over the British Government's release of Litvinov, but they were finally allowed to cross the frontier and bid their farewells to Bolshevik Russia.

Lockhart would never return. Eight weeks later, at a spectacular show trial, he and Reilly were tried and sentenced to death in absentia.

CHAPTER ELEVEN

A DEADLY GAME

TOP SECRET

Mansfield Cumming's spy network had fallen apart at the seams. The recklessness of Sidney Reilly, coupled with the treachery of René Marchand, had led to the exposure and expulsion of almost all his agents.

Both Reilly and George Hill were back in England. So, too, was Ernest Boyce, having suffered the indignity of being incarcerated in the fortress of Peter and Paul in Petrograd. The only good news was that his role as Cumming's chief spymaster inside Russia had not been unmasked.

John Scale, head of the Stockholm bureau, was also in England. His return, at least, was a voluntary one. There were many pressing issues that needed to be resolved before attempting to smuggle spies back into Russia.

Cumming might have been forgiven for despairing at the situation in which he now found himself. Yet he was able to find lines of comfort in the disastrous situation that had unfolded inside Russia. The past two years had shown him and his men a dangerous new world. Agents like Hill, Reilly and Rayner had proved that professional spies, with resources and backup, could operate with impunity inside an enemy country.

The killing of Rasputin was one of the successes. So was the gathering of military intelligence, which had enabled Cumming to form an accurate assessment of the strengths and weaknesses of the Red Army. And although Reilly's plot had been foolhardy, it had come remarkably close to succeeding.

Other successes were less tangible but no less real. Mansfield Cumming's agents had managed to supply London with an accurate profile of a wholly new regime that was led by men whose ultimate goal was to export their revolution across the globe. Reilly and Hill had proved themselves particularly adept at working undercover and acquiring highly classified information.

Arthur Ransome had meanwhile chosen a different approach, forging close (and often amicable) relationships with Russia's revolutionary leaders.

Cumming's team had proved something else that was to be of great importance in the future. They had been adept at linking up with anti-Bolshevik activists who, under the pretence of working for the regime, were in fact doing every-thing possible to undermine it. This use of fifth-column insid-ers was a new tactic and it was to prove of the greatest value in the years to come.

Although Cumming's Russian network had been crippled by the mass arrests, it had not been entirely destroyed. His agents had long made use of the British expatriate commu-nity of Petrograd; men and women who spoke fluent Russian and could pass themselves off as native Russians. Among these unofficial operatives was John Merrett, the British-born owner of a Petrograd engineering firm.

Merrett was no stranger to the world of deception. He had spent much of the previous year collecting secret information for Captain Cromie and had relished the dangers of espionage.

After Cromie was killed, Merrett 'discontinued his visits [to the embassy] in order to avoid detection,' wrote acting consul Arthur Woodhouse, 'having altered his appearance by growing a beard and wearing non-descript clothes.'

On one occasion, Woodhouse had bumped into him in the street and mistaken him for a stranger. 'I met him accidentally and failed to recognise him. I knew he was employed in some risky enterprises, but refrained from enquiring his object . . . rumours of a modern Scarlet Pimpernel had reached us, but only subsequently were we able to confirm this.'

Woodhouse was not the only person to be fooled by Merrett's disguise. 'What was my surprise on entering Mr Merrett's house to see my host transformed into a bearded, shabbily dressed Russian in top boots, who contrasted very much with the well dressed Englishman of two years ago.' So wrote one member of the expatriate community.

Merrett was a born adventurer who welcomed situations of grave danger. Now, as a result of discussions between Mansfield Cumming and John Scale, he was to be assigned a more important role. He was charged with keeping the organisational structure of the courier system operating until such time as new agents could be infiltrated into Russia.

He was also to lead an audacious plan to smuggle out of Russia all the remaining British nationals living in the country. These were primarily businessmen and bankers who had declined to leave with the diplomats and whose companies had now been confiscated by the Bolsheviks. There were rumours that they were to be held hostage by the regime.

One of these businessmen asked Merrett if he was not worried about being caught by the Cheka, given that it would almost certainly lead to his execution. Merrett shrugged off the risk. 'He laughingly replied that while the Bolsheviks were busy arresting him at the Moika, he was to be found in the country, and when they were after him in the country, he was to be found somewhere else.'

He was in fact arrested by Red Guards on at least one occasion, but managed to slip from their clutches. 'Fortunately, I succeeded in escaping on my way to prison and was thereafter only able to avoid re-arrest by adopting disguises and sleeping in ever-changing and out of the way quarters,' he wrote.

Amid all this evasion, Merrett started smuggling British nationals out of the country, right under the eyes of the Cheka. He would assemble little groups of them at a safe house in Petrograd and then place them in the hands of trusted couriers. These couriers, the surviving remnants of George Hill's network, would lead them over the border into Finland.

One of the escaping businessmen asked Merrett what he should do if anyone stood in his way. Merrett's response was characteristically blunt: 'Knife him,' he said.

Merrett eventually helped 247 British nationals to flee the country. His work became increasingly dangerous, for Cheka officers were continually on his trail. It was clear that he could not operate indefinitely in Russia without the backup of a trained operative.

★

The collapse of Mansfield Cumming's Russian operations was soon to be followed by a further blow. Armistice was declared in November 1918, and in the weeks that followed, senior figures in Whitehall argued that there was no longer any need for an autonomous secret service.

Lord Curzon, Acting Foreign Secretary, was one of the sceptics. He informed his colleagues that Cumming's organisation was 'a luxury we could not afford in the present state of our finances as it did not produce value for the money spent on it.'

In the aftermath of war, Cumming's bureau was increasingly targeted by the heavy guns. Both the Admiralty and the War Office proposed that his foreign espionage operations should now be combined with domestic security. There would be one amalgamated organisation that was to be dominated by military intelligence: Cumming would be demoted to a junior partner.

Cumming played his hand with skill in this crucial round. In a robust defence of his organisation, he argued that military intelligence officers were wholly unequipped to deal with peacetime espionage. 'They have no knowledge or expertise of the matter at all,' he wrote, 'and are competent only to say what the military requirements will be.'

Nor did Cumming want to have anything to do with the War Office, whose staff had continued to poach his best agents throughout the final years of war. He was adamant that his secret service should remain as an autonomous bureau run by himself and answerable only to the Foreign Office.

A number of parliamentary committees met to discuss the issue. It was a critical time for Cumming for the very existence of his organisation was at stake. The first glimmer of good news came in January 1919, when the most important Cabinet sub-committee reported on its findings. It had made a close investigation into Cumming's operations over the previous years and pronounced them to have been a success. Under his tenure, it concluded, 'there was an enormous growth in all kinds of secret operations abroad, involving the expenditure of very large sums of money.'

The expense had been justified by the results. The committee heaped praise upon Cumming, saying that information obtained by his agents 'has been equal, if not superior, to that obtained by any other country engaged in the war.'

Vindicated by one committee, Cumming now found himself attacked by another. The Treasury was intent on tightening the purse strings and senior officials had set their sights on Whitehall Court. Cumming's budget had been running at about £80,000 a month during wartime. Now, he was told that it would be slashed to just £65,000 a year.

This proved too much for Winston Churchill, the Secretary of State for War. He had a high opinion of Cumming's organisation and told his colleagues that 'with the world in its present condition of extreme unrest and changing friendships and antagonisms . . . it is more than ever vital for us to have good and timely information.'

He reminded ministers that it had taken years for Cumming to build up his organisation. If the proposed budget cuts took place, all the hard work would be 'swept away by the stroke of a pen.' Furthermore, it would be 'an act of the utmost imprudence to cripple our arrangements at the present, most critical time.'

Cumming's undercover operations in Russia proved a critical factor when ministers finally came to take decisions. The world was indeed embarked on an uncertain course, as Churchill had said, and Bolshevik Russia remained a threat to global peace. It seemed foolhardy to jeopardise the existence of an organisation that had proved adept at acquiring intelligence from inside an enemy country.

It was decided that Cumming's bureau would be left untouched and that 'all anti-Bolshevik work abroad' – including all underground operations in Russia – would be his responsibility alone.

Cumming had been fortunate to secure Churchill's backing; he also had the continued support of Charles Hardinge, the Permanent Under-Secretary for Foreign Affairs. Hardinge reminded sceptical ministers that Cumming's work was 'exceedingly technical, requiring very special qualities which are not easy to find.' He added that the Foreign Office had been fortunate to find a chief who had 'a unique experience of secret service both in peace and war.'

Cumming had won a decisive victory and he looked to the future with renewed optimism. Just a few months later, he was able to inform Compton Mackenzie that 'far from closing down, as we thought we should have to do after the war, we are actually expanding and we have any amount of work to do in the immediate future.'

There was to be one lasting change. In the aftermath of the war, Cumming's organisation began increasingly to be referred to as the Secret Intelligence Service. The name was eventually officially adopted, and is retained by the service to this day (although it is more usually referred to as MI6 or Military Intelligence 6, the name it had first acquired during the First World War).

★

George Hill's return to London in November 1918 gave him his first opportunity to meet 'the Chief'. He felt unusually nervous as he climbed the stairs to the top floor of Whitehall Court and knocked on Cumming's door. He had been forewarned that Cumming had a formidable presence. Now, as he entered the room, that presence quickly made itself felt.

'For half a minute, he leisurely surveyed me and I have never been so thoroughly looked over before or since in my life.' After an uncomfortably long silence, Cumming suddenly stood up, shook Hill's hand and asked him to report on his work.

Cumming expressed his admiration for what Hill had achieved. He had proved a model agent, working undercover for many months without arousing any suspicion. Cumming's reward was to recommend him for the Military Cross, and he also ensured that he was made a Companion of the Distinguished Service Order.

'He has attended Bolshevik meetings at night when street fighting was at its height,' read the citation that accompanied Hill's award, 'passing back and forth through the Bolshevik fighting lines, and has been almost daily under fire without protection.'

Hill was invited back to Mansfield Cumming's offices within a few days of his first meeting. This time, Sidney Reilly was also present – his first meeting with C since his return to England.

Reilly feared that he would be censured for his reckless behaviour in Moscow. Indeed, he had gone so far as to beg Lockhart to report favourably on his behalf.

Now he was relieved to discover that he had no need to worry about Cumming's disapproval. Cumming remained impressed by the amount of intelligence that had been smuggled out of Russia and ensured that Reilly, like Hill, was awarded the Military Cross.

Cumming had summoned the two men to his offices because he had a new mission for them to undertake, one that would take them back onto Russian soil. The victorious Allies were about to begin delicate negotiations at the Paris Peace

Conference and urgently required information on the fighting that was taking place in Southern Russia.

It was well known that an anti-Bolshevik army led by General Denikin was engaged in a violent offensive against Lenin's Revolutionary forces. What Cumming needed was an accurate assessment of Denikin's prospects. He also wanted to know the likelihood of him uniting forces with Admiral Kolchak, who was leading a second anti-Bolshevik army in Eastern Russia.

Hill asked Cumming when he and Reilly would need to leave England. He was looking forward to relaxing in England after such a stressful stint abroad and hoped to have at least a couple of weeks to catch up with friends and family. Cumming told him that their train was departing in two hours. There was no time to pack and precious little time for farewells.

Hill had a rare moment of hesitation, one that Cumming was quick to notice. He discussed the situation with him 'much more like a friend than a senior officer' and his kindness finally convinced Hill to go. Two hours later, he and Reilly were aboard the train and bound for Odessa. For Reilly, in particular, it was a most dangerous undertaking. If caught by the Bolsheviks, he would be executed.

★

Sidney Reilly and George Hill were not heading back to Russia alone: Cumming had recently hired a new recruit to his organisation, someone he had first met four months previously. His name was Paul Dukes and he was charged with the task of rebuilding Cumming's shattered network inside Russia.

Dukes was a talented musician and former conductor with the Imperial Mariinsky Opera. He had been living in Russia since 1908 and had witnessed first-hand the revolution that had swept the Bolsheviks to power. Indeed he had been one of the trio of Englishmen who had first glimpsed Lenin on his return to Petrograd in 1917. He had also seen the civil unrest that accompanied Lenin's first months in government.

Dukes's intense eyes hinted at an inner sharpness, an ability to think on his feet and take clear decisions in moments of crisis. This natural intelligence, coupled with his fluency in the language, had already earned him unofficial employment in the service of the Foreign Office. It was almost certainly his vivid despatches about the Bolshevik revolution that brought him to the attention of Mansfield Cumming.

'One day, when in Moscow,' wrote Dukes, 'I was handed an unexpected telegram. "Urgent" – from the British Foreign Office. "You are wanted at once in London", it ran.'

He wasted no time in heeding the call. He took the train to Norway, bought himself passage across the North Sea and eventually arrived in Aberdeen. Here, he was met by a passport control officer who put him on the first train to London where a car was awaiting him.

Dukes was mystified by the summons. 'Knowing neither my destination, nor the cause of my recall, I was driven to a building in a side street in the vicinity of Trafalgar Square. "This way," said the chauffeur, leaving the car.'

Dukes was led into a labyrinthine building with 'rabbit-burrow-like passages, corridors, nooks and alcoves, piled higgledy-piggledy on the roof.' He was eventually ushered into a tiny room, the office of a colonel in uniform.

Dukes was not at liberty to provide his name when he came to publish his account, but it may well have been Colonel Freddie Browning, who was still employed as Cumming's unofficial deputy.

After a warm handshake, the colonel informed Dukes that he was being offered a job in the Secret Intelligence Service. He was to return to Russia and remain there, 'to keep us informed of the march of events.'

Dukes was taken aback by the unexpected job offer and blurted a series of objections. The colonel brushed these aside with a wave of his hand and told him to return to Whitehall Court on the following day. The arrival of a young secretary heralded the end of the interview: a bewildered Dukes was led back through the maze of passages.

'Burning with curiosity and fascinated already by the mysticism of this elevated labyrinth, I ventured a query to my young female guide. "What sort of an establishment is this?" I said.'

Dukes noticed a twinkle in her eye. 'She shrugged her shoulders and without replying pressed the button for the elevator. "Good afternoon," was all she said as I passed in.'

Dukes's induction into the Secret Intelligence Service was to become a great deal more mysterious on the following day. He was escorted back to the colonel's office and provided with a more precise brief. He was to gather intelligence on Bolshevik policy and was also to investigate the level of popular support for Lenin's regime.

'As to the means whereby you gain access to the country,' said the colonel, 'under what cover you will live there, and how you will send out reports, we shall leave it to you . . . to make suggestions.'

The colonel excused himself and left the room for a moment in order to see if 'the Chief' was ready to give Dukes a more detailed brief. In the few minutes that he was left alone, Dukes had the opportunity to admire the bound volumes that adorned the shelves. Among them was a complete edition of Thackeray's works in a decorative binding of green morocco. He took down *Henry Esmond* in order to look at the title page.

'To my bewilderment, the cover did not open, until, passing my finger accidentally along what I thought was the edge of the pages, the front suddenly flew open of itself, disclosing a box.'

Dukes almost dropped the volume in astonishment. As he clutched it to prevent it falling from his hands, a sheet of paper slipped out. 'I picked it up hastily and glanced at it. It was headed Kriegsministerium, Berlin, had the German Imperial arms imprinted on it and was covered with minute handwriting in German.'

Dukes hastily stuffed it back into the box and replaced the book on the shelf. He did so in the nick of time, for the colonel re-entered the room at that very moment. 'A – the – er – Chief is not in,' he told Dukes. 'But you may see him tomorrow.'

He then proceeded to chat about his little library, informing him that the only volume of value was a book on Cardinal Richelieu. It was directly above *Henry Esmond* and Dukes warily pulled it from the shelf 'expecting something uncommon to occur, but it was only a musty old volume in French with torn leaves and soiled pages.'

Dukes returned to the building for a third time on the following day and was ushered back to the colonel's room. The colonel was keen to talk more about his book collection, telling Dukes that he was particularly proud of his Thackeray volumes. He asked him if he would care to look at them.

'I looked at the colonel very hard, but his face was a mask . . . I rose quietly and took down *Henry Esmond*, which was in exactly the same place as it had been the day before. To my utter confusion, it opened quite naturally and I found in my hands nothing more than an *edition de luxe* printed on Indian paper and profusely illustrated.'

Dukes was utterly mystified. There was no other copy of *Henry Esmond* and the volume of Cardinal Richelieu stood directly above it, as it had done on the previous day. ' "It's a beautiful edition," he repeated, as if wearily. "Now, if you are ready, we will go and see – er – the Chief." '

Dukes was led through a maze of corridors and passages until he was totally confused as to where he was. 'From the suddenness with which the angle of view changed, I concluded that in reality we were simply gyrating in one very limited space, and when suddenly we entered a spacious study – the sanctum of "er – the Chief" – I had an irresistible sentiment that we had moved only a few yards.'

Dukes still had no clue as to Cumming's identity and was unsure as to how he should introduce himself. The colonel knocked and then opened the door. 'From the threshold, the room seemed bathed in semi-obscurity,' wrote Dukes. 'The writing desk was so placed with the window behind it that on entering, everything appeared only in silhouette.'

In the long silence that followed, he was able to make a brief survey of the room. 'A row of half-a-dozen extending telephones stood at the left of a big desk littered with papers. On a side table were numerous maps and drawings, with models of aeroplanes, submarines and mechanical devices, while a row of bottles of various colours and a distilling outfit with a rack of test tubes bore witness to chemical experiments and operations.'

Dukes was not at liberty to name Cumming in his memoirs, for C's identity was at that time still a closely guarded secret. 'I may not describe him,' he wrote, 'nor mention even one of his twenty-odd names.' Yet he managed to convey the aura with which Cumming liked to cloak himself.

'In silhouette I saw myself motioned to a chair. The Chief wrote for a moment then suddenly turned with the unexpected remark, "So, I understand you want to go back to Soviet Russia, do you?" as if it had been my own suggestion.'

Cumming proceeded to brief Dukes on what he would be required to do once he was back inside Russia. He was to travel alone and would be expected to create his own network of couriers to smuggle out his reports.

' "Don't go and get killed," said the Chief in conclusion, smiling. "You will put him through the ciphers," he added to the colonel, "and take him to the laboratory to learn the inks and all that." '

It was the end of the meeting. Dukes was escorted back out of the room and given a brief training in codes and secret inks. Three weeks later, he was on his way back to Soviet Russia.

★

Paul Dukes was not the only new recruit to Cumming's revamped Russian network. For the previous two years, Arthur Ransome had been passing information to the Secret Intelligence Service, although always in an unofficial capacity. Now, that was about to change. Ransome was an obvious candidate to be sent back to Soviet Russia as an officially employed spy.

There were, however, problems with his appointment. Ransome's close personal friendship with the Bolshevik leaders and his intimate relationship with Trotsky's secretary had made him a suspect person. The publication of his pamphlet, *On Behalf of Russia: An Open Letter to America* had hardly helped matters. It was an attempt to reconcile the American government to the new political reality inside Russia. Its tone, similar to that of his newspaper despatches, particularly offended officers from MI5.

'His articles have been, I consider, most detrimental,' wrote one of those officers, 'as he has frequently applauded the Bolshevik Government and one is forced to the conclusion that he has become a Bolshevik himself.'

The head of Military Intelligence, William Thwaites, also mistrusted Ransome, labelling him 'a Bolshevik agent'. He said that his articles were 'nothing but Bolshevik propaganda' and added: 'personally, I cannot understand the *Daily News* or any other paper being prepared to pay for the rubbish he telegraphs.'

Matters would eventually reach a head. The editor of the *Daily News*, A.G. Gardiner, had also become increasingly irritated by Ransome's articles. He told colleagues that his erstwhile correspondent had 'gone native' and decided to recall him from his current base in Stockholm.

There was a swift response when this news reached Whitehall Court. A senior member of Cumming's team paid a visit to Gardiner and quietly informed him that it was essential for Ransome to remain at his post. His work was so vital to British interests that the Secret Intelligence Service offered to cover all his costs.

Officers from MI5 were also warned to stop attacking Ransome. 'We expect to get a lot of most valuable stuff from him,' they were told. 'It is hoped that you will see your way, so to speak, to leave him alone for a bit and give him a chance.'

Ransome's rehabilitation was facilitated by Robert Bruce Lockhart. After his expulsion from Russia, Lockhart had met up with Ransome in Stockholm. He took the opportunity to introduce him to Clifford Sharp, who was working for Cumming's Stockholm bureau under the acronym S8.

Lockhart held Ransome in high esteem, having become friends with him when the two of them were living at the Elite

Hotel in Moscow. He told Sharp that Ransome 'was on excellent terms with the Bolsheviks and frequently brought us information of the greatest value.'

He also dismissed suggestions that he was not to be trusted and showed considerable insight in appreciating Ransome for what he was: a radical thinker with a sentimental streak.

'[He] was a Don Quixote with a walrus moustache,' he wrote, 'a sentimentalist who could always be relied upon to champion the underdog, and a visionary whose imagination had been fired by the revolution.'

Lockhart was infuriated by those who claimed that Ransome was unpatriotic: 'I championed him resolutely against the secret service idiots who later tried to denounce him as a Bolshevik agent.'

George Hill joined Lockhart in testifying to Ransome's trustworthiness. 'He was extremely well informed, intimate with the Bolsheviks and masterly in summing up a situation,' he said.

Hill had also spent time at the Elite Hotel and had at one point even shared a bathroom with Ransome. 'Our profoundest discussions and most heated arguments took place when Ransome was sitting in the bath and I wandering up and down my room dressing,' he recalled.

Ransome hated losing their verbal sparring matches. 'Sometimes, when I had the better of an argument and his feelings were more than usually outraged, he would jump out of the water and beat himself dry like an angry gorilla.'

Ransome would then disappear and Hill would not see him for two or three days. 'Then we would meet and grin at each other, I would ask after the pet snake which lived in a large cigar box in his room, and the following morning he would come in as usual and we would begin arguing again, the best of friends.'

Clifford Sharp heard enough about Ransome to be convinced that he could be trusted. '[He] may be regarded as absolutely honest,' he wrote in a report to London. 'His reports about conditions in Russia may be relied upon absolutely with only the proviso that his view tends to be coloured by his personal sympathies.'

Cumming's Stockholm bureau chief, John Scale, had also changed his opinion of Ransome. He conceded that he had been 'badly handled' and informed London that 'he is quite loyal and willing to help by giving information, and that this appearance of working against us is due to his friendship with the Bolshevik leaders, not by any means to any sympathy with the regime, which the Terror had made him detest.'

This was true enough. In a private letter to his mother, Ransome admitted that although he enjoyed the company of a handful of senior Bolsheviks – men like Karl Radek – the rest were 'a pig-headed, narrow-minded set of energetic lunatics, energetic as if possessed by seven devils apiece.'

Cumming had heard enough to believe that Ransome could be trusted and now formally enrolled him on his books, giving him the acronym ST76. There remained one logistical problem: how to get him and Shelepina back into Russia. Both had fled the country just before the Allied intervention and were unlikely to be granted permission to return.

Two events saved the day. The first was a widely reported speech given by Lockhart, quite possibly at the behest of the Secret Intelligence Service. Lockhart publicly denounced Ransome's journalism as erratic and untrustworthy.

The second, more dramatic, event was orchestrated by John Scale. He persuaded the Swedish authorities to expel

Ransome and Shelepina from the country, along with eleven others, on the grounds that they were revolutionary Bolsheviks.

These two developments were enough to convince the regime in Moscow that Ransome could still be trusted. Within weeks he was on a boat bound for Petrograd, travelling legitimately under his own name. But to Cumming's team in London, he was now Agent ST76.

CHAPTER TWELVE

TOXIC THREAT

In the great southern underbelly of Soviet Russia, Frederick Bailey was still living an undercover double life disguised as Andrei Kekechi, an Austrian chef. He had to tread with care for he was a wanted man with a price on his head. Anyone found harbouring him risked being shot.

The authorities were so desperate to catch Bailey that they assigned agents from both the Cheka and the counter-espionage department to his case. 'Some amusement was caused when the counter-espionage spies arrested the Inquiry Commission [Cheka] spies on suspicion of being enemy agents,' wrote Bailey.

His most important task was to gather intelligence on the threat that Tashkent's Moscow-backed regime posed to British India. He also needed to discover the extent of Bolshevik rule in the bleak plains and mountain ranges of Russian Central Asia.

He soon learned that not all of Turkestan had fallen to the Bolsheviks. Little islands of resistance remained and these were becoming rallying points for all who opposed Lenin's regime. The caravan cities of Bokhara and Khiva remained hostile, as did the remote Ferghana Valley.

But the independence of such places was looking shaky. Bailey knew that if these little bastions fell to the Bolsheviks, then Afghanistan and Chinese Turkestan would be likely to follow suit. If so, Lenin's realm would extend to the gates of India.

Bailey tried to travel to one of these enclaves but it proved well-nigh impossible. All of the routes were controlled by forces loyal to the Bolsheviks. This was a blow, but there was far worse to come. On his way back to Tashkent, he lost his balance in the deep snow and plunged more than two hundred feet down the side of a mountain, smashing his leg on a rocky outcrop and severely dislocating his knee. Only a large dose of self-administered opium enabled him to bear the excruciating pain.

'The accident upset all my plans,' he wrote from his temporary refuge in a mountain cave. As the snow stacked up against the vertical peaks that encircled him, he could do nothing but gaze helplessly at the gunmetal sky. He was to be out of action for several months.

Only at this point did the dangers of being a lone operator become acutely apparent. Unlike Mansfield Cumming's agents, who were rarely more than two days' journey from the Russian border with Finland, Bailey was hundreds of miles from safety. Worse still, he was entirely without backup or support. His life would have been in grave danger in the aftermath of the accident had it not been for a group of local tribesmen who protected him and brought him food.

Back in England, Bailey's elderly mother, Florence, was growing increasingly alarmed by the lack of news from her intrepid son. She had no idea why he had been sent to Tashkent and nor did she know how long he was to be away. The only certainty was that he was engaged in an operation that entailed great danger.

She had last heard from him in September, when she received an unsigned letter containing the cryptic lines: 'Nothing I can write, but things are pretty interesting for us.' This did little to reassure Florence. 'When we know what that word implies these days,' she wrote to John Shuckburgh, Secretary to the Political Department of the India Office, 'you will scarcely wonder at my anxiety. He has been in many a tight hole and extricated himself, but I fear circumstances must be against him now.'

Shuckburgh could say little to put Mrs Bailey's mind at rest. A wire transmission from Kashgar revealed that Bailey had disappeared without trace. The only good news was that he seemed to have escaped capture.

'Had anything untoward happened . . .' the wire read, 'some rumour of it would almost certainly have reached us by now and [the] probability is that he is in hiding.'

Mrs Bailey was right to be concerned for her son. Although Bailey's shattered knee eventually healed, his return to Tashkent was thwarted by a brutal anti-Bolshevik uprising. In a report that he managed to send to Percy Etherton, he described how the rebellion was crushed amid scenes of grotesque violence. The renegades were arrested by Bolshevik soldiers, stripped naked and shot in cold blood.

'Some of the Red Guards were drunk and missed or wounded their victims, who had to wait until someone finished them off, usually with a bayonet.' One man bragged of having slaughtered more than 750 rebels.

Bailey eventually smuggled himself back into Tashkent, only to find himself with another problem. For months he had been living under the identity of an Austrian named Andre Kekeshi. He had even been able to acquire identity papers bearing Kekeshi's name; papers that had seen him through several sticky situations.

'I had always imagined that Kekeshi must have been one of the many thousands of prisoners of war who had died,' wrote Bailey. But now, on his return to Tashkent, he discovered that Kekeshi 'was very much alive and was incommoded by the absence of his passport which he had lent to a friend for a short time.'

Bailey was fortunate in acquiring a new set of papers that had formerly belonged to a Romanian soldier named Georgi Chuka. He disposed of his Austrian uniform and kitted himself out with civilian clothes. 'I also obtained a pair of plain (non-magnifying) pince-nez as a further disguise,' he wrote. These, together with his bushy beard, made him look convincingly Romanian.

Even so, he often found himself in a tight corner. He was lodging with a Tashkent landlord who kept asking him questions about his assumed homeland. 'If we had a melon on the table, I was asked if such things grew in Romania. If we had fish for dinner, I was asked about fish in Romania.' Bailey derived some amusement from inventing answers, 'knowing full well that what I said would be soon forgotten.'

★

Frederick Bailey's return to Tashkent coincided with two connected events that were to prove of immense political significance. These events were not only destined to affect Central Asia; they would also send shockwaves right around the globe.

In March, the railway line to Moscow was finally reopened, enabling a direct connection between Tashkent and the Russian capital for the first time since the revolution. Among the first people to arrive from Moscow was a team of hardline Bolshevik commissars, determined to bring order to unruly Turkestan.

They also brought a three-point plan for revolutionary action. This plan called for aggressive propaganda against British India, the establishment of agents inside the Raj and the organisation of crack military units. Turkestan was called to create 'special battalions from among the Russian Muslims in order to render active assistance to the East in its struggle against the British imperialists.'

Lenin sent a personal letter of support to the Tashkent commissars. He was intent on starting a whole new round of the Great Game, the struggle for control of Central Asia, only this time the goal was to spark violent revolution right across the East.

'Cossacks' spears appearing on the Himalayan summits were Britain's nightmare in the past,' declared an official Bolshevik document published at the time. 'Now, these will be the spears of Russian proletarian Muslims.'

Bailey learned of the arrival of the Bolshevik commissars within hours of them entering Tashkent. He also heard news that they were accompanied by a small band of Indian revolutionaries.

The threat to the Raj from home-grown revolutionaries was nothing new. For almost a decade, Mansfield Cumming had been working closely with Indian Political Intelligence on this very danger. His agents in New York, Berlin and else-where had been keeping close tabs on these men, monitoring their movements and intercepting their mail.

Among those they had been tracking was Abdul Hafiz Mohamed Barkatullah, who had established an Indian government-in-exile in the spring of 1916. Now, Barkatullah pitched up in Tashkent in order to forge closer links with the Bolsheviks.

'The ideas advanced by the Bolsheviks have already taken root in the Indian masses,' he told a journalist from *Izvestia*, 'and a small spark of active propaganda would be sufficient to set aflame a huge revolutionary fire in middle Asia.'

Bailey learned that the Indian revolutionaries had been given access to Tashkent's printing presses and were preparing inflammatory propaganda leaflets for distribution inside India. He managed to obtain one of these leaflets and was shocked by the lies that were being peddled. It said that the British had forcibly closed all mosques and Hindu temples, that education had been forbidden to Indians and that slave labour had been reintroduced.

'The Bolshevik plans for India were to start disturbances by any means possible,' wrote Bailey. 'The professed plan in the East was to exploit countries considered ripe for revolution' – India and Afghanistan – 'and compel them to adopt Communism.'

Bailey was witness to a most alarming menace; one that was wholly new. The rulers of Bolshevik Russia were intent on forging an alliance with the Islamic tribes of Afghanistan, Chinese Turkestan and the frontier regions of India. Their idea was to bring together Islamic extremists and revolutionary Bolsheviks, thereby creating a highly inflammatory movement that would be capable of engulfing British India.

The scale of their project was not merely local or regional but of global significance. 'The complete Bolshevism of Asia,' warned Bailey, 'was the key to World Revolution.'

Bailey's most urgent goal was to inform India of the plot that was taking place. But sending information from Tashkent – never easy – had become almost impossible.

'Road to Kashgar is closed by robbers,' he wrote in one report that would eventually reach Percy Etherton in Kashgar. 'I may possibly be able to send occasional messages by wireless and will only try in case of urgency. Please warn stations. Messages will be in my cipher and unsigned.'

Etherton forwarded Bailey's note to operational headquarters in Simla, adding that all of the recent messages received from Tashkent had been extremely difficult to read. 'Owing to the faintness of the invisible ink used, portions of the above message are quite illegible, repeated attempts having failed to decipher them.'

Bailey became increasingly inventive in transmitting his messages. One important report was written in invisible ink inside a book of old lithographs of Samarkand. Etherton received a message from a third party alerting him to the fact that the book 'should be rubbed with ammonia. It contains messages in invisible ink.'

Bailey's reports were picked up not only by intelligence officers in Simla but also by Mansfield Cumming's men as well. The Stockholm bureau had a particularly deep reach and its officers were, on occasion, able to transmit news of Bailey's movements to their colleagues in India.

'Colonel F M Bailey, Tashkent, sends his best salaams to [Sir Arthur] Hirtzel and [Sir John] Shuckburgh, India Office,' read one message picked up by Major Scale. 'He is at present disguised.'

Another memorandum informed the India Office that Bailey was using the key: 'Where three empires meet'. A third revealed that Bailey was 'trying to send short code messages interpolated in Bolshevik wireless from Tashkent'. Such messages had to be sent sparingly: Bailey placed himself in considerable danger each time he tried to contact his colleagues.

★

Frederick Bailey's work was not only dangerous but also extremely complex. He was attempting to uncover intelligence on a rapidly changing situation that involved people whose movements and communications were by necessity kept secret.

His task was further complicated by an unexpected development that took place in the spring of 1919. The ruler of Afghanistan, Amir Amanullah, declared a holy war against British India. His proclamation of *jihad* was primarily intended to deflect from domestic difficulties, but this was cold comfort to the poorly armed soldiers guarding the remote North West Frontier of India.

'Make their hearts tremble with your Islamic war cries,' shouted the amir in an address to his troops, 'and destroy them with your flashing swords.'

The rhetoric was fiery, but still it was pretty standard fare. More alarming was the uncompromising decree issued by the Indian revolutionaries in Tashkent. 'Murder the English wherever you find them, cut the telegraphic lines, destroy the railways lines and the railway bridges and help in all respects the liberating armies.'

The Afghans fought well, seizing several towns inside India and highlighting the extreme weakness of the British forces guarding the mountainous frontier. The first British counter-attack stalled, then failed in the stifling 40 degree heat.

Superior weaponry and the judicious use of Handley Page bombers eventually won the day. The amir's forces were driven back over the frontier. But the invasion rang warning bells in Simla and led British and Indian intelligence agents to redouble their efforts to intercept the telegraphic transmissions between Moscow and Tashkent.

These intercepted telegraphs shed much light on the alarming new threat that Bailey had witnessed in Tashkent. In the same month as the amir's invasion, a top-secret message was intercepted while it was being sent from Moscow to Tashkent.

'Islam is in imminent danger of extinction,' it warned, 'and all Mohammedan races who value their religion as well as their own existence as independent peoples should rise and join us in the struggle for world freedom.'

Such a rallying cry would have made for disturbing reading if it had come from the pen of an Islamic ruler. Far more alarming was the fact that it had been written by a Bolshevik commissar. It revealed Moscow's intention of harnessing radical Islam to its own revolutionary movement.

Shortly afterwards, Tashkent's government began issuing propaganda sheets calling upon Islamic warriors across Asia to join forces with the Bolsheviks. It urged the Muslim world to launch a violent crusade against British interests.

'The British are bleeding to death 300 million Indians . . . they have raised to the ground the tomb of the prophet . . . they have converted the Golden Shrine [in Meshed] into a cow-shed.'

Bailey did his best to monitor the negotiations between Moscow, Tashkent and Afghanistan. One of his agents managed to intercept a number of letters between Lenin and the Afghan ruler. In these letters, Lenin proposed the opening of formal and friendly relations between the two countries. What's more, he also offered military assistance to Afghanistan.

Shortly after this, Bailey witnessed a meeting in Tashkent between Afghan officials and Bolshevik commissars. 'They are treated royally,' he wrote, 'bedecked with flowers and they were received with salutes; afterwards, there was a gala performance at the theatre.'

Bolshevik leaders in Moscow had awoken to the importance of Islam to the revolutionary struggle in Central Asia. Stalin himself addressed a Muslim-Communist congress that had met in Moscow just a few months earlier. He stressed the need to spread revolutionary doctrine into the mosques and madrasahs of the Islamic world. 'No one can erect a bridge between the West and East as easily and quickly as you can,' he told the delegates.

In the autumn of 1919, those same delegates met for a second time in Tashkent and consecrated their lives to insurrection. They sent a resolution to Moscow declaring that 'Soviet Turkestan is becoming a revolutionary school for the whole East. Revolutionaries of neighbouring states are coming to us in droves . . . through them and with their help we are taking all measures for the spread of the Communist idea in the East.'

★

Frederick Bailey's work was extremely dangerous and he lived in constant fear of being caught. 'The danger of arrest was still as great as ever,' he wrote. 'It was impossible not to allow at least a few people to know who and where I was, but I kept the circle as small as possible.'

The Moscow authorities had established a 'Special Department' in Tashkent, whose task was to root out spies and traitors. 'This department posted notices in the streets asking all work people to report at once on the evil doings of the bourgeoisie, speculators, sabotagists and hooligans,' wrote Bailey. It felt like there were hidden eyes everywhere.

After a long period of no news from Bailey, British Indian officials contacted a Danish Red Cross representative named Captain Brun who was known to have met with him in Tashkent. The captain spoke of his concerns for Bailey's safety.

'With my knowledge of his pluck and energy, I hope that he has managed to escape and baffle the energetic pursuit of the government,' he wrote. 'But in case they should succeed in finding him, I am afraid his life would be in great danger.'

For some weeks Bailey had been living at the house of an anti-Bolshevik engineer named Andreyev. Now, this lodging became too dangerous. He was helped to find new accommodation by Miss Houston, the indefatigable Irish governess who had remained in Tashkent despite the turmoil.

'Stand on the corner of Romanovsky and Voronsovsky at five-thirty,' she told him, 'and you will see a grey-haired lady coming along from our house direction with a bundle wrapped in a red tablecloth under her arm.'

This was to be his new landlady. 'She will stop at the Town Hall for a minute and light a cigarette, then go on walking. You must follow; then, when she will go into her house, you pass and afterwards come back and go in yourself.'

Bailey changed his identity on several occasions in order to avoid discovery. But the house-to-house searches that were being daily conducted by the Cheka meant that even his new lodgings had become too dangerous.

'For a few days, I carried on my old plan of sleeping a single night in different houses,' he wrote. He travelled light, carrying only a small bundle of clothes, and sought shelter with the few contacts that he knew could be trusted. But this peripatetic life required a large network of safe lodgings. 'Finding fresh quarters ... was proving difficult,' he wrote, '[and] for the rest of my time in Tashkent, I flitted from house to house.'

He knew that his days in the city were numbered and that it would soon be time to make his escape.

PART THREE
THE PROFESSIONAL SPY

TOP SECRET

CHAPTER THIRTEEN

MASTER OF DISGUISE

The night was thick with frost and the moon hung low in the sky.

On the banks of the River Sestro, which marked the frontier between Finland and Russia, a lone figure could be seen crouching in the shadows. When he was sure that no one was watching, he slipped into a nearby boat and rowed in silence across the fast-flowing water.

As he jumped out on the opposite bank, he missed the shore and crashed through a sheet of ice, plunging into the freezing water. Dripping and shivering, he pulled himself onto the snowy banks. It was November 1918, and Paul Dukes – Mansfield Cumming's newest recruit – had just crossed over into Soviet Russia.

Scarcely had he recovered his breath than he heard gunshots. A Red Army border patrol had been disturbed by the crack of breaking ice and the men began firing wildly into the night.

Dukes pushed himself deep into the snow and waited. 'Finally, all was silent again,' he later recalled. After spending the rest of the night in the bitter chill, he made his way to the local station at Beloostrov and bought himself a ticket to Petrograd.

The task facing Dukes was a daunting one. Cumming urgently required intelligence on the intentions of the Bolshevik Government. Lenin's regime was now overtly hostile, that much was clear, but it was not yet known if it had the wherewithal to pursue its goal of creating lasting military alliances in Central Asia and then setting the East on fire.

Cumming also needed information about the Baltic fleet and Red Army, as well as on conditions inside the country. The Bolsheviks were under attack from three separate White armies. British ministers needed to know whether or not these forces should be backed with military hardware and troops.

To fulfil all these tasks was a tall order for one man. Dukes knew he would have to locate anti-Bolshevik insiders in the government commissariats and persuade them to hand over secret documents. If discovered, he – and they – would be shot.

Dukes had learned much from Sidney Reilly about the advantages of having several different aliases. Long before he crossed back into Soviet Russia, he had begun creating a host of false identities. Not for nothing would he later be known as 'The Man with a Hundred Faces'.

'To go back as an Englishman was totally out of the question,' he wrote. 'I resolved at Archangel to transform myself into a Russian and a Bolshevik.'

He had already switched identity twice on route to Russia, arriving at the Finnish border post as Sergei Ilitch, a Serbian businessman. Now, he changed into the clothes he had bought in Vyborg's bustling flea market: 'a Russian *rubashka* (shirt), black leather breeches, black knee boots, a shabby tunic and an old leather cap with a fur brim and a little tassel on top.' When he glanced at himself in the mirror, he saw what he described as 'a thoroughly undesirable alien.'

The Finnish guards manning the border post with Russia had been forewarned about Dukes's mission. As agreed, they helped him to create yet another fake identity. He was to enter Russia as a Ukrainian by the name of Joseph Ilitch Afirenko – the nationality had been chosen in order to explain his slight foreign accent when he spoke Russian.

The guards handed him a newly forged passport and identity papers. One of the men then opened a cupboard 'and took out a box full of rubber stamps of various sizes and shapes with black handles.

' "Soviet seals," he said, laughing at my amazement. "We keep ourselves up to date, you see." '

The seals were an important element in making the identity papers look authentic: Dukes said they were 'a talisman that levelled all obstacles.' Many Bolshevik officials were illiterate and only inspected the seals. If these were in order, the bearer was allowed to pass.

Dukes was even more surprised when one of the border guards handed him a freshly typed certificate on official paper that read as follows: 'This is to certify that Joseph Afirenko is in the service of the Extraordinary Commissar.' The document attested to his employment by the Cheka.

Dukes felt that this was taking deception a step too far, but the guards said that it would afford him the greatest possible protection once he was inside Russia. He would have carte blanche to travel wherever he wanted.

An important aim of Dukes's mission was to supply low-level intelligence on conditions inside Russia. This was the oft-forgotten (and less glamorous) side of espionage, yet it was vitally important. The exodus of British nationals from Russia meant there was very little news of what was taking place inside the country. Information about daily life was urgently required. To this end, Dukes began supplying Mansfield Cumming with monthly reports describing the hardships faced by the populace.

The catastrophic decline in living standards became apparent as soon as he stepped off the train in Petrograd. The streets were strewn with garbage and pervaded with the stench of dead and decaying corpses of horses. The inhabitants presented a picture of human misery. 'Lines of wretched people standing patiently, disposing of personal belongings or of food got by foraging in the country.'

The opulent palaces that lined the Moika lay deserted, for the dynastic families had either fled or been shot in the Red Terror. The city's liberal intelligentsia, along with its writers and journalists, had met with a similar fate. So had the wealthiest business magnates.

Felix Dzerzhinsky himself had encouraged his Cheka officers to devote all their energies to a ruthless class war. He called for 'the extermination of the enemies of the revolution on the basis of their class affiliation or of their pre-revolutionary roles.' He said that up to ten million people would have to be annihilated – all those who had actively supported the old order.

Dukes had grown up in pre-revolutionary St Petersburg and had known the city at the height if its imperial splendour. Now he got to see first-hand the Soviet system that Lenin was determined to impose on the city, the vast country and ultimately the rest of the world.

'The market places of Petrograd are crowded daily with thousands selling every imaginable sort of goods . . .' he wrote, 'people with a few herrings in filthy pieces of newspaper, a number of individuals displaying on their open palms lumps of sugar at 6 or 7 roubles per lump.' It was tangible evidence of a growing economic catastrophe.

Dukes had decided to remain incognito during his entire time in Russia, for he had no wish to implicate any of his former friends. But he did make contact with John Merrett, who had been keeping Mansfield Cumming's espionage operations alive ever since the departure of Reilly, Hill and Lockhart.

Merrett told him how the secret police had been on his trail for many weeks. Just a few days earlier he had managed to make 'a larky getaway' as they burst into his apartment. He escaped from their clutches by 'slithering down a drainpipe outside his kitchen window.'

On that occasion he had managed to disappear into the night, but he knew they would soon be back on his trail. 'The blighters are looking for me everywhere,' he told Dukes. 'I was held up one evening by one of their damned spies under a lamppost, so I screwed up my face into a grimace and asked him for a light. Then I knocked him down.'

Merrett provided Dukes with a graphic account of the dangers of life in Russia. He also told him of his intention to leave the country immediately, for he had been warned that the Cheka were closing in on him.

He gave Dukes a list of all his underground contacts and agents, including several employed by the Ministry of War. He also gave him the addresses of all the safe houses in the city.

Then, after a brief farewell, Merrett fled the city in disguise: 'With his face smudged with dirt and decorated with three days' growth of reddish beard, a driver's cap that covered his ears and a big sack on his back, Murometz [Dukes's code-name for Merrett] looked – well, like nothing on earth.'

Dukes tentatively made contact with known anti-Bolshevik agents living in Petrograd – men and women whose names were so secretive that he only ever referred to them by their professions: The Banker, The Policeman, The Journalist. He made it known that his first requirement was intelligence on the state of the Baltic fleet.

It was not long before he was brought a top-secret report that had been intercepted while it was being transmitted to Trotsky from the commander in chief of the Bolshevik Navy. It revealed that coal was in such short supply that the fleet could no longer put to sea.

Dukes also obtained the confidential minutes of a meeting of the Revolutionary Military Soviet, chaired by Trotsky himself. This provided many more revelations about the state of the fleet and included an amusing anecdote about Trotsky's fury on learning that officers were being forced to clean the lavatories.

'[He] thumped his fist on the table, smashing an ink-stand, and declared in an excited voice: "I dare not call this sort of thing by its right name, as there is a lady present." '

The most important piece of intelligence was a plan of the minefields that surrounded the fort of Kronstadt in the Gulf of Finland. This included an instruction to the mine-layers that was to prove critical to Dukes's own survival in the months to come. 'The mines,' it said, 'must be laid at a depth of 2½ to 3 feet from the surface.'

When Mansfield Cumming read these lines, he realised that any future naval operation in the Gulf of Finland would require a wholly new type of vessel – flat bottomed and of shallow draught – if they were to avoid being blown up by mines.

In a short space of time, Dukes managed to forge contacts inside various commissariats and thereby provide Cumming with a steady supply of intelligence documents. His work was much appreciated in London. He received a message of praise from Whitehall and learned from the Stockholm bureau that he would be given every possible support.

'The whole of the Baltic area was told to be ready to render me assistance . . . my name was kept a strict secret and if ever I needed to use an English name, I was told to use Captain McNeill.'

Cumming himself ordered that Dukes be helped in every possible way. 'Supply ST25 with everything he wants,' he told his men in Stockholm, 'and convey thanks.'

Dukes spent part of his time mingling with the local Petrograd dockworkers in order to gauge morale in the fleet. He invented a whole new biography of himself, telling the sailors that his hostility to the old regime had led him to be banished from Russia. He even spun a tale about being imprisoned in England, '[where] the brutality and starvation to which I had been subjected in the English jail had reduced me both physically and mentally and I was a confirmed invalid for a long time to come.'

He relished the deceit, limping along with a stick and wincing with every step. The sailors took pity on him and repeated his stories to their comrades, telling them that he had been a 'victim of capitalist maltreatment'.

Dukes continued to use the persona of Joseph Ilitch Afirenko throughout the spring of 1919. But he also adopted a second disguise, that of Joseph Krylenko, having managed to forge papers in Krylenko's name.

He would later assume a third identity, Alexander Vasilievitch Markovitch, a clerical assistant at the head postal-telegraph office. He even acquired a uniform and a set of blank post-office identity papers that he filled in with Markovitch's personal details.

'Tracing the signatures carefully, and inserting a recent date, I managed to produce a document indistinguishable as regards authenticity from the original.'

Dukes was proud of his various personas and had himself photographed in disguise. His pose as Afirenko saw him sporting a wispy moustache and beard, a missing front tooth and oval framed glasses. It gave him the air of an impoverished mathematician.

As Markovitch, he cut a quite different figure. With his neatly trimmed beard, smart fur hat and round glasses, he looked like a provincial but well-educated functionary.

Dukes would later become Alexander Bankau, who bore no resemblance to his other incarnations. For this role, he shaved his beard and discarded the fur hat. As Bankau, he would sport a razor-sharp moustache, a peaked cap and workers' smock. He looked the perfect Bolshevik revolutionary.

He felt so confident in his various disguises that he decided to return to the apartment in which he had lived before the revolution. He had left some belongings there and wanted to know if they were still there.

He visited the flat in the guise of Alexander Markovitch, hoping that the friendly old housekeeper, Martha Timofeievna, would not recognise him. When she opened the door, he told her that he was a friend of Paul Dukes and had come to pick up some of his belongings. His disguise worked to perfection. Martha had no clue as to his real identity.

Dukes got a surprise when he looked through his remaining possessions. 'I came upon my own photograph taken two or three years before,' he wrote. 'For the first time, I fully and clearly realised how complete was my present disguise, how absolutely different I now appeared in a beard, long hair and glasses.'

He passed the photo to Martha in order to gauge her reaction. 'Was he not a nice man,' she sighed. 'I wonder where he is now and what he is doing?'

Dukes concealed his smile. ' "I wonder," I repeated, diving again into the muck on the floor. To save my life, I could not have looked at Martha Timofeievna at that moment and kept a straight face.'

★

While Paul Dukes was living his undercover life in the northern city of Petrograd, Arthur Ransome was reporting to Mansfield Cumming on the situation in Moscow.

Ransome had no need for false identity papers for he had crossed the frontier quite openly, after being expelled from Stockholm on suspicion of being a Bolshevik. He and Evgenia travelled by train to Moscow, arriving on 'a rare cold day' and paying over the odds for a sledge-driver to take them to the Metropol. The hotel was full, but Ransome's old friend Lev Karakhan, Commissar for Foreign Affairs, came to the rescue and secured him rooms in the Hotel National.

Ransome had told the Bolshevik leadership (truthfully, as it later transpired) that he was intending to write a history of the Bolshevik revolution. This opened many doors. Over the weeks that followed, Ransome was given free rein to attend meetings of the Executive Committee and interview all the most important political players.

In his 'Report on the State of Russia', written for Mansfield Cumming and the Foreign Office, he said he was given unlimited access to ministries and meetings. 'I was entirely uncontrolled . . .' he wrote. 'The Bolsheviks, knowing I am writing a history of the revolution, gave me every possible assistance.'

Trotsky suspected him of being a spy, as did Grigori Zinoviev. Indeed Ransome would later confess that he had 'run considerable risks of detection at the hands of the Bolsheviks.' Yet he was always protected by Lenin, who trusted him as a supporter of the revolution.

The book that Ransome eventually published, *Six Weeks in Russia*, contained pithy descriptive portraits of the most important commissars. These were often satirical and always irreverent: only Lenin escaped censure. 'This little, bald-headed wrinkled man who tilts his chair this way and that, laughing over one thing or another . . .'

The two men liked to banter about the revolutionary struggle. Lenin genuinely enjoyed Ransome's company 'and paid me the compliment of saying that "although English", I had more or less succeeded in understanding what they were at.'

Ransome insisted that England was not ripe for revolution, but Lenin refused to listen. 'We have a saying that a man may have typhoid while still on his legs,' he said. 'Twenty, maybe thirty years ago, I had abortive typhoid and was going about with it, [and] had had it some days before it knocked me over . . . England may seem to you untouched, but the microbe is already there.'

Lenin was convinced that the entire world was tipping inexorably towards revolution and told Ransome of his conviction that one extra push would bring the old order crashing down.

He had good reason for his optimism, for a glance around the globe revealed a world in upheaval. The Ottoman Empire was on the brink of collapse and the Hapsburg Empire lay in ruins. Berlin was in revolutionary turmoil and even the victorious Allied powers faced massive social unrest in the aftermath of war.

In the first week of March 1919, Ransome was privy to some sensational news. It might never have reached his ears had it not been for the unguarded comments of the senior Bolshevik functionary, Nikolai Bucharin.

Bucharin had heard that Ransome was thinking of leaving Russia. Never doubting that he was anything but a loyal Bolshevik, he offered a piece of advice.

'Wait a few days longer,' he said, 'because something of international importance is going to happen which will almost certainly be of interest for your history.'

Ransome was intrigued. No one else had spoken of this event. Indeed officials had been studiously careful not to mention it in his presence. 'Only once,' he would later write, 'I found them hiding something from me.'

This 'something' was indeed to prove of immense significance. That very week, a meeting in Moscow saw the founding of a new body, the Comintern, which was dedicated to fomenting global revolution.

This was no hypothetical goal. The new organisation had been created in order to struggle 'by all available means, including armed force, for the overthrow of the international bourgeoisie and the creation of an international Soviet republic.' The meeting was to bring together revolutionary activists from around the world, with more than two dozen countries represented.

Arthur Ransome eventually obtained permission to attend the opening session of the Comintern. On his way to the meeting, he bought the local newspapers and noted with interest that they made no mention of it whatsoever. 'It was still a secret,' he wrote.

He made his way to the Kremlin, where the gathering was being held, and watched as the delegates assembled in the Courts of Justice built by Catherine the Great. The décor had been elaborately prepared for the occasion: 'the whole room, including the floor, was decorated in red.' The walls were festooned with revolutionary banners in different languages and the principal Soviet delegates were already in their seats.

'Everyone of importance was there,' noted Ransome, including Lenin and Trotsky. The latter had come in full military garb: 'leather coat, military breeches and gaiters, with a fur hat with the sign of the Red Army in front.'

The audience was waiting in great expectation; waiting for Lenin to issue his rallying cry for global revolution. Eventually the great man rose to his feet and prepared to launch into his speech. As he did so, the delegates leapt from their seats in frenzied excitement and began cheering and whistling in support of their leader.

'Everybody [was] standing and drowning his attempts to speak, with roar after roar of applause,' wrote Ransome. They were so loud and enthusiastic that it was a long time before Lenin could make himself heard.

Ransome was blown away by the experience, not least because of the secrecy that surrounded the meeting. 'It was an extraordinary, overwhelming scene, tier after tier crowded with workmen, the parterre filled, the whole platform and the wings.'

When the crowd finally fell silent, Lenin launched into a wild invective, promising that the Comintern would export revolution around the globe. 'Let the bourgeoisie of the world rage, let them drive away, imprison, and even kill the

[Bolsheviks]. All this is of no avail.' He said that Soviet Russia was the leader of an international struggle in which there could be only one winner.

No one was in any doubt that Lenin was in earnest when he spoke of unleashing terror around the world. His words were uttered with such chilling conviction that Ransome listened wide-eyed.

'It was really an extraordinary affair . . .' he wrote, '[and] I could not help realising that I was present at something that will go down in the histories of socialism.'

Ransome met with Lenin in private on the day that followed the conference and pressed him further on the founding of the Comintern and its drive for world revolution. He particularly wanted to know the implications for Britain.

'We are at war,' was Lenin's blunt reply. 'And just as during your war, you tried to make revolution in Germany . . . so we, while we are at war with you, adopt the measures that are open to us.' These 'measures' included invasion, insurrection and militant propaganda.

Lenin chatted candidly with Ransome, unaware that his words were being sent directly to Mansfield Cumming. The report that Ransome eventually compiled was detailed, covering political and economic aspects of life in Russia. He also acquired a number of documents from the Commissariats of Labour, Trade and Education: 'practically all the printed matter that was available,' he wrote. This was all despatched to London.

Ransome warned that the Bolshevik government had been 'very much strengthened' over the preceding months. He also stressed that Lenin and Trotsky were committed to global revolution. Both men had long spoken of their intention of spreading revolutionary mayhem around the world. Now, with the establishment of the Comintern, they had a tool with which to achieve this.

★

Paul Dukes was still in Petrograd when the Comintern was established 'amid circumstances of great secrecy'. Shortly after the Moscow meeting, he learned that several key delegates were due to visit Petrograd. Aware of the significance of what was taking place, he made it his business to meet them. Among them was Grigori Zinoviev, the first chairman of the Comintern.

Dukes had first met Zinoviev before the revolution and had viewed him as a firebrand. Now Dukes heard his acid tongue in action once again. His position in the upper hierarchy of Bolsheviks had done nothing to improve his oratory. He had become 'a gutter demagogue of low type, with bloated features and a vicious tongue.'

Dukes's goal was to investigate the aims of the Comintern and he soon laid his hands on a report, written by Lev Karakhan, the Assistant Commissar for Foreign Affairs. This set out Bolshevik policy towards the East and gave details of a special mission that was being established to promote revolution and civil unrest.

'The main object of the Mission,' according to the report, 'is to form connexions with revolutionary societies, to establish a centre in Turkestan for revolutionary activities in the East, where literature may be published, agents recruited and where it will be easier to keep in touch with affairs and direct the work according to the demands of the moment.'

The report made for such disturbing reading that it would (at a much later date) be published in *The Times*. Dukes noted that the Bolshevik mission had been provided with 'an enormous sum' to foment trouble. 'It was decided to do everything possible to excite anti-British feelings in India, working at the same time on the fanatical religious sentiment of the natives.' The Comintern wanted to harness militant Islam to its own revolutionary goals.

Dukes always tried to send original documents to Mansfield Cumming. But this was not always possible and he often had to make notes in secret and at short notice.

Some reports were so sensitive that they had to be copied in invisible ink. 'I made the ink by – oh, it doesn't matter how,' wrote Dukes in his memoir. He had presumably been briefed about using semen when reporting highly sensitive information.

Dukes hid all his reports in his apartment until such time as they were ready to be transmitted to Stockholm. 'I wrote mostly at night, in minute handwriting on tracing paper, with a small caoutchouc [rubber] bag about four inches in length, weighted with lead, ready at my side.'

He was constantly listening out for the Cheka. 'In case of alarm, all my papers could be slipped into this bag and within thirty seconds be transferred to the bottom of a tub of washing or the cistern of the water-closet.'

It was the perfect hiding place. Dukes said he had seen Cheka officials turn entire apartments upside down in their quest to find hidden documents, 'but it never occurred to anybody to search through a pail of washing or thrust his hand into the water closet.'

It was one thing to prepare his reports for transmission to London, quite another to smuggle them out of the country. Dukes inherited John Merrett's courier system but it proved far from perfect. One of the key couriers was executed in January 1919, and Dukes urgently needed to find a new one.

He eventually found the perfect candidate, a man whom he referred to as Peter Petrovitch. His real name was Pyotr Sokoloff, an imposing figure who was 'tall and muscular, slightly round-shouldered, with thick fair hair and a good humoured but somewhat shy expression.' He was well equipped for danger: 'a crack revolver shot and a prize boxer.'

Sokoloff's preferred method of transporting documents to Finland (and thence to Sweden) was on foot. 'The first time he took my despatches, it was in winter and he went on skis,' recalled Dukes. 'He was to run out at night onto the frozen sea near Sestroretsk, opposite Kronstadt, and ski across the snow-covered ice to Finland.'

It was a hazardous trip, for the coastline was under constant observation by Red Guards. On one occasion, Dukes himself made the journey, only to end up being chased by Red Army soldiers. 'Suddenly there was a flash and a crack, then another and another,' he wrote. 'They were firing with carbines, against which a pistol was useless . . . a bullet whipped close to my ear.'

Dukes flung himself out of his dog-sledge and slid across the ice, clutching his precious reports. His pursuers did not notice his escape: they continued to chase after the empty sledge while Dukes hid in the craters of rough sea ice. When the soldiers were no longer in sight, he trekked across the frozen bay until he reached the ice-bound harbour of Terijoki in Finland.

'It must have been a weird, bedraggled creature that stumbled several hours later, up the steep bank of the Finnish shore,' he wrote.

CHAPTER FOURTEEN

THE LETHAL M DEVICE

He had only been recently appointed Secretary of State for
War, yet he was outspoken in his approach to Bolshevik
Russia. He viewed Lenin and his commissars as an enemy
that needed to be fought and crushed before it was too late.

'Of all the tyrannies in history,' he said, 'the Bolshevist
tyranny is the worst, the most destructive, and most
degrading.'

He surprised many in his audience by declaring that 'it is
sheer humbug to pretend that it [Bolshevism] is not far worse
than German militarism.'

He contended that the revolutionary atrocities being
committed by Lenin and his comrades were 'incomparably
more hideous, on a larger scale and more numerous than any
for which the Kaiser is responsible.' Now they were intending
to export those atrocities right around the globe.

Churchill would have liked to send large numbers of British
troops into Soviet Russia with immediate effect, but his

F ive weeks after the founding of the Comintern, Winston
Churchill made a keynote speech at the Connaught
Rooms in London.

ministerial colleagues demurred. They had little appetite for renewed warfare and they were acutely aware that public opinion would not support large-scale military intervention. Prime Minister David Lloyd George listened to Churchill's Connaught speech with consternation: 'He has Bolshevism on the brain,' he later remarked, '[and] he is mad for operations in Russia.'

Churchill's anti-Bolshevik speeches were to grow increasingly strident in the months to come as he sought to persuade colleagues of the absolute necessity of major intervention in Russia, including the deployment of ground troops.

'Bolshevism is not a policy, it is a disease,' he told the House of Commons shortly after his Connaught speech. In an address to his constituents he went even further, warning that 'civilisation is being completely extinguished over gigantic areas while Bolsheviks hop and caper like troops of ferocious baboons amid the ruins of cities and the corpses of their victims.'

Churchill warmed to his baboon theme and used it on a number of occasions. 'I will not submit to be beaten by the baboons,' he thundered to one audience; he also spoke of the need to fight 'against the foul baboonery of Bolshevism.'

In another speech, equally colourful, he described the new regime in Russia as 'a league of failures, the criminals, the morbid, the deranged and the distraught', while those who supported them were 'typhus-bearing vermin.'

Churchill's choice of language offended many. Even *The Times* baulked at his turn of phrase. Churchill was unrepentant. 'I did not expect to encounter the hostile criticism of *The Times*,' he wrote in a haughty response to their lead article.

Churchill continued to argue the case for armed intervention: he said it was Britain's moral duty to throw military support behind the White armies that were locked in a desperate struggle against the Bolsheviks. In Churchill's eyes, they represented the last hope of destroying the dangerous regime in Russia. But he also knew that parliament could not consider any intervention until it had a hard-headed assessment of the strengths and qualities of the White armies.

Military intelligence now became a priority. Britain had already landed small numbers of troops in both Archangel and Siberia and a delegation had been sent to serve alongside General Denikin, the commander of the Volunteer Army in the Ukraine.

It was in order to gather intelligence on these latter forces that Mansfield Cumming had sent Sidney Reilly and George Hill back into Russia at the same time as Paul Dukes. Their task was to report on General Denikin's strengths and weaknesses and determine if he was the right horse to back in the battle against Bolshevism.

★

Reilly was under sentence of death when he made his way back to Russia in the company of George Hill. The Bolshevik Revolutionary Tribunal had tried him in absentia in November 1918, along with everyone else involved in the attempted coup. Reilly (together with Lockhart) was found guilty of conspiring to overthrow the Bolshevik government. He knew that he too would be executed if ever he were to be apprehended on Soviet territory.

Reilly was unfazed by the death sentence; indeed, he was rather looking forward to returning to Russia. George Hill was less enthusiastic, if only because he had been given so little time to prepare for the voyage.

Reilly had noticed Hill's reluctance to leave England and chided him for it. 'Hill,' he said, 'I don't believe you want to catch that train. I bet you fifty pounds you won't be on it.' In the event, Hill jumped onto the train just seconds before it was due to pull out of Victoria station. Ever the sportsman, Reilly paid up the fifty pounds.

There was a brief stop in Paris, where the two men indulged themselves with a gastronomic dinner 'with marvellous wine and the oldest brandies served as brandy should be served, in crystal goblets.' They then continued southwards to Marseilles, Malta and Constantinople before eventually arriving in Rostov in Southern Russia.

There was no need for them to travel in disguise, for the area they were visiting was firmly under the control of General Denikin's anti-Bolshevik Volunteer Army. Yet the situation remained volatile and they faced considerable danger. Reilly and Hill followed Mansfield Cumming's advice and posed as English merchants attempting to forge trading links with Russia's Black Sea ports. It gave them a cover of sorts.

General Denikin's ultimate goal was to sweep the Bolsheviks from power and install a new government in their place. He was not alone in fighting for such an outcome. In Siberia, a second army headed by Admiral Aleksandr Kolchak (formerly of the Tsarist navy) was also hoping to drive the Bolsheviks from power. It numbered some 200,000 men, almost a quarter of whom were nationals of the Allied powers, including 7,500 Americans and 1,600 British.

The British had been landed in batches over the previous six months. They were not there to fight; rather they were 'to assist the orderly elements of Russian society to organise themselves under a national government.'

Most of the troops were hopelessly unfit for active service: they nicknamed themselves the Hernia Battalion. It was a far cry from the sort of intervention being suggested by Churchill.

There would soon be a third White Russian general fighting the Bolsheviks. Nikolai Yudenitch had his headquarters in the Baltic States and presented a serious threat to Petrograd. He was hoping to advance on the city and capture it before the Red Army could reinforce its defences.

At the time of Reilly and Hill's arrival in Southern Russia, British interests were focussed on General Denikin. He seemed to represent the best hope for a future, non-Bolshevik Russia, and Reilly and Hill were keen to meet him as soon as possible. But they were told that any meeting would have to wait until the New Year festivities had come to an end.

The two men took themselves to the Palace Hotel in Rostov where they joined a glittering soirée in the hotel's spectacular ballroom. Arriving at the dance amid a sea of fur and diamonds, Hill had a sudden flashback to pre-revolutionary Russia. The revellers were dancing to a lively rendition of 'The Merry Widow' and in the centre of the ballroom a fountain splashed water into a carp-filled pool.

Some of the men were in imperial evening dress, dusted off for the evening and last worn at the pre-war winter balls of St Petersburg. But the turmoil of revolution had left its mark on everyone present. 'Beautiful women wore threadbare blouses [and] down-at-heel shoes,' wrote Hill, 'yet on their fingers displayed rings, or on their necks collars that would have made even a Cartier's assistant's mouth water.'

The glamour of these former ladies of the court was rarely more than skin deep. Most had forsaken all their worldly belongings when they had fled their palaces in fear of their lives. They had 'the air of duchesses', wrote Hill, and wore 'luxurious fur coats', but they 'took good care to keep [them] fastened, for in most cases anything worn beneath was scanty and painfully shabby.'

Hill welled up with melancholy as he gazed upon the faded glory. Reilly, however, was heartened to see that the old ways had not been entirely extinguished. He clicked his heels and stood to attention as the band gave a rousing performance of the Russian national anthem.

'I watched Reilly's face,' wrote Hill, 'with its long, straight nose, dark penetrating eyes, large mouth and black hair brushed back from his forehead – as he sipped Turkish coffee, took an occasional drink of iced water and with precision smoked one Russian cigarette after another.'

Hill noticed that Reilly was observing everyone like a hawk and making a mental record of everything he saw. 'These, I knew on the morrow, would appear carefully analysed in his meticulous written reports.'

As midnight approached, the trumpets of the united Cossack regiments saluted the New Year and suckling pigs were released into the ballroom to increase the merriment. Hill eventually staggered to his room, bleary eyed and much the worse for wear. But as he was preparing to go to bed, he heard the strains of 'The Old Hunters' March', the regimental tune of the Preobrajensky regiment, which revived happy memories. He dashed downstairs to the ballroom dressed in only pyjamas and a Jaeger dressing gown.

'Something possessed me,' he later recalled. 'Without a word, I beckoned to the leader of the band to follow me. Which explains how it came about that the massed bands of the Don Cossacks, followed by a crowd of visitors, marched up and down the corridors and stairs, into the attics and through the kitchens of the Palace Hotel, Rostov, led by a short, plump Englishman in a flowing Jaeger dressing gown, on New Year's morn, 1919.'

No one among the crowd of revellers would ever have guessed that this short, plump Englishman was in the employ of Britain's Secret Intelligence Service.

★

Still reeling from the New Year festivities, Reilly and Hill headed to Ekaterinodar in order to meet with General Denikin and his senior staff.

Reilly was immediately struck by the fifty-year-old general's demeanour. He was dignified, cultivated and spoke with great clarity. 'He gives one the impression of a broad-minded, high-thinking, determined and well-balanced man,' wrote Reilly. Yet he had his doubts about Denikin's leadership qualities and wondered whether he could control his subordinate generals who were constantly jostling for power.

Most troublesome was General Krasnoff, leader of the formidable Don Cossack regiments. A high-minded and egocentric autocrat, Krasnoff had been persuaded into an uneasy alliance with Denikin.

Reilly feared that the alliance would not last. 'Louis XIVs maxim, *l'etat, c'est moi*, has been so completely assimilated by General Krasnoff...' he wrote, 'that any attempt at portraying the situation must naturally start from him.'

Reilly and Hill investigated many of the key people serving under Denikin and grew increasingly concerned by their sheer ineptitude. There was widespread evidence of torture throughout the general's fiefdom and abuses of power were everywhere to be found.

'Such a state of things,' concluded Reilly, 'cannot be viewed otherwise than with grave apprehension.'

Not included in his report, but later given much attention, was the malignant antisemitism of Denikin's senior officers. Pogroms were justified on the grounds that many of the leading Bolsheviks came from Jewish backgrounds.

Reilly and Hill travelled widely during their time in Southern Russia. Their reports for Mansfield Cumming, written mostly by Reilly, were accurate and balanced. They provided an excellent assessment of Denikin's requirements and his chances of victory.

The general had told the two men that he needed no fewer than fifteen British divisions to fight alongside him, as well as Whippet tanks and aeroplanes.

Hill agreed that aeroplanes would benefit Denikin's forces. 'The effects of bombing, contour chasing and machine-gun strafing would be of the greatest value,' he wrote. 'The risks to our pilots' life would, in view of the primitive state of aviation amongst the Bolsheviks, be practically nil.'

The British ground forces requested by General Denikin would, however, have faced considerable risks on the battlefield. The Red Army had swelled significantly over the previous months and now had some 500,000 men under arms. 'Mobilisation of troops is in full blast,' wrote Reilly, 'and by spring an army of over 1,000,000 is expected to take to the field.' The majority of these were to be thrust against General Denikin's Volunteer Army.

Reilly's sober report did nothing to dampen Churchill's enthusiasm for military intervention in Russia. Over the months to come, he managed to persuade the government to ship large quantities of munitions and supplies to all three of the White Russian armies fighting the Bolsheviks. The British press, overwhelmingly hostile to intervention, dubbed it 'Mr Churchill's private war.'

Yet only a tiny inner circle of people knew quite how private – indeed secret – his war had become. For at the same time as Reilly and Hill were compiling their reports, Churchill took the highly controversial decision to sanction the use of chemical weapons against the Bolsheviks.

Scientists at the governmental laboratories at Porton in Wiltshire – known to insiders as the Experimental Station – had recently developed the top secret 'M Device', an exploding shell that released a highly toxic gas derived from arsenic. The man in charge of developing the M Device, Major General Charles Foukes, called it 'the most effective chemical weapon ever devised.'

The active ingredient in the M Device was diphenylaminechloroarsine, a highly toxic chemical. A thermogenerator was used to convert this chemical into a dense smoke that would incapacitate any soldier unfortunate enough to inhale it.

Trials at Porton suggested that the M Device was indeed a terrible new weapon. The symptoms were violent and deeply unpleasant. Uncontrollable vomiting, coughing up blood and instant and crippling fatigue were the most common features.

'The pain in the head is described as like that caused when fresh water gets into the nose when bathing, but infinitely more severe . . . accompanied by the most appalling mental distress and misery.' So wrote the biologist J.B.S. Haldane in his boldly titled book, *Callinicus: A Defence of Chemical Warfare*. Victims who were not killed outright were struck down by lassitude and left depressed for long periods.

Major-General Foukes had originally hoped to use his deadly new weapon against the German Army. Indeed his 'favourite plan', as he termed it, '[was] the discharge of gas on a stupendous scale.' This was to be followed by a British attack, bypassing the trenches filled with suffocating and dying men.

The war came to an end before Foukes could use his weapons. He was left with a stockpile of chemicals and thermogenerators. Churchill now wanted the British forces stationed in small numbers in the ports of Northern Russia to deploy this stockpile against the Bolsheviks.

In the greatest secrecy, 50,000 M Devices were shipped to Archangel, along with the weaponry required to fire them. 'Fullest use is now to be made of gas shell with your forces, or supplied by us to [White] Russian forces,' wrote Churchill to the commander in chief in Archangel, Major-General Ironside.

One member of Britain's Imperial General Staff expressed concern about the use of such weapons becoming public knowledge. Churchill was also anxious about secrecy, but he was prepared to take the risk. He said that he would 'very much like the Bolsheviks to have it [a chemical attack], if we can afford the disclosure.' He believed it to be the quickest and most efficient means to crush the Bolshevik enemy before it was too late.

His head of chemical warfare production, Sir Keith Price, was in full agreement. He declared it to be '[the] right medicine for the Bolshevist' and said that in the forests of Northern Russia 'it will drift along very nicely.'

Like Churchill, he thought it could lead to the rapid collapse of the Bolshevik regime. 'I believe if you got home only once with the Gas you would find no more Bolshies this side of Vologda.'

There was considerable hostility in the Cabinet to the use of chemical weapons, much to Churchill's irritation. He wanted the M Devices used not only in Russia but also against the rebellious tribes of Northern India, to prevent them entering into a pact with the Bolsheviks.

'I am strongly in favour of using poisoned gas against uncivilised tribes,' he declared in one memorandum written at the time. He criticised his colleagues for their 'squeamishness', declaring that 'the objections of the India Office to the use of gas against natives are unreasonable. Gas is a more merciful weapon than [the] high explosive shell, and compels an enemy to accept a decision with less loss of life than any other agency of war.'

He ended his memo on a note of ill-placed black humour: 'Why is it not fair for a British artilleryman to fire a shell which makes the said native sneeze?' he asked. 'It is really too silly.'

Churchill ignored the concerns of his colleagues and instructed the government's Chemical Warfare Department to press on with their research into creating weapons suitable for use in the mountainous areas of the North-West Frontier. According to an internal War Office memo, 'experiments are to continue with a view to discovering a suitable gas bomb for use in India against insurgent tribes.'

India could not be dealt with immediately; Russia could. British aerial attacks using chemical weapons commenced at 12.30 p.m. on 27 August 1919, targeting Emtsa Station, 120 miles to the south of Archangel. Fifty-three M Devices were dropped at lunchtime and a further sixty-two in the evening. The Bolshevik soldiers on the ground were seen fleeing in panic as thick green clouds of toxic chemical gas drifted towards them.

More M Devices were dropped on the next day, followed by a chemical attack on nearby Plesetzkaya Station. One of the devices landed close to a Russian soldier named Private Boctroff of the 49th Regiment. He managed to escape from the looming gas cloud, but not before inhaling some of its poison. Captured by the British, Boctroff described the effect that the gas had on him.

According to his medical notes, he was 'affected with giddiness in head, running from ears, bled from nose and cough with blood, eyes watered and difficulty in breathing. Said he was very ill for 24 hours.'

Private Boctroff reported that a number of his comrades had been very close to the spot where the M Device had landed. 'They did not know what the cloud was and ran into it and some were overpowered in the cloud and died there; the others staggered about for a short time and then fell down and died.'

Boctroff claimed that twenty-five of his comrades had been killed. The gas also drifted through the adjacent village and hung in the air for fifteen minutes before eventually dispersing.

The attacks continued throughout the month of September, with chemical strikes on the Bolshevik-held villages of Chunova, Vikhtova, Pocha, Chorga, Tavoigor and Zapolki, along with a number of other places. Some of these attacks used large quantities of M Devices: 183 canisters were dropped on Vikhtova.

As soon as the gas had dissipated, British and White Russian troops (equipped with gas masks) would attack and drive out any remaining Bolshevik soldiers. They were warned to avoid skin contact with the earth and not to drink any water. If they were unfortunate enough to inhale any residual gas, they were told that smoking would bring relief.

One British lieutenant, Donald Grantham, later questioned many Bolshevik prisoners about the attacks. They described their gassed comrades as 'lying practically helpless on the ground and the usual symptoms of bleeding from the nose and mouth.' In extreme cases, the men coughed up large quantities of blood.

The use of chemical weapons was said to have caused widespread demoralisation on the battlefield, even among those who had not inhaled the gas. Yet they proved less effective than Churchill had hoped. Chemical attacks did not lead to the collapse of the Red Army, as he believed they would. Nor did they lead to any major breakthrough on the Northern Front. The weather was primarily to blame. Toxic gas proved ineffectual in the damp and misty conditions of an early Russian autumn.

By September, as British forces prepared to withdraw from Archangel and Murmansk, the chemical attacks were halted and then permanently stopped. According to a report written for the War Office, a total of 2,718 M Devices had been dropped on Bolshevik positions; 47,282 remained unused.

It was deemed too dangerous to ship these remaining devices back to England. In mid-September, the decision was taken to dump them in the White Sea. A military tug took them to a position thirty miles north of the Dvina Estuary and they were tipped overboard.

They remain on the sea bed to this day in forty fathoms of water.

★

Sidney Reilly and George Hill had hurried back to London after their meetings with General Denikin and presented their findings to Mansfield Cumming and other Whitehall officials. 'A fund of useful information,' was how one Foreign Office mandarin described their mission.

Their warnings about the failings of the White Army leadership did little to deter Churchill from persisting in supporting those armies throughout the autumn of 1919. There were times when it seemed as if his gamble would pay off. Admiral

Kolchak made sweeping westward advances across Siberia and General Denikin's war machine rolled relentlessly northwards, capturing a string of towns and cities. Before long, he was just 250 miles from Moscow and looked certain to vanquish the Red Army. 'We were deciding which horses we should ride during the triumphal entry into Moscow,' recalled a British lieutenant who was serving with the general.

In the North-West of Russia, General Yudenitch also seemed unstoppable. He marched his army towards Petrograd, sweeping all before it: by October 1919 his troops were just twelve miles from the city. Lenin panicked. 'Finish him off,' he wrote in a desperate telegraph to Trotsky. 'Despatch him.'

Trotsky launched his dramatic counter-attack in the third week of October and succeeded in pushing Yudenitch's army back from the gates of Petrograd. In the same week, General Denikin suffered a series of serious reverses. The Red Army smashed through his front line just a short time after a powerful rebel leader had seized control of three major towns in his rear.

A few days later, the Red Army was also victorious in Siberia, making sweeping advances against Admiral Kolchak. The admiral's end came shortly afterwards. After being decisively beaten on the battlefield, he was captured by the Bolsheviks at Irkutsk. There he was shot in cold blood, and his corpse ignominiously tipped into the river; it quickly disappeared under the ice.

On the same day as Kolchak's execution, the Bolsheviks triumphantly entered Odessa on the Black Sea coast, having recovered almost all of the territory seized by General Denikin.

George Hill happened to be back in Odessa when the Red Army rode into the city. He was woken by a breathless friend who urged him to flee before he was captured. 'The Reds have broken through!' he was told. There was no time to be lost.

Hill reacted with magnificent calm. He had a leisurely wash and shave before putting on a newly cleaned pair of spats and checking out of his hotel. He made his exit just as the Bolshevik soldiers entered the city.

By the time Odessa was in Bolshevik hands, General Yudenitch had also been defeated in the north-west of the country. He had got tantalisingly close to Petrograd – close enough to catch the glint of the city's domes and spires. But Trotsky's Red Army ultimately proved unstoppable. Yudenitch was driven back to the Baltic States from whence he had come.

British military intervention against the Bolsheviks had never been on the scale that Churchill wanted. Nevertheless, his support for the anti-Bolshevik forces had cost 329 British lives. It had also cost the government a staggering £100,000,000. Over the previous year, numerous shipments of munitions had been sent to the three White generals who were fighting Lenin's regime. The 'final packet' to Denikin was more modest than most, yet it nevertheless contained eighty field guns, twenty-five aeroplane engines and a vast quantity of winter clothing, including a million pairs of socks and 85,000 pairs of trousers.

The Chief of Imperial General Staff, Sir Henry Wilson, surveyed the wreckage of Churchill's Russian policy and was damning in his assessment. 'So ends in practical disaster another of Winston's military attempts ...' he wrote. 'His judgement is always at fault and he is hopeless when in power.'

Churchill himself was unrepentant. 'I am convinced that very great evils will come upon the world and particularly upon Great Britain,' he wrote in a letter to the American president, Woodrow Wilson. 'We shall find ourselves confronted almost immediately with a united Bolshevik Russia, highly militarised and building itself up on victories easily won over opponents in disarray.' He feared more than ever for the frontiers of British India. But he also feared for the world at large.

Mansfield Cumming had a rather different concern. His finest agent, Paul Dukes, had gone missing. There was every possibility that he had been captured by the Cheka.

CHAPTER FIFTEEN

AGENT IN DANGER

Paul Dukes had sent regular despatches to London during his early months in Russia. These had included military and political reports as well as monthly updates on the state of the country. But by the spring of 1919, they were arriving with less frequency and soon they dried up altogether.

There was no explanation for the breakdown in communication. Dukes had not signalled that he was in danger and the regime had given no indication that he had been captured. Nor could the Stockholm bureau shed any light on the matter. Cumming was as mystified as he was concerned. After a few more weeks of no contact, he took the unprecedented decision to send a mission to find out what was wrong.

The person selected to lead this mission was a young naval captain named Augustus Agar. He was on leave and pottering in his room at the Waldorf Hotel in London when he received an unexpected call from his commanding officer.

'Agar?' he said, 'I've got a proposition for you and want you back at once.'

Agar was excited by the summons and hoped it would lead to adventure. He was finding it hard to adapt to peacetime after four long years of conflict. 'I was still keen to take part in more of our war activities . . .' he wrote. '[It] meant excitement, adventure and something out of the ordinary dull routine.' He packed his clothes and hurried to the train station. By lunchtime, he was back at his base on Osea Island in Essex.

Agar had previously been working for special operations in the secretive Coastal Motor Boats division. The boats were known as skimmers and they combined revolutionary design with advanced engineering.

They looked like elongated kayaks and were powered by two massive petrol-drawn engines that enabled the craft to attain hitherto unimaginable speeds. Their hydroplane hulls weighed next to nothing and there was no onboard equipment. All they carried was two torpedoes.

The armistice had led to the cancellation of a planned attack on the German fleet and the skimmers were put into storage. Agar bemoaned the fact that all his training had been in vain.

Now, with his summons back to Osea Island, his life was about to take an unexpected turn. 'Well, Agar,' said his commanding officer, 'would you like to go on Special Service?'

Agar pricked up his ears and asked what it involved, at which point the officer asked the secretary to leave the room.

'No one must know where you are going until you are under way,' he said. 'Not even your crew . . . It is of the utmost importance that not a soul, either here in England, on the journey out, or even when you arrive in those waters, shall have any suspicions of your activities.'

Agar listened with growing excitement as the officer continued. 'I need hardly add that your mission is of great political importance and for this reason secrecy is vital.' The officer then told him to report to the London Admiralty on the following morning, where he would be given clearer instructions.

Agar headed back to London the next day and was briskly escorted from the Admiralty to Naval Intelligence. But this was not his final destination that morning.

'I was taken to another building, through more corridors, up many flights of stairs, through a small passage and yet into a third building.'

Finally, a young secretary emerged and told him to knock on the door in front of him and enter immediately. Agar did as instructed. 'Seated at a large desk with his back to the window and apparently absorbed in reading a document was the most remarkable man I have ever met in my life.' Agar was struck by his huge head, intelligent features and the fact that he did not even look up from his work.

'Then, with startling suddenness, he put his papers aside and banging the desk with his hand said, "Sit down, my boy, I think you will do."'

Agar still had no idea of the purpose of his mission and nor did he know his destination. But one thing was clear: 'Something really eventful had come into my life. This was my first introduction to C – the name by which this man was known to all who came in official contact with him.'

Over the course of the next hour, Cumming briefed Agar on the mission for which he had been selected. His destination was Soviet Russia – ' a closed book,' he was told, 'and hostile country with which we were virtually at war.'

Cumming told Agar that his finest agent had been keeping a close eye on the Soviet leadership and had managed to infiltrate a number of government agencies.

'He said there was a certain Englishman – unnamed, and with regard to whom no details were given – who had remained in Russia to conduct Intelligence, whose work was regarded of vital importance and with whom it was essential to get in touch.'

It was necessary to bring this agent out alive, 'as he was the only man who had first-hand reliable information on certain things which was required urgently by our government.'

There was one problem. The Bolsheviks had turned the Gulf of Finland into a giant minefield, with a sweep of mines to the north and south of Kotlin Island. These surrounded Petrograd in an extending arc, making naval access to the city almost impossible.

It was hoped that Agar's skimmers could overcome this dangerous obstacle. Dukes's reports had revealed that the Russian minefields lay at a depth of no more than three feet below the surface. This made the gulf impassable for any conventional vessel. But the skimmers were designed to draw just 2'9" of water; in theory, they would pass over the top of the mines. It was a high-risk undertaking, for their lives would be dependent on those three inches of water.

Cumming provided a few more details of the planned mission. Agar was to pick a small group of young men, all of whom would be transferred from the Navy to the Secret Intelligence Service. The only stipulation was that they should be unmarried and without ties.

They would travel to Finland 'in the guise of yachtsmen', with the ostensible object of promoting the sale of British motor-boats. But their real task was to cross the Gulf of Finland and make contact with Dukes. 'That was the general plan,' Cumming told Agar, adding that the details had yet to be worked out.

'He paused for a moment and looking me straight in the face said: "Well, my boy, what do you think of it?"'

Then, without giving Agar the chance to reply, he added: 'I won't ask you to take it on, for I know you will.'

Agar left the room in a state of high excitement and almost walked into the arms of the same pretty secretary who had accompanied him to Cumming's office.

'You look rather bewildered,' she said. 'Come in here and have a cigarette.'

★

Agar began planning his mission the following day. He picked six young officers, all as 'keen as mustard'. He then selected two of the 40ft skimmers and began refitting their engines. The craft were painted white to make them look like pleasure craft. All supplies were to be acquired in Finland, with the exception of a special charging plant for compressed air which was needed to start the engines.

Two days after his first meeting with Cumming, Agar was back in Whitehall Court. Cumming quizzed him about the skimmers and then asked how much money he needed.

Agar had not considered the cost of the operation. He said the first sum that came into his head – a thousand pounds – before realising that this was a vast amount of money. Cumming did not bat an eyelid. 'I could hardly believe my ears when the old man pressed a button to call a secretary and I heard him say quite simply: "Make a cheque to bearer, pay cash, for one thousand pounds."'

Agar had supposed that his mission would be conducted without backup and support. But Cumming now revealed that he had a complex system of agents at work in Scandinavia.

'Each contact had a number,' wrote Agar. 'I myself would be given one and would only be known by that number, with which I was to communicate with headquarters.'

Agar's number was ST34 and he was told that the Stockholm bureau would help him plan his mission.

Cumming stressed that the operation would be extremely dangerous. He said that 'if we were caught "on the wrong side of the line", it would be our own funeral, for in the circumstance, nothing officially could be done to save us.'

When the meeting came to an end, Agar was ushered to a training room at the top of the building. 'I was shown how to make use of a most ingenious rough and ready cipher code . . . [and] methods of using invisible ink on various kinds of the thinnest of thin paper.' Messages, he was told, were to be carried in boots, 'if possible, between the soles.'

On the day before Agar was due to leave London for Finland, he was whisked to a farewell luncheon at one of Cumming's clubs. 'We drove there in his large Rolls-Royce, himself at the wheel, and I remember the boyish delight he took in driving at terrific speed past the sentries and through the arch of the Horse Guards Parade.' Cumming was one of only five Londoners who had been granted this privilege.

Russia was not mentioned during lunch. Nor was there any dramatic farewell when the time came for Agar to leave. 'He just gave me a pat on the back and said: "Well, my boy, good luck to you" – and he was gone.'

On the following morning, Agar and his team left for Hull and thence for the Baltic. When he stepped off the ship at the port of Abo in Finland, two of Cumming's agents – ST30 and ST31 – were waiting to greet him.

Mansfield Cumming had been right to be concerned for Paul Dukes's safety. He was living a perilous existence in Petrograd and had been lucky to escape arrest by the Cheka.

The first danger had come when he picked up rumours that his closest collaborator, Colonel Zorinsky, was actually on the Cheka's payroll. To minimise the risk of capture, Dukes moved to a new safe house on Vasili Island owned by a friendly doctor.

He then set about changing his look. First, he shaved off the shaggy beard he had worn for the previous six months. This alone, he noted, 'altered my appearance to a remarkable degree.'

He also cut his hair and dyed it black. There was one last detail to complete his disguise. For many months, Dukes had been missing a front tooth; it made him instantly recognisable and it was how Colonel Zorinsky had known him. Now, he reinserted the missing tooth and closed the gaping aperture. His 'diabolic leer' was transformed back into a regular smile.

Dukes studied himself in the mirror and was pleased by what he saw. 'Attired in a suit of [the doctor's] old clothes, and wearing eye-glasses, I now presented the appearance of a clean shaven, short-haired, tidy but indigent, ailing and unfed "intellectual."' He looked very different from the 'shaggy-haired, limping maniac of the previous days.'

Dukes and the doctor together concocted a story as to why he was lodging in the building: he was to pretend to be an epileptic suffering from such life-threatening fits that he needed a doctor on call at all times.

Dukes practised having fits until he had perfected the art. It stood him in good stead when the Cheka arrived unexpectedly one night and raided the apartment.

'A loud groan from beneath the bedclothes – a violent jerk

– and I made my body rigid, except for tortuous motions of the head and clenched fists.'

He even managed to foam at the mouth. The Cheka officers glanced at him anxiously and made a hasty exit.

Dukes continued to gather intelligence in spite of the difficulties. 'From Moscow, I received regular reports regarding Soviet internal policy and the special reports submitted to Trotsky on the state of the Red Army.'

At one point, Dukes even considered moving to Moscow in order to be nearer the centre of decision-making. But when he learned that Petrograd was to be made the headquarters of the Comintern, he realised that this northern city was 'of greater importance to me as a base of operations.'

After a second raid on the doctor's apartment, Dukes deemed it prudent to leave. Homeless and adrift, he was reduced to spending his nights in Volkovo Cemetery where he hid in the neglected tomb of an Old Believer.

His precarious existence made it increasingly difficult to smuggle his reports out of the country. 'I was completely isolated,' he confessed, '. . . for although I found couriers to carry my despatches out, none returned to me and I was ignorant as to whether my messages were being delivered.'

Dukes's chief courier remained Pyotr Sokoloff, who had carried many reports from Petrograd to Finland (and thence to Stockholm). But one day Sokoloff failed to return. Dukes made discreet enquiries but could discover no news of what had happened to him.

'When a month passed and there was no sign of him, I became anxious, but when two months and more passed and there was still no sign of him, I began to fear the worst.'

Dukes made strenuous efforts to get his reports out of the country by other means; he even tried to bribe an operator at the Petrograd wireless station, but the man wanted too much money. Dukes found himself in the galling position of having to destroy some of his hard-won intelligence reports to prevent them falling into the wrong hands.

Isolated and alone, he was at a loss to know what to do.

★

Augustus Agar chose the Finnish fishing port of Terijoki as his base for rescuing Dukes. In pre-revolutionary days it had been used as a sailing club by the aristocracy of St Petersburg. Now the village had fallen into decay and its wooden dachas were abandoned. Agar could conduct his operations untroubled by prying eyes.

The skimmers arrived in Terijoki within a few days, having been specially transported across the North Sea. Agar could set to work on the detailed planning of his mission.

His first task was to acquire a Russian chart of the minefields that lay between Terijoki and Petrograd. This proved very easy. 'Like a magician, ST30 produced one on a Russian document.' It revealed all of the submerged breakwaters that linked the forts and batteries in the Gulf of Finland.

Cumming's agents had also managed to track down Dukes's courier, Pyotr Sokoloff. He had been forced to seek temporary refuge in Finland after a particularly hazardous mission. Now, he was brought to Terijoki and solicited for information that might lead to Dukes's rescue. Agar immediately warmed to Sokoloff, finding him 'full of guts and courage.' The feeling was mutual: Pyotr agreed to participate in Agar's mission, even though it would place him back in danger.

Agar's plan was to cross the Russian minefields in the skimmer and deposit Sokoloff on the thickly wooded shores to the north-west of Petrograd. Sokoloff would then head to the city on foot, make contact with Dukes and bring him back to the same stretch of shoreline. Both men would then be plucked off by Agar a few days later. The outbound mission was scheduled to take place on the night of 10 June, just before the white nights of midsummer.

On the evening in question, the men synchronised their watches and checked their revolvers before pushing off into the night. It was exactly 10 p.m. and the sky was dark, but they knew that the summer nights were so short that they had only a few hours to complete their mission.

The journey across the Gulf of Finland was extremely treacherous. They had to pass through the chain of heavily armed forts and breakwaters that linked Kronstadt with the mainland and they also had to cross the minefield.

Agar silenced the engines as they approached the forts and they inched forwards at an agonisingly slow speed. They did not even whisper to each other, lest they alert the Russian garrison to their presence. Soon, the naval battlements loomed large in the darkness, black silhouettes against a grey night sky.

'Four pairs of eyes were glued on them as if hypnotised,' wrote Agar. 'Every nerve was tense, every muscle taut. Would these suddenly flash out the beam of a searchlight?'

If so, Agar knew what to do. He would slam the skimmer into full throttle and attempt to outrun the gunfire that would be sure to follow.

In the event, they slipped through the forts unnoticed and were soon nearing the circular minefield. Only now did Agar thrust the engine into full speed. The little craft reacted in an instant, lurching forwards and then skimming across the surface of the water leaving the mines beneath undisturbed.

They travelled so fast that they reached the Neva Delta in less than fifteen minutes. Agar then cut the engines and helped Sokoloff unlash the tiny boat that had been strapped to the skimmer. This was to be his means of reaching the rocky shore.

'I waited there for his signal,' wrote Agar. 'It came soon, three short flashes on his electric torch from the direction of the rushes.' Sokoloff was safely ashore and the first stage of the mission had gone like clockwork.

Agar fired the engines and headed back to Terijoki. His plan was to return in three days to pick up Dukes.

★

Paul Dukes was reunited with Sokoloff quite by chance while he was strolling through the gardens of the Winter Palace. He caught sight of a familiar figure seated on a park bench.

'I peered – and my heart gave a bound – for to my unspeakable joy and surprise I recognised my courier for whom I had so long been waiting.'

Sokoloff tried to explain about Agar and his high-speed skimmers but it made no sense whatsoever to Dukes. He spoke of 'some mysterious kind of motor-boat' and of strange British operations in the Gulf of Finland. 'But throughout the jumble there constantly recurred a name – "Eggar-Eggar-Eggar" and I gathered at once that this man "Eggar" as Peter pronounced it, was the man who by some quite miraculous means had deposited him here in Petrograd in the early hours of that morning.'

Dukes stopped him in mid-sentence and asked him to start from the beginning. Sokoloff repeated what he had said, explaining how Agar had arrived from England with the most extraordinary boats he had ever seen. They were so fast that they flew across the water, throwing out a mountainous wave on either side.

'I listened spellbound to this amazing story,' wrote Dukes, 'punctuating it with innumerable questions as incident after incident, each more incredible than the last, was unfolded.' He was especially astonished that 'Eggar' had managed to cross the mine-strewn Gulf of Finland.

Sokoloff was carrying a letter from Mansfield Cumming: this informed Dukes that he should remain in Russia if at all possible, 'but that if I found it necessary to leave, I could return with the bearer.' Sokoloff was also intending to remain in Petrograd for the foreseeable future.

Dukes was keen to stay longer in Russia but was hampered by a lack of money. Now, Sokoloff came to the rescue. He handed him a large stack of Russian roubles that had been carefully forged by Cumming's team in London. This clinched it for Dukes. He decided to spend a further month in Petrograd before being taken out by Agar in July.

★

Augustus Agar and his skimmers were not the only British naval forces in Baltic waters at this time. In January 1919, Admiral Sir Walter Cowan had been sent with a fleet of ships to patrol the coastline of the newly independent Estonia and Latvia. His orders were to keep the sea-lanes open to merchant shipping.

Agar had contacted Admiral Cowan on his arrival in the Baltic, just as Mansfield Cumming had requested. The admiral was friendly and asked if he could be of any assistance. Agar did indeed have a request and it was one that Cowan was not expecting. He asked if he could have a couple of torpedoes with which to arm his skimmers.

'I explained that although in London I had been told quite definitely that I was to avoid all operations which would involve us in a hostile act . . . yet these torpedoes might come in very useful in self-defence.'

Cowan was hesitant: the torpedoes on his flagship were among the most powerful ever produced and could easily sink a large vessel. But such was Agar's persistence that the admiral eventually agreed to his request.

Agar may have indeed intended to use the torpedoes for self-defence. But his time in Terijoki coincided with the mutiny of the huge Russian garrison in Kronstadt. This presented a serious threat to the Bolshevik regime and Trotsky's response was characteristically brutal. He ordered the fortress to be bombed into submission.

Agar felt a very British sense of indignation: the bombardment was not fair play, and he began toying with a bold if reckless retort. 'Should I or should I not single-handed and without orders, set out to attack the bombarding battleships?'

He knew he could wreak havoc with his torpedoes but he also knew that to attack the Soviet fleet would be to go against orders from London. He therefore decided to request permission to attack, sending a cipher to Sweden and thence to Whitehall.

The answer arrived within hours. 'BOATS TO BE USED FOR INTELLIGENCE PURPOSES ONLY – STOP – TAKE NO ACTION UNLESS SPECIALLY DIRECTED BY S[ENIOR].N[AVAL].O[FFICER]. BALTIC.'

The note was clear and unambiguous: the requested permission had not been forthcoming. But Agar felt that the last sentence gave him room for manoeuvre. He was sure that Admiral Cowan would wish to encourage the mutinous troops and therefore took the momentous decision to attack the Bolshevik vessels that very evening.

He set out in a single skimmer at around 11 p.m. on 17 June, when it was completely dark. He and his crew were nervous as they inched towards the Russian fleet; they kept their engine on the lowest throttle so that no one might be alerted to their presence. Agar had already selected his target: he intended to fire his torpedo at the biggest ship at anchor, the armoured cruiser, *Oleg*. The only drawback was that she was fenced in with destroyers and patrol vessels. Agar needed to penetrate this cordon before he could strike.

In the darkness of the night, the skimmer slipped silently through the cordon of ships. All was quiet on the Russian fleet and the sentries, weary after the day's bombardment, had fallen asleep at their posts.

Agar's eyes were fixed on the looming silhouette in front of him. It grew larger in the darkness and soon he could pick out details of the vessel. He knew that the time had come to launch his attack and felt a sudden rush of adrenaline.

With a decisive flick of his wrist, he slammed hard on the throttle. As he did so, the front end of the skimmer rose high in the water and the twin petrol engines roared into action. Within seconds, they were alongside the *Oleg*, firing their torpedo at point-blank range and then spinning the skimmer on its nose in order to shoot away at full speed.

'We looked back to see if our torpedo had hit and saw a large flash abreast the cruiser's foremast funnel, followed almost immediately by a huge column of black smoke reaching up to the top of her mast.'

They would have surveyed the damage more carefully had it not been for the burst of machine-gun fire that raked their path. Only the speed of the skimmer saved them from catastrophe: within seconds, they were beyond range of the Russian guns.

Agar returned to Terijoki in jubilant spirits: he had crippled the *Oleg*. He was not prone to self doubt and was convinced he had done the right thing. But he experienced an uncharacteristic flutter of nerves as he prepared to inform Admiral Cowan of his nocturnal attack.

He need not have worried: Cowan was delighted and said that the attack had boosted his own stature. 'This enables me to show them [the Bolsheviks] that I have a sting which I can always use if they ever show their noses out of Kronstadt.'

Agar confessed his concerns about the reaction in London, but he was reassured by Cowan. 'He told me he approved absolutely of everything I had done and that if there was trouble with the Foreign Office about exceeding my instructions he would make my position quite clear and stand by me.'

Agar was extremely relieved. 'I went in feeling depressed, apprehensive and a little frightened – and I left in an exactly opposite mood.'

Later that evening Admiral Cowan invited him to a champagne dinner and two days later, when he returned to Cowan's flagship once again, he was given a hero's welcome. Every vessel in the fleet was lined with cheering sailors. 'Such moments as these can never be forgotten,' wrote Agar.

Agar was fortunate in having Cowan's support, for his actions caused uproar in Whitehall. Not for the first time, one of Mansfield Cumming's agents had wildly exceeded his brief.

Cumming himself was delighted when he heard of Agar's attack. It was exactly the sort of operation he loved – bold, hastily improvised and completely outlandish. He was already thinking about how to reward Agar.

The Bolsheviks were rather less amused. They put a price of

£5,000 on Agar's head and let it be known that he would be executed if caught by the Cheka.

★

Paul Dukes had hoped that the fake banknotes brought by Pyotr Sokoloff would bring him new opportunities for espionage. But he soon discovered they were useless.

'[They] had the correct design and wording, but the paper was thin, its dye was not good and the inscription on some of them was smudged. The sheets were not of uniform thickness or colour.' He knew that using them would carry unacceptable risks.

Dukes could not operate without money. He needed to pay his contacts and he also needed funds 'for lodging, food, clothing, travelling, sending couriers, paying "sackmen" [private bootleggers] and agents, purchasing information, tipping, bribing and all kinds of emergencies.'

He now turned to the only available means of getting money: the last remaining English nationals in Petrograd. They had stayed behind in a forlorn bid to save their businesses. Now, Dukes hoped they would be able to advance him some cash.

Among those still living in the city was George Gibson of the United Shipping Company. Gibson was constantly trailed by the Cheka and had already endured one spell in a Petrograd prison. The strain of living under observation had made him suspicious of everyone. Little wonder that he was extremely sceptical when a bearded Red Army officer pitched up at his office and whispered that his real name was Paul Dukes.

Gibson had not seen Dukes for many months: indeed he had no idea that he was still living in the city. He was about to slam the door on this uninvited visitor when he heard the words 'Henry Earles' slip from Dukes's lips. Gibson peered more closely at his visitor. Henry Earles was a password agreed between the Foreign Office and the residue of British nationals in Petrograd: it denoted an agent in need of help. Only now was Dukes invited inside.

He told Gibson that he was in desperate need of money. Gibson responded with extreme generosity, advancing Dukes a total of 375,000 roubles – some £250,000 in today's money. In return, Dukes gave him a receipt signed 'Captain McNeill'; it was one of his Secret Intelligence Service cover names. He assured Gibson that the money would be refunded within two months. (In the event, it took rather longer, but Gibson was eventually repaid.)

Now that Dukes had money, he could once again set to work and he did so with customary aplomb. For months there had been a concerted drive by the Bolsheviks to recruit people into the party. Now, it was realised that many had joined in the hope that a party ticket would bring them employment. Trotsky called such people 'radishes' – red on the outside only.

In the summer of 1919 the party was purged on a dramatic scale. The majority quit when it was decreed that all party members were subject to mobilisation at the battlefront. 'The cowards and good-for-nothings have run away from the party,' said Lenin. 'Good riddance.'

Dukes saw the purge as an opportunity. With his new identity papers he now applied to join the party of the faithful. Acceptance brought him the status of a trusted loyalist.

'My party ticket was everywhere an Open Sesame,' he wrote. 'I passed with the first, wherever documents had to be shown. I travelled free on trams and railways.'

Determined to profit from his remaining time in Russia, he also applied to join the Red Army. This would enable him to gather intelligence on soldier loyalty and how the army functioned. He was recruited into the automobile section of the Eighth Army, whose commander was one of his key contacts.

'Enlistment brought enormous advantages in its train,' he wrote. As well as being able to observe the inside workings of the army, 'the Red Army soldier received rations greatly superior to those issued to the civilian population.' After months of hunger, Dukes could finally fill his stomach.

Dukes learned that the closed meetings of the Petrograd Soviet were always attended by elected representatives of the Red Army. He now put forward his candidacy and was duly elected as a delegate. He was privately jubilant, having managed to 'achieve the peak of my ambition, which was to be delegated to attend meetings of the Soviet . . . I was deputed as the official guest for my regiment.'

Dukes also travelled to Moscow at this time and made contact with a secret anti-Bolshevik organisation called the National Centre. It was while he was in the capital that he picked up a dramatic rumour. The Comintern was in the process of establishing a terror school for revolutionary activists. Its principal task was in 'training agitators to go abroad and stir up class warfare, foment strikes and preach seditious propaganda in the defence forces of all western countries.'

This school was to devote the greater part of its resources to spearheading attacks on the Raj. 'In particular,' wrote Dukes, 'numerous highly paid agitators were being despatched to aggravate the trouble in India.' They intended to strike first in the most volatile areas of the North-West Frontier province, where British rule was facing severe difficulties.

Dukes was unaware that Frederick Bailey was sending similar intelligence to Simla. He was completely cut off from news of the outside world and felt that it was time to leave Russia and provide a briefing to Mansfield Cumming in London, especially as he had achieved so much in the previous few weeks.

'I will not say that the strain of many months' disguised existence, with all its adventures, had left no mark on my nerves. I was tired and fully realised that I could not keep it up indefinitely, or even for much longer.'

But getting out of the country was to prove considerably more difficult than getting in.

★

Augustus Agar's original plan had been to take his skimmer back across the Gulf of Finland and await Dukes's arrival at a pre-arranged rendezvous. Dukes himself would then row out to the skimmer in the boat left behind by Sokoloff. But the boat had been discovered by a Red Army patrol and Agar had been obliged to send a second courier (and boat) to make contact with Dukes.

This time, everything went according to plan. The courier, a man named Gefter, made contact with Dukes in Petrograd and informed him that the rendezvous with Agar had been changed: it was now set for the night of 14 August. He and Dukes would row out into the Gulf of Finland and meet with the skimmer at a previously agreed rendezvous.

At around 10 p.m., under a sky still streaked with light, the two men clambered into the boat and began rowing out into the gulf. They glanced anxiously at the skyline for both had noticed that banks of angry clouds were rolling towards them.

'After a while the sky blackened, the wind freshened, the wavelets became waves, their caressing grew into lashings,' wrote Dukes.

No less alarming was the fact that the boat was much lower in the water than normal. Gefter investigated what was wrong and discovered that there was a serious problem.

He had forgotten to close the fish well – a basin in the centre of the boat that could be filled with water to keep the catch fresh. By the time he tried to plug the opening it was too late. Seawater was gushing in with tremendous force, dragging the boat deeper and deeper into the water.

A waterlogged boat would have presented major difficulties in any weather conditions, but it was to prove a disaster in the face of an advancing storm. The breeze had stiffened into a gale, sloshing even more water into the boat. Soon Dukes and Gefter were up to their waists in water and no amount of bailing could save them.

As the gunwale slipped below the waterline, both men must have realised that they were deeply in trouble.

★

Augustus Agar and his crew were on their way to the rendezvous in the Gulf of Finland at the very moment when Dukes and Gefter's boat slipped beneath the waves.

Agar steered the skimmer through the chain of forts and successfully crossed the minefield. Soon, he could see the dark silhouette of the lightship that was anchored permanently in the gulf. He steered half a mile towards the Lissy Nos Point and then cut the engines. He had reached the rendezvous exactly on time.

He scanned the water in the hope of seeing Dukes's prearranged flashlight signal. There was no sign of it and he glanced anxiously at the mounting waves. He feared for the two men in their little boat.

After a long wait, he flashed a signal in the direction of the shore. It was a dangerous thing to do, for it would expose the skimmer's position to any Russian lookout. But he hoped it would help to guide Dukes towards them.

Five minutes passed – then ten – but still there was no sign of Dukes. Agar and his men continued to scan the water for another forty minutes. But when the first rays of light began to streak low across the eastern sky, Agar reluctantly restarted the skimmer's engines and swung the boat in the direction of Terijoki. He needed to pass the chain of forts before daybreak.

Agar was depressed by his failure to rendezvous with Dukes and Gefter and feared that they had been caught by the Cheka. In fact, their plight had been even more dramatic.

The two men had been in sight of Agar's skimmer when their rowing boat slipped beneath the waves. But with a strong current against them, and a mounting sea, they had no option but to swim for the shore.

The water was icy and the spray made rapid progress impossible. Dukes was a strong swimmer and eventually reached the shore exhausted and close to collapse. Gefter was washed up in an even more critical condition. His skin was white and he was suffering from acute hypothermia.

The two men attempted to walk to safety. Gefter was barefoot for he had kicked off his boots in the water to stop himself from drowning. Now, the sharp rocks lacerated his feet and they were soon bleeding badly. Dukes attempted to carry him, but he was too heavy and the two men sat down exhausted. As they shivered in the chill air, Gefter suddenly slumped forwards and collapsed. He had stopped breathing.

'In sudden terror I began to rub him with great energy,' wrote Dukes. 'I lay down beside him, covered his mouth with mine and blew down his throat. Alternately, I filled his lungs and pressed on his belly.'

After a terrifying few minutes, Gefter vomited a bucketful of seawater. His eyes flickered and his hands stirred. He eventually managed to sit himself upright and a little colour returned to his face. Once dawn had broken through the pewter sky, Dukes carried him to a fisherman's cottage and left him there to be nursed. He then made his return to Petrograd.

★

Agar made one last attempt to pluck Dukes from Bolshevik Russia. It was a disaster. His skimmer crashed into a mine-field and was almost blown apart. He and his men were lucky to limp back to Terijoki in one piece.

Any future rescue mission was scuttled by Admiral Cowan's actions in the Gulf of Finland. He had ordered more skimmers to be sent from England and had then used them to launch a devastating attack on the Soviet fleet. The *Petropavlosk, Andrei Pervozvanni* and the submarine depot ship *Pamiat Azova* were all either sunk or crippled.

Shortly after the attack, Agar returned to London in order to report to Mansfield Cumming on everything that had happened. When he arrived at Whitehall Court, he was met by the same secretary that he had last seen on the eve of his departure for Finland. She told him that Cumming had asked him to wait in the corridor outside his office.

The door soon opened and a tall, dark-haired man emerged from the room. 'Something about him and his manner arrested my attention and seemed to me to be familiar, but whether it was the eager look in his eyes, or a certain tense expression in his face, I cannot say.'

Agar hesitated for a moment: he could not take his eyes off the man.

'Then, in a flash of intuition, a thought came to my mind. "Yes," I said to myself, "it must be him."

'I was the first to speak.

' "Are you Dukes?"

' "Yes," he replied.'

Agar introduced himself, bringing a smile to Dukes's face.

' "C has a habit of arranging these little matters like this." At which point we both laughed and shook hands and entered C's office together.'

Cumming had already heard Dukes's account of his dramatic escape. He had waded through a vast bog to reach the shores of Lake Lubans, which marked the frontier between Russia and Latvia. Braving Red Army patrols, he stole a half-derelict boat and rowed across to the Latvian shore where he was promptly arrested. He was eventually released by the border officials and made his way to Stockholm and thence to London.

Cumming had delighted in Dukes's tale of high adventure. Now, he was keen to hear Agar's stories as well. He was not disappointed. 'He laughed heartily over the amusing episodes and commended us for all we had done,' wrote Agar.

Agar had feared censure for his role in the raid on Kronstadt. Instead, Cumming wanted to reward him. 'When it came to accounting for the thousand pounds I was given when we started our venture . . . I was told not to bother about accounts, but just hand back any balance left over after our expenses were paid.'

Shortly after his meeting with Cumming, Agar was whisked to Buckingham Palace for an audience with King George V. The king had also expressed a wish to hear about his exploits in the Gulf of Finland.

Agar recounted his tale once again, to the king's evident relish. He presented Agar with the Victoria Cross and also awarded him the Distinguished Service Order. He told Agar that Dukes also deserved a Victoria Cross, but this was not possible since it was a purely military decoration. 'He said he would make sure that some suitable recognition would be made for the services he had rendered.'

This he duly did. Dukes was knighted just a few months later, the only person ever to be so honoured for services to espionage.

Mansfield Cumming was proud of what had been achieved by Agar and Dukes. Dukes in particular had exceeded all his expectations: he had also helped to justify the growing expense of the Secret Intelligence Service. Now, in a modest way, Cumming wanted to thank both Agar and Dukes.

'C and some of his staff, whom he always referred to as his "top mates" . . . gave a small dinner party at the Savoy Hotel to Paul Dukes and myself,' wrote Agar.

As the assembled company swilled their goblets of brandy, Cumming presented Agar with a silver salver. It was inscribed with four words: 'From his top mates'.

'After dinner,' recalled Agar, 'we adjourned to the supper rooms to watch the dancing and I can recollect the old man picking out the prettiest girl in the room – to us a complete stranger – and insisting on her dancing with me.'

Agar was never one to turn down a pretty girl. He clutched her tightly as he led her onto the dance floor, just as Cumming had wished.

'He always managed to get his own way,' wrote Agar.

CHAPTER SIXTEEN

DIRTY TRICKS

P aul Dukes had been lucky to have got out of Petrograd alive. He had been helped by the fact that the city was close to the border with Latvia. He had also had the support of the Stockholm bureau, which could supply him with whatever he needed once he had crossed the frontier.

It was a very different situation for Frederick Bailey, who had spent almost fourteen months hiding in Tashkent. He had to cross some of the world's most inhospitable terrain if he was to make a safe return to British India. All of this land was now under Bolshevik control.

There was by now a very real urgency to his getting out of Turkestan. He had collected vital information on the threat that was facing British India, which now needed to be transmitted to Indian intelligence. Bailey also faced an increased risk of capture from the 'Special Department' whose primary task was to root out traitors. He felt as if there were hidden eyes in every wall, especially when he learned that the Cheka 'were making renewed efforts to find me.'

But escape brought its own dangers. Just a few days earlier, a French agent named Captain Capdeville had tried to flee the city. The Cheka were soon on his trail and he was finally caught in the town of Osh, halfway to Kashgar. The captain's arrest had potentially serious ramifications for Bailey; he had entrusted Capdeville with a batch of secret documents in the hope of getting them delivered to British India.

It was fortunate that the Cheka officers did not realise that the rolls of rice paper in the Frenchman's baggage contained Bailey's secret messages. They used them to make hand-rolled cigarettes.

'The paper was thin, clean and of a suitable thickness,' wrote Bailey. 'What would have happened if my secret ink had responded to heat it is interesting to imagine.'

Bailey had already adopted six different identities during his time in Tashkent. He now changed into his final disguise – the one he would use to flee the city. He transformed himself into an Albanian prisoner of war named Joseph Kastamuni and invented a fictional autobiography to go with the disguise.

He pretended that Kastamuni had been serving as an Albanian mercenary attached to the Serbian Volunteer Corps. The Albanian nationality was a clever choice, as Bailey knew all too well. He was most unlikely to meet anyone in Turkestan who could speak the language.

The creation of an identity photograph of Kastamuni in service uniform proved more of a challenge. 'There were no Serbian uniforms in Tashkent,' explained Bailey, '. . . but we found that [they] could be sufficiently well copied from a photograph by cutting the shoulder straps off the Austrian uniform and turning the kepi back to front.'

A friend helped him make special badges for the cap, fabricating them from paper and card. 'We had no paste, so these were temporarily fixed for the purpose of the photo with the only sticky thing we had at hand, a kind of apricot preserve.'

Bailey took the passport to a trusted contact of his who had formerly served in the Russian imperial police. 'He said it would not have deceived him for a moment, but was good enough for the casual glance of a Soviet policeman or government official.'

Bailey knew that leaving a country was far harder than entering it. There were two routes out of Tashkent: the eastern one to Kashgar or the western one to Meshed. The overland journey to either of these cities presented grave difficulties. Both involved hundreds of miles of travel and Bailey knew that every road, train station and railway junction was under heavy guard.

After much consideration, he decided to head first for the ancient caravan city of Bokhara, which lay some 300 miles to the west of Tashkent. Bokhara was ruled by a British-friendly amir who Bailey could solicit for help in traversing the great Karakum Desert. If he managed to cross both the desert and the Persian frontier, he would at long last be back in friendly territory.

Bailey hit upon a second idea to help him in his escape attempt, one that was characteristically bold. He decided to apply for a job with the counter-espionage branch of the Cheka, known as *Voivne Kontrol* or Military Control Department. Its function was to track down foreign spies working inside Turkestan.

Acceptance into this organisation would bring him the special permit that was needed to travel with complete freedom. But he knew that applying for the job also carried huge risks.

The department was headed by a thuggish Bolshevik commissar named Dunkov, a man who was infamous in Tashkent for killing all who crossed him. Bailey described him as 'a most dangerous type', someone who despised everyone who was not a Bolshevik. His fanaticism 'led him to hunt out people suspected of opposite views and have them executed.'

Bailey had closely investigated the activities of the Military Control Department and knew that he had one factor in his favour. Commissar Dunkov was urgently trying to substantiate rumours that the British were training anti-Bolshevik forces in Bokhara. He had already sent fifteen agents to the city with the hope of gathering intelligence. All fifteen had been executed. Not surprisingly, he was finding it difficult to find a sixteenth volunteer.

This is where Bailey sniffed his opportunity. He knew that he stood a high chance of being accepted into the ranks of the Military Control Department if he offered to undertake a mission to Bokhara. But he also knew that he would have to meet Commissar Dunkov in person, and this would expose him to considerable risk.

'I would have to walk down a long room where all the hottest Soviet spies were working at their desks,' he wrote. 'Some of these men had been specially on the lookout for me for months. I would then have to carry out a difficult and detailed conversation with Dunkov who might be suspicious.'

In the event, he managed to avoid being scrutinised by these Soviet spies. With the aid of an intermediary, he set up an informal meeting with the commissar and was able to offer his services without being officially interviewed.

Commissar Dunkov was as surprised as he was delighted by Bailey's willingness to undertake a mission to Bokhara. 'You must go at once and see what truth there is in these stories of British officers,' he said.

Within hours, Bailey was supplied with all the papers he needed. These included an open permit that allowed him to leave Tashkent and travel wherever and whenever he wanted.

★

In mid-October, Bailey boarded a train at Tashkent and began the long journey to Bokhara.

He wore the costume of a Military Control Officer and carried the identity papers of Joseph Kastamuni. His clothes were made of coarse woollen cloth cut in the Bolshevik fashion and on his cap was a red star decorated with a hammer and sickle, the badge of the Red Army.

He alighted at the Bolshevik-controlled town of Kagan, which lay just a couple of miles to the south-east of Bokhara. Within minutes of arriving, he received a telegram from the Chief of the General Staff in Tashkent: 'Please communicate all information you have regarding the Anglo-Indian Service Colonel Bailey.' Bailey allowed himself an inner smile: he was being asked to spy on himself.

The Bolshevik leaders in Kagan were impressed by the bravado of this newly arrived Military Control Officer. '[They] looked on me as a very brave man who, for the Soviet cause, was about to meet an unpleasant death in Bokhara.'

In reality, Bokhara was to provide him with his first safe haven since leaving British India. He smuggled himself into the walled city and managed to gain an audience with the Amir of Bokhara, a grizzled autocrat whose age and infirmity prevented him from taking advantage of the 400 concubines in his harem.

Bailey was still undecided as to whether to take the western or eastern route out of Turkestan. Now, the amir's offer of assistance in crossing the Karakum Desert convinced him to continue heading west. It would enable him to reach Meshed, where a British officer named Wilfrid Malleson was busily establishing a highly subversive operation against the Bolsheviks. Bailey had already been sending reports to Malleson. If all went according to plan, he would soon meet him face to face.

The amir offered Bailey five guides to help him cross the desert. In return, Bailey was asked to assist in the escape of seven White Russian officers who were fleeing from the Bolsheviks and two Indian Army officers on route to Persia. Also in the party was a Serbian renegade named Manditch and his new bride. Far from travelling light as Bailey had hoped, his entourage now numbered twelve, in addition to the five guides.

The party set off under the cover of darkness on 18 December 1919, a far later date than anticipated. They were disguised as Turkman tribesmen, dressed in large sheepskin hats and woollen *khalats*. They hoped that the peasant costumes would prevent them from being molested by the bands of wild Turkman brigands who roamed the desert in search of easy prey. Bailey wore his corduroy riding breeches underneath the tribal garb, an extra layer against the bitter Bokharan winter.

They travelled by pony, reaching the mighty Oxus River on Christmas Day. From this point on, they were entering the barren Karakum where there were no settlements and precious few wells.

The desert crossing was to prove more arduous than any of them had imagined and it left them close to collapse. The freezing wind whipped dust and gravel into their eyes, causing constant pain. It also delivered a ferocious blizzard that arrived from nowhere. Five inches of snow fell in a matter of minutes and obliterated the few distinguishing landmarks.

'The steppe . . . was rough,' wrote Bailey, 'rather like a stormy sea, the waves of which had been frozen.'

The snow made their progress even more wearisome. 'We had had practically nothing to eat for several days, except the ponies' food, which we either parched or boiled according to the individual's taste.'

They were soon suffering from severe hypothermia and might easily have died a lonely death in the desert had it not been for a chance encounter with some nomads. They managed to acquire three sheep that were promptly slaughtered and then roasted on the cleaning rods of their rifles.

In spite of the gruelling hardship, Bailey's fascination with native flora and fauna was undiminished. He was hoping to shoot a rare specimen of gazelle, *Gazella subgutturosa*, that he knew to inhabit this area of desert. Unable to get close enough to kill one, he eventually stumbled across the carcass of an animal that had recently died. 'I took the horns,' he later wrote, 'and they are now in the Bombay History Society's Museum.'

Finally, almost three weeks after setting out from Bokhara, Bailey's party glimpsed the snow-topped mountains of Persia. They were glinting in the winter sunshine and brought a renewed sense of optimism to the weary travellers. 'The feelings for all of us at the sight of a free land, even in the distance, is hard to describe,' wrote Bailey.

There was a brief skirmish with Red Army border guards at the frontier with Persia, leading to an exchange of bullets. This might have proved deadly, were it not for the fact that the guards were poor shots. The only loss was Mrs Manditch's saddle bag containing dozens of Bokharan silk dresses. Unable to recover them (to Mrs Manditch's great distress), the party rode on to the town of Sarakhs inside Persia. Here, Bailey was able to telegraph Wilfrid Malleson with the news that he was alive and safe. Soon after, he rode triumphantly into Malleson's headquarters in Meshed.

The British sentries initially refused him entry to the compound: they took one look at his Soviet-made clothes and assumed he was a Russian Bolshevik. But Bailey soon convinced them of his real identity and he was promptly whisked into the staff mess for a hearty luncheon.

'My difficulties and dangers were over,' he wrote. 'It was pleasant to see the Union Jack waving over the barracks after such a long time under other colours.'

The story of Bailey's escapades in Turkestan were so colourful that it would eventually be published in *The Times*, albeit in an edited and carefully censored form. Under the headline 'A Central Asian Romance' the article gleefully recounted how Bailey had outwitted Bolshevik spies for many months.

The Soviet press took an altogether different line. They announced Bailey's death in a shoot-out on the Persian frontier and said that he had been given a military funeral.

Bailey's lengthy mission to Tashkent had once again highlighted both the strengths and weaknesses of solo operations in hostile lands. He had found it relatively easy to gather intelligence on the growing alliance between Soviet and Indian revolutionaries. It had proved altogether more difficult to smuggle this information out of the country.

Now that he was in Persia, he was able to debrief Wilfrid Malleson more fully on the disturbing new threat. He also warned that the ultimate goal of Bolshevism remained global revolution.

'The Bolsheviks cannot sit still,' he wrote in the conclusion to his intelligence report. 'Their object has always been world revolution . . . When the East has adopted Soviet government, the whole world will be compelled to adopt the same principles.'

★

Agents such as Frederick Bailey, Paul Dukes and Arthur Ransome had proved themselves masters at laying their hands on secret information. Wilfrid Malleson was to prove no less masterful at using this information for his own nefarious purposes.

Malleson had long harboured a pathological hatred of Bolshevism and had privately vowed to devote all his energies to unpicking their dream of world revolution. He was to prove a formidable enemy.

He had originally been sent to Persia as commander of the British and Indian troops stationed along the Afghan-Persian border – a small defensive unit known as the East Persian Cordon.

Changing circumstances had led to a dramatic change of brief. The intelligence obtained from Moscow and Tashkent now presented Malleson with a very different challenge. He was to spy on the Bolsheviks, eavesdrop on their communications and do whatever he could to prevent the spread of revolution into British India. 'The times were critical,' he would later write. 'The Government of India hardly slept at nights.'

The growing strength of the Bolsheviks had led Malleson to conclude that something dramatic needed to be done. But before he launched himself into his new mission, he sent a telegram to British India asking for clarification as to the extent of his powers.

The reply informed him 'that I was on the spot and had a free hand.' He was allowed to act in any way he chose.

In a speech that he later made to the Royal Central Asian Society, he wryly noted that being given a free hand was 'in the nature of a gift from the Greeks.' If he were successful in his work, then 'some gentlemen in easy chairs on a hilltop 2,000 miles away would appropriate the credit.' If he failed, on the other hand, he would be 'spurned and repudiated and thrown remorselessly to the wolves.'

Malleson was not in the habit of failing. Nor did he intend to fail on this occasion. Sabotaging the fledgling alliance between the Soviets and the Indian revolutionaries was to prove his most difficult mission to date, but he was well equipped for the task ahead. He had the use of a small army, the 28th Light Cavalry and the 19th Punjabis, whom he described as 'magnificent material'. He also had an effective channel of communications with British India and a team of highly dependable agents.

Surviving photographs of Malleson suggest an archetypal military commander. He sports a handsome upturned moustache and his eyes sparkle brightly at the camera. But there is an icy chill to the gaze, perhaps hinting at the adamantine core within. Malleson's men were terrified by his 'hard-boiled temperament' and they were also fearful of his fierce lack of sentiment.

'His attitude was determined by the task he had undertaken . . .' wrote one officer, 'with very little regard for the teeming life going on around him.'

He collected sporting guns and revolvers and spent his leisure hours blasting game birds from the skies above Ashkabad. Those serving under him described him as 'unorthodox', 'critical of authority' and 'cynical', especially in his dealings with others. He was also a lonely man 'who could unbend only when discussing something of particular interest to himself.'

Malleson was employed by neither Indian Political Intelligence nor Mansfield Cumming. His ostensible boss was the government of India, but he operated in the fashion of an Elizabethan privateer, wreaking chaos in a spirit of patriotic duty. Except instead of gathering booty, he distributed lies and falsehoods among his enemies.

A measure of his ruthlessness can be detected in his decision, taken in August 1918, to lead a private military offensive against the Bolsheviks. He led his cavalry across the frontier into Turkestan, where a much larger force of Red Army troops were fomenting unrest. After two nights of gruelling marching, his men spotted the Bolsheviks at the desert town of Dushak.

Malleson had long displayed a cavalier approach to warfare. Now, he ordered his troops to attack at dawn and told them to show no mercy. The men advanced against heavy machine-gun fire from the entrenched Bolsheviks and displayed considerable bravery in the face of sustained shooting.

The Punjabi forces were first to reach the enemy trenches and they attacked with their bayonets, causing the Bolshevik soldiers to flee in panic to the hills behind the town. Here, they were decimated by Malleson's hidden cavalry forces.

The fight was costly in human life. Malleson lost sixty of his men, while more than a thousand Bolsheviks were killed.

The government of India was alarmed that Malleson had interpreted their offer of a carte blanche with quite such freedom. They told him not to launch any more attacks and they also forbade him from advancing any further. They did not want to provoke a full-scale war against Soviet Turkestan.

Malleson halted his offensive but he kept his forces inside Turkestan for much of the winter before finally returning to Meshed. It was from his Meshed headquarters that he now set about planning his next round of dirty tricks.

★

Wilfrid Malleson had known about the arrival of the Indian revolutionaries in Tashkent for several months, for he'd received copies of Frederick Bailey's intelligence reports. Now he was brought news of a far more alarming nature.

One of his agents handed him a widely circulated pamphlet written by the revolutionary agitator, Abdul Hafiz Barkatulla. As Malleson studied it, he was shocked to discover that it was nothing short of a rallying cry for a Soviet-backed *jihad*. It informed Islamic warriors that the Bolsheviks wanted to enter into a crusading alliance against 'the usurpers and despots, the British.'

'Oh Muhammedans!' it began. 'Listen to this divine cry: respond to this call of liberty, equality and brothership which brother Lenin and the Soviet Government of Russia are offering you.'

There were two principal reasons why the pamphlet was so toxic. One was its highly provocative language, designed to inflame Islamic sensibilities against the British. The second was the fact that it stressed the common goal of Bolshevism and Islam – namely, the destruction of British India. This, it said, would bring about the defeat of 'the savage wolves who stand ready to conquer countries and enslave people.'

There was a third pernicious element to the pamphlet, one that did not go unnoticed by Malleson. The writer stressed the similarities between the followers of the Prophet Mohammed and the followers of Lenin. There was no mention of Bolshevism's inherent atheism. Instead, the pamphlet compared Lenin's economic policies to the Islamic institution of Bait-ul-Mal, a charitable body for the relief of the poor.

Malleson was appalled by what he was reading. It was a gross distortion of the truth and he immediately forwarded the document to British India, where it was also greeted with grave concern.

'The pamphlet is of a very dangerous nature,' wrote a senior government secretary. Malleson was ordered to intercept and destroy as many copies as possible.

Malleson undertook this task to the best of his ability, instructing his agents to seize copies wherever they were being printed. But he also decided to take the offensive. If the Soviets were prepared to finance inflammatory propaganda, then so was he. He hired the services of the distinguished Islamic scholar Jalaluddin al Hussaini, and paid him to write a vitriolic rebuttal to the pamphlet.

Jalaluddin excelled himself, pouring scorn on the notion of holy Islam entering into an alliance with 'the pig-eating infidels of Russia.' He also rubbished the claim that Bolshevism and the Bait-ul-Mal shared the same economic goal. He reminded Muslims that the latter was one of Islam's most noble institutions – a treasury of money that had been used to care for the needy for many centuries.

Bolshevism, by contrast, was simply 'an institution for plunder' and one that attracted 'the very dregs of Russians and irreligious, unpatriotic, sinful people, Jews, Kafirs, robbers, pick-pockets and blood-thirsty assassins.'

Warming to his theme, he thundered that Bolshevism was an atheistic creed that was 'against the regulations and decrees of Islam'. Its leaders were not to be trusted, for they were 'accursed, vicious, irreligious tyrants.'

Jalaluddin invoked the holy name of the Prophet in order to forbid the Muslims of Central Asia to 'unite and combine with these tyrannical heathens.'

Jalaluddin's authorship of the pamphlet gave it considerable weight and ensured that it received widespread attention.

It also provided Malleson with much food for thought. He now realised that it was no longer enough to remain on the defensive when dealing with the Bolsheviks.

If he was to protect the world from the Soviet threat, then he would have to play an even more devious game.

★

Wilfrid Malleson's most pressing concern at this time was the number of enemy agents managing to infiltrate his headquarters.

'Bolshevik spies and counter-espionage agents are becoming more and more numerous in Persia,' he wrote. '[They] come in freely and even when known to be spies, I have little or no power to deal with them.'

Two of his own spies had recently been shot by Bolsheviks. Now, he asked India for the authority to execute the spies that he had managed to capture.

He received no reply and nor did he press the issue. His preferred mode of action was to act first and inform India afterwards: this gave him the greatest possible freedom.

Malleson now began to expand dramatically his own network of agents and informers. These were always men of dubious probity whom he, in common with Mansfield Cumming, referred to as 'his ruffians'. They were often well-educated local men who showed great ability in infiltrating Bolshevik organisations and acquiring intelligence directly from the source.

A number of them also managed to infiltrate key telegraphic exchanges, enabling Malleson to intercept hundreds of top-secret messages. They included telegrams sent from Lenin and Trotsky to the Tashkent government, the Indian revolutionaries and the Amir of Afghanistan.

Malleson was staggered by the content of these intercepts: they detailed everything from troop movements and the export of weaponry to decrees from the Comintern and the Soviet regime. As such, they were intelligence gold dust.

The despatches that Malleson sent to British India give some inkling of the extent and reach of his network. In one month alone, he received comprehensive reports from his agents in towns right across the region, including Kuskh, Kabul, Yulatan, Sarakhs, Kerki, Bokhara, Tejend and Daragaz, as well as every frontier post on the borders of Turkestan.

'The mission is well adapted for providing advanced information of events in Central Asia,' he wrote to India, 'but the work is rapidly increasing. Fifty pages of foolscap daily is required for the wireless intercepts, and to go through them takes hours.'

Malleson was justifiably proud of his vast team. 'I had some most excellent officers speaking numerous languages,' he said. 'I had agents up to distances of a thousand miles or more, even in the Government Offices of the Bolsheviks. I had relays of men constantly coming and going in areas which I deemed important.'

He kept a particularly close eye on the movement of suspect people. 'There was hardly a train on the Central Asian Railway which had not one of our agents on board, and there was no important railway centre which had not two or three men on the spot.'

Just as Malleson had been given carte blanche by British India, so he gave his men the freedom to arrest and interrogate suspects in the manner that they thought best. None of his agents would ever be punished for using heavy-handed tactics when questioning their subjects.

'Travellers of every sort and description were cross-examined at scores of different places. Intelligence cannot well be improvised. It needs to be slowly built up. But we started with nothing beyond a few agents and ended with a great deal.'

The quantity of information reaching Malleson continued to grow with every week that passed. 'We sent [to British India] . . . a stream of information from every part of the huge area for which we were responsible. It was a veritable *tour de force* for the officers I have in mind to have organised and to have brought to such a state of efficiency in so short a time so excellent an intelligence system.'

This system enabled Malleson to build a highly accurate picture of what was taking place inside Turkestan. More than that, it revealed the tightening links between Soviet Russia and Afghanistan. A Soviet-Afghan alliance presented a serious threat to British India, for it would enable the Bolsheviks to establish military bases on the very frontiers of the Raj.

Malleson's first inkling of the close relationship between Moscow and Kabul had come during the amir's invasion of British India in the spring of 1919. His agents intercepted a number of secret telegrams that revealed the Soviet intention of supporting the invasion.

One of these telegrams, sent to the governor of Kabul, informed the Afghans that '500 camel loads of munitions, including bombs and aircraft parts, would soon arrive at Kushk for Herat, with seven aircraft mechanics.'

The delivery of this military hardware was being co-ordinated by a professional revolutionary known as Bravin, a man already being tracked by Malleson.

The Afghans were defeated long before the Soviet weaponry could be used but it was clear that the dangers of a co-ordinated Bolshevik-Islamic assault were growing by the day. Malleson intercepted scores of Afghan orders for Soviet weaponry, many of which read like extended shopping lists: 'Seven airplanes, 24 machine-guns, 2,000 hand grenades, 50,000 rifles . . .'

Telegraphic intercepts also confirmed that senior Bolshevik figures were intending to boost their support for Afghanistan. One of these telegrams, sent from Moscow's Commissar for Foreign Affairs to his counterpart in Turkestan, made for particularly perturbing reading.

'Military help to Afghanistan will be given free of charge as soon as railway communications are established with Tashkent . . . Aeroplanes will be despatched in the immediate future.'

The wireless correspondence between Lenin and the Amir of Afghanistan was also intercepted; British India found itself with tangible proof of the warm relations between the two leaders.

'Now [that] the standard of Bolshevism has been raised by Russia,' declared the Afghan leader, 'the Amir hastens to declare that she has earned the gratitude of the whole world.'

Lenin responded by telling the amir that 'the long awaited flame in the East has flared up and the fire is gathering all shades of Muhammedans in its trail.'

In distant Moscow, Cheka officers were quick to realise that Malleson was eavesdropping on these secret communications. They warned senior-ranking commissars to take additional precautions when sending telegrams.

'In future, answers to our coded telegrams must be coded, as non-coded telegrams are intercepted by the English.' The Soviet transmissions were henceforth coded as requested, but it made little difference for Malleson's team of code-breakers managed to crack the cipher within days.

Malleson was by now fully alerted to the dangers of a Soviet-Afghan pact. His response was to begin a proxy war against the Bolsheviks, providing their Turkic enemies with secret military information. This enabled the Turkman fighters to take effective action for the first time since the revolution reached Turkestan.

The town of Tejend was a case in point. When Malleson discovered that the Bolshevik garrison was understrength, he passed this information to his allies. '[They] promptly fell on Tejend . . . slaughtered its garrison and wrecked the station.' Attacks such as this were repeated right across the region and seriously rattled the Bolsheviks.

Malleson was convinced that the Soviets and Afghans were unlikely comrades and he set himself the task of destroying their friendship. Like a puppeteer, he stood in the shadows and pulled the strings.

'We laid ourselves out to "queer the pitch",' he admitted with customary lack of scruple. With access to the secret communications of both camps – and a talent for dirty diplomacy – Malleson was able to 'queer the pitch' with remarkable effect.

'It became our task to do everything possible to prevent the consummation of Afghan and Bolshevik plans for an offensive and defensive alliance,' he wrote.

His first task was to sow discord in the Afghan camp, exploiting the tensions between the country's different Muslim factions: the Shia West and the Sunni East.

When a bloody massacre of Shias took place in Kandahar, Malleson's propaganda team distributed thousands of highly inflammatory leaflets in Shia areas of the country. These blamed the Sunnis for the acts of violence and expressed outrage at the humiliating treatment of the minority Shia population. 'We were able to make much capital of this,' wrote a gleeful Malleson.

His propaganda campaign proved so successful that he began poisoning relations between the Afghans and their new Soviet allies. He printed vicious leaflets about the militant atheism of the Bolsheviks and had them smuggled across the border into Afghanistan.

'[They] invariably circulated freely amongst the people we desired they should reach' – the tribal chieftains and mullahs – and provided many examples of the 'notorious faithlessness of the Bolsheviks'.

Malleson's next trick was to instruct his Kabul-based agents to make contact with senior figures in the Afghan elite. Masquerading as advisors, they warned that Afghanistan would be wise to extract territorial pledges from Moscow before striking an alliance with 'such dangerous people to the God-granted kingdom'.

Malleson knew exactly the territorial pledge that would delight the Afghans as much as it would infuriate the Soviets. It was the return to Afghan rule of the Panjdeh district of the country, a slab of Afghanistan that had been forcibly seized by Russia in 1885. The land now formed a part of Soviet Turkestan and the Bolsheviks had no intention of ever giving it back.

Malleson had found an open wound in which to pour his poison. Within weeks, the issue was being openly discussed by the Afghan government. Shortly afterwards, a senior envoy was sent to Moscow with a demand for the restitution of the Panjdeh. This was to be an essential prerequisite of any formal alliance between the two countries.

The Bolshevik Government squirmed. They gave a woolly response to the amir, holding out 'strong hopes of such a concession' and making vague promises of establishing 'a frontier commission and a plebiscite of the people of the area.'

The Afghan Government was unhappy with this and promptly upped its demands. It now demanded not only the Panjdeh, but also the entire area to the east of Merv – a vast slab of additional territory.

Furthermore, they insisted on a realignment of their entire western border with Turkestan. To show that they meant business, they despatched a team of hardline mullahs to these areas in order to ensure that the outcome of any plebiscite was certain to go in their favour.

These mullahs already mistrusted the Bolsheviks. Now, they used the occasion to lambaste Lenin's godless policies. They told the local population that they should sever all links with the Soviets and they also spoke of their determination 'to extirpate from Central Asia . . . not only all infidels, but especially the Bolsheviks.'

From his headquarters in Meshed, Malleson watched the breakdown in relations with considerable satisfaction. 'Having, through numerous agents in both camps, a very fairly accurate notion of what was going on,' he wrote, 'and of how these two interesting parties were seeking how best to take each other in, we made it our business to keep each side unofficially informed of the perfidy of the other.'

When the Afghan Government learned of a serious anti-Bolshevik rebellion in the mountains to the east of Tashkent, it sent emissaries with gifts for the leaders of the insurgents.

Malleson learned this from his spies in Kabul. It was yet another piece of highly useful intelligence. 'This information,' he wrote, 'we felt it our duty to bring to the notice of the Bolsheviks.'

Lenin and Trotsky were seriously troubled by the rupture in relations. They now invited an Afghan mission to Moscow in the hope of bolstering an alliance that was fast slipping through their fingers. They promised the restitution of Afghan territory and offered grants of munitions and money in return for a pact of military co-operation.

Malleson's agents in Kabul made great play of what many Afghans perceived to be a diplomatic triumph. They printed leaflets portraying the Soviets as being in need of Afghan assistance, fully aware that this would embolden the Afghans still further. 'Hence more Afghan arrogance and further demands,' wrote Malleson.

The Afghan Army now joined the fray. It marched north-east towards Kushk, with Afghan mullahs following in its wake. 'As a result of our bringing these matters to Bolshevik notice, there was considerable anxiety.'

The Bolsheviks responded by sending their own troops to Kushk, along with the head of Turkestan's government. On his arrival in the city, he was threatened by a mob of angry Afghans. It was exactly as Malleson had intended. 'And so the game went on,' he wrote.

Malleson was instigating a twentieth-century version of the Great Game and he was playing his hands with aplomb. Over the months that followed, his agents continued to set the Afghans against the Bolsheviks with remarkable efficacy.

The Soviet Government could not understand why their alliance with Afghanistan had so quickly turned sour. They were unaware of the extent of Malleson's deviousness and remained puzzled as to why the Afghans had so rapidly switched from friend to foe.

Malleson continued to play his game for many months to come, until the vaunted Soviet-Afghan military alliance collapsed in the spring of 1920. Malleson justifiably claimed much of the credit. He said that his Machiavellian exposés of Afghan diplomacy 'had materially chilled the Bolsheviks' former enthusiasm for them.'

This, in turn, had averted a war 'that would certainly have cost millions . . . [and] cost many lives from battle and many more from disease.'

Malleson hoped for official recognition for the role that he and his undercover agents had played. He petitioned the commander in chief of the British Army, the British Government of India, the India Office and the Army Council, but all to no avail.

'None of the rewards so richly deserved by the officers whose services I brought to notice have been gazetted,' he informed an audience at London's Royal Central Asian Society when he finally returned home.

British India was embarrassed by his work and wished to disassociate itself from his ungentlemanly tactics. Malleson had torn up the rulebook and devised his own, more cunning version.

But he had also proved what the British Government was only just beginning to understand: that an enemy could be more convincingly trounced by espionage and dirty tricks than it could by conventional warfare. It was a lesson to be heeded in the months to come.

CHAPTER SEVENTEEN

ARMY OF GOD

In November 1920, just a few days after the third anniversary of the Bolshevik revolution, a huge military entourage slipped unnoticed out of Moscow's Pavelestsky station.

The trains were heavily camouflaged and under armed guard. As they left the capital and trundled southwards across an increasingly bleak landscape, a team of lookouts scanned the skies for any sign of trouble from the air. Three of the carriages had machine-guns installed on the roofs, a precaution against attack.

Only a handful of top-ranking commissars knew the purpose of the mission. It had been organised in absolute secrecy and had required months of planning. The trains were equipped with a large stockpile of military hardware that was being transported from Moscow to Tashkent.

'Our party travelled in two trains,' wrote the leader of this clandestine party, 'one composed of twenty-seven 30-ton wagons carrying arms (pistols, rifles, machine-guns, hand-grenades, light artillery, etc.) adequate supplies of ammunition and military stores, and field equipment which included several wireless receivers and transmitters.'

The second train contained gold coins and bullion, the staff of a military training school and a large number of dismantled aeroplanes, including the entire supply depot of an air-force battalion. Seven other wagons were filled with military personnel.

The reason for the secrecy was obvious to everyone on board. Their task was to raise a Soviet-Islamic 'Army of Liberation' and thrust deep into British India. They intended to sweep over the mountainous North-West Frontier and occupy the territory inhabited by rebellious tribesmen.

This liberated area would then be used as a base to spearhead terrorist attacks on other Indian cities. Lenin himself had argued that setting India aflame was the only way to guarantee the long-term destruction of the West. 'Successful revolt of the colonial peoples,' he said, 'was a condition for the overthrow of capitalism in Europe.'

The person in overall command of the liberation army was not Russian and nor could he even speak the language. He answered to the name of Roberto Allen, although this was only one of his numerous aliases. His comrades knew him as Manabendra Nath Roy and he was a professional revolutionary who had been on the run since 1918, when he was indicted in absentia for plotting revolution in India.

Roy had achieved further notoriety in Mexico, where he founded the first Communist Party outside Russia. Invited to Moscow in the spring of 1920, he was immediately embraced by the Soviet inner circle.

Foreign Commissar Lev Karakhan was the first to meet with Roy. The two men spoke about stoking violent unrest in India, a subject which Roy had given a great deal of thought. Karakhan was impressed by Roy's insight and told him that 'the Soviet Government was prepared to help me in every possible manner.'

Roy was next introduced to Chicherin, head of the Soviet Foreign Ministry. Chicherin was a reviled figure in the West, but Roy was impressed by the man. He reminded him of a patrician gangster: 'The picture of the highly cultivated European gentleman,' he wrote, '[and] so very conscious of his inner self as made him oblivious of his physical appearance.'

Chicherin was no less impressed with Roy. He seemed to combine intelligence with an inner drive, making him the perfect candidate for thrusting the revolution beyond Russia's frontiers. His arrival in Moscow was also timely. Chicherin told him that 'the colonial world was in flames', and said that it was time to pour petrol onto those flames. 'Revolution must be spread eastwards; a second front of the world revolution must be opened in Asia.'

Roy could scarcely have wished for more. The destruction of British India had been his ambition for almost a decade and he informed the two commissars of his desire to join forces with the Comintern.

He also expressed his belief that revolution could only be achieved through a wave of bloodshed. Indeed he would later say that a non-violent revolution was as grotesque as a vegetarian tiger. 'The Indian struggle for freedom is a revolutionary struggle,' he wrote. 'It will never be successful without the final stage of violence.'

The two commissars were impressed by the bravado of this young revolutionary. After giving him an impromptu tour of the Comintern headquarters, they took him directly to meet with Lenin. Without Lenin's blessing, Roy could not begin consultation with the two bodies whose support he would need: the Comintern and the Revolutionary Military Council.

Roy confessed to an attack of nerves as he entered Lenin's office. Not yet twenty-eight years of age, he revered Lenin as his revolutionary hero. Now, he found himself being ushered into his private study.

'My attention was immediately attracted by the bald dome of a head stooping very low on the top of a big desk placed right in the middle of the room. I was nervous and walked towards the desk, not knowing what else to do.'

Suddenly, Lenin jumped to his feet and bounded across to greet him. He shook Roy's hand and then peered at him more closely, as if he wanted to inspect him at close quarters. 'Nearly a head shorter, he tilted his red goatee almost to a horizontal position to look at my face quizzically.'

Roy smiled weakly. 'I was embarrassed [and] did not know what to say. He helped me out with a banter. "You are so young! I expected a bearded wise man from the East." '

Lenin's quip broke the ice. The two men warmed to each other immediately and within minutes they were deep in conversation about colonialism and the best means to bring about the destruction of British rule in India.

Roy explained his strategy to Lenin. It was a two-fold strategy for revolution that involved both internal and external attacks on India. The first stage was to smuggle small teams of highly trained operatives into key cities. They would create 'fighting cells' which could receive illicit supplies of weapons and start co-ordinating centres of resistance.

He would simultaneously raise an army of liberation in Tashkent and lead it through Afghanistan and across the frontier of British India. Once it had reached the troubled territory around Peshawar, the army commanders would forge links with the rebellious Islamic tribes who were already stoking unrest.

'Using the frontier territories as the base of operations and with the mercenary support of the tribesmen,' explained Roy, 'the liberation army would march into India and occupy some territory where a civil government should be established as soon as possible.'

The timing of Roy's proposed invasion could scarcely have been more opportune. Gandhi's civil disobedience campaign had already united Hindus and Muslims against the British ruling elite. Several key cities had erupted into rebellion and the British response to the continual unrest had been disastrous. The Amritsar Massacre of the previous spring, in which more than 1,300 civilians had been gunned down by the forces of the Raj, had cast a long shadow over Northern India. Roy's army was assured of an enthusiastic welcome from the local population.

Nor was his strategy as fanciful at it sounded. In the previous few months, some 50,000 militant Islamic tribesmen living along the volatile North-West Frontier had crossed the border into Afghanistan and Turkestan.

They were incensed by the dismemberment of the Ottoman Empire by Great Britain and her allies and fearful that the caliphate, traditionally invested in the Turkish sultan, would be abolished. Now, they intended to travel overland to Turkey – a journey of more than 2,000 miles – where they would fight the British.

These were the men who Roy intended to draft into his army. They were fanatically anti-British and fired by religious fervour. They were also highly experienced in guerrilla warfare, especially in the treacherous passes of the Hindu Kush. Roy knew they could cause mayhem if they were professionally trained and then sent back into India to fight.

Roy's strategy, coming after the collapse of the military alliance with Afghanistan, made a deep impression on everyone he met in Moscow. He was introduced to the inner circle of the Comintern and given every possible assistance in turning his vision into reality. The Comintern was to provide money, leadership and technical know-how. It would also help Roy to establish a Central Asiatic Bureau, which was to be directly responsible for planning the assault on India.

Roy was installed as the bureau's most prominent member, 'charged with the responsibility ... of carrying through the revolution in Turkestan and Bokhara' – where there were still pockets of resistance – 'and then spreading it to the adjacent countries.' India was the principal goal, but the Comintern also had Chinese Turkestan in its sights.

The support of the Comintern brought many benefits. Roy was able to call upon the services of key figures in the Soviet regime, including Grigori Sokolnikov, the commander in chief of Soviet forces in Central Asia. His presence on the board of the Central Asiatic Bureau ensured that Roy could lay his hands on whatever supplies and hardware he needed for his army.

Roy was aware that he needed to move fast if he was to have any hope of success. 'The war in Europe was over,' he wrote. 'Before long, the British-Indian army would again be available for the defence of the North-West Frontier.'

He worked around the clock on planning the logistics for his invasion, acquiring a huge quantity of military hardware. This included a 'large quantity of arms, field equipment, training personnel and plenty of money.'

By November 1920, everything was ready. The weaponry was secretly loaded onto trains, along with two companies of crack Red Army troops. Their Soviet commander was a veritable giant: 'nearly seven foot tall,' wrote Roy, 'and proportionately broad.'

The initial destination of this travelling force was Tashkent; this was to become Roy's principal base. But once the nucleus of his Army of Liberation had been recruited and trained, he would move swiftly to stage two of the planned invasion: 'the establishment of the advance base at Kabul, and operational bases on the Indian frontier.'

After months of secret talks and shady negotiations, the offensive was finally under way.

★

While Roy was busily acquiring equipment for his army, the Comintern had been engaged in propaganda warfare on a scale never hitherto undertaken. It organised a conference at Baku, on the shores of the Caspian, with the aim of bringing together Soviet revolutionaries and Islamic jihadis and uniting them in a common purpose.

Some 1,800 delegates were invited to the week-long rally which opened in September, 1920. Grigori Zinoviev, head of the Comintern, travelled from Moscow to Baku in order to declare the beginnings of a holy crusade that was intended to sweep away the democracies of the West.

Zinoviev was already infamous as a fiery demagogue, one whose speeches could set a crowd alight. In Baku, he surpassed all his previous performances with an oration that electrified his audience. Rising from his seat on the rostrum, he cast his eyes over an auditorium that was heaving with expectant delegates. Some were dressed in the khaki uniform of the Red Army. Many more were decked in the colourful *khalats* and headscarves of Central Asia. All fell silent as Zinoviev launched into his speech with a rousing call to arms.

'Comrades! Brothers!' he roared. 'The time has now come when you can set about organising a true people's holy war against the robbers and oppressors. The Communist International [Comintern] turns today to the peoples of the East and says to them: "Brothers, we summon you to a holy war, in the first place against British imperialism!" '

His war cry was greeted with tumultuous applause. Indeed, the shouting and cheering was so loud that his voice was completely drowned out and it was some minutes before he could continue.

'May this declaration made today be heard in London, in Paris, and in all the cities where the capitalists are still in power,' he thundered. 'May they heed this solemn oath sworn by the representatives of tens of millions of toilers of the East, that the rule of the British oppressors shall be no more in the East.'

This was greeted by another roar of approval. Fired with enthusiasm, the delegates unsheathed their swords and scimitars. Some even pulled out their revolvers and started brandishing them in the air. As the roar of the crowd increased in volume, the band pumped out 'The Internationale', playing it three times in succession. As it did so, the delegates shouted 'Long live the Comintern! Long live those who have united the East!'

The Times would later carry a report on the alarming nature of the congress. Sneering in its tone, it warned of the threat that the Comintern posed to the world at large and reserved much of its contempt for Zinoviev and Bela Kun, the Hungarian revolutionary who had accompanied him to Baku.

'Of all the strange things which have happened in the last few years,' it said, 'none has been stranger than the spectacle of two Jews, one of them a convicted pickpocket, summoning the world of Islam to a jihad.'

★

Roy and his Red Army troops faced a long and dangerous train journey to Tashkent, for parts of the route were only nominally under the control of Bolshevik forces.

'Roving detachments of White Guards, who had taken to banditry, still infested the steppes beyond the Ural River,' wrote Roy. 'They frequently tore up the railway line and held up trains to plunder.' He was only too aware that his own trains, with their cargo of weaponry and money, would make an enticing target.

It took two days to reach the Volga River and another day and a half before they arrived at Orenburg, on the border with Turkestan. From here, it was a further one thousand miles across the bleak landscape of the Kirghiz Steppes.

Roy had been granted the rare privilege of travelling in the salon car of the Russian Imperial Train, now reserved for senior commissars and dignitaries. Its velvet drapes and luxurious cushions gave the illusion of comfort, but afforded little protection against the biting cold. He was relieved when they finally pulled into Tashkent after seven days of travel.

Roy stepped onto the platform and was greeted by General Sokolnikov. The general was to help him establish a military base and training camp for his projected army.

But first, Roy was taken to the building that was to be his Tashkent headquarters. It was centrally located and large enough to house his staff. But like so many of the city's larger villas, it had been ransacked and gutted in the violence that followed the revolution. The furniture had been smashed, the electric wires cut and the water pipes had ruptured in the freezing weather.

'A few kerosene lamps, feebly aided by flickering candles, tried in vain to dispel the sepulchral darkness of a deserted house,' wrote Roy. 'The vast porcelain stoves had not been lit since the arrival of the intense winter cold.'

He and his men were undeterred by the lack of comfort. In fact, they derived an ascetic pleasure from the hardships of revolution. 'The joy of participating in the liberation of peoples downtrodden for centuries . . .' wrote Roy, 'added to the richness of life.'

His first task was to open a Tashkent office of the Comintern. This was a key ingredient for future success, since the Comintern was funding his revolutionary activity. Its central role was signalled by the building selected as its headquarters. It was the mansion that had formerly belonged to the Russian Imperial Bank, a building whose vaults still contained the viceregal crown jewels and all the most precious (and now requisitioned) possessions of the court nobility.

Roy found a profound significance in the choice of such a building. '[It was] as if the valuable booty of the Revolution was placed under the custody of the world proletariat, and the honour of holding the trust fell on me.'

Roy himself presided over the weekly meetings of the Comintern, occupying the throne of the deposed imperial dignitary for whom it had originally been made. It was richly carved in rare wood, upholstered in crimson velvet and bore the Romanov coat of arms embroidered in gold.

Roy was all too aware that he was working to an extremely tight time frame. He wanted his army ready within months, so that the thrust into India could begin while the country's defences were still weak. He immediately set to work on establishing a military academy with training facilities, firing ranges and lecture rooms for teaching propaganda. This was achieved within a matter of weeks and Roy soon found himself his first set of recruits. They were a group of Pathan deserters from the Indian Army, along with a small band of Persian revolutionaries.

The men were swiftly enrolled into the Tashkent academy and trained to use Soviet light artillery. 'Formidable with rifles, they quickly learned to handle machine-guns and operate the artillery.'

Within weeks, they were formed into an irregular brigade. 'It was the first International Brigade of the Red Army,' wrote Roy, 'and the experiment was a success.'

Other deserters were also enlisted and drafted into an irregular force that began patrolling the Trans-Caspian railway.

Many expressed the desire to train as pilots for Roy's planned air force. He had brought a large number of dismantled planes to Tashkent, aware that they were certain to play an important role in any assault by land. The havoc wreaked by British planes in the Anglo-Afghan war of 1919 had demonstrated the efficacy of airborne attack in the treacherous terrain of the North-West Frontier.

'To learn aviation was the general craze,' wrote Roy. 'There was a general scramble; everyone wanted to learn flying.' At least one of those who received training at Tashkent later went on to become a flying ace in the Red Army's aviation unit.

Roy was delighted by the progress that was being made. 'A step was taken towards the creation of a nucleus of the army to liberate India,' he wrote. This 'nucleus' was initially commanded by Russians but it was not long before Indians were also raised to officer rank, encouraging yet more deserters to sign up.

'The International Brigade soon became an effective auxiliary of the Red Army,' wrote Roy. Armed with machine-guns, they began ambushing and killing British Indian troops on the Persian border and proved highly skilled in guerrilla warfare.

'Persian groups of the International Brigade could penetrate deep into their country in various disguises and harass the flank of the British Army on the road south of Meshed.' These were exactly the skills needed for waging war inside India.

Roy was filled with confidence and now set to work on recruiting from the ranks of the 50,000 itinerant *Muhajir* that were drifting through the region. These were from a very different background to the deserters from the British-Indian Army.

'A refractory lot,' wrote Roy, 'moved only by religious fanaticism.' He drafted an initial group of fifty into his growing army and was taken aback by their Islamic fervour. They had little interest in the revolutionary struggle. Rather, their motivation for fighting the hated British was 'the possibility of going to heaven by laying down their lives in jihad.'

They were so diligent in their prayers that one of Roy's officers quipped that they were not creating an 'Army of Liberation' but an 'Army of God'. The name stuck. Henceforth, even Roy began to refer to his army as the Army of God. It gave the impression that destiny was on their side.

Roy's energies were focussed on British India, but he had also been charged with helping the Red Army to mop up resistance in the vast hinterlands of Turkestan. The emirate of Bokhara, to which Frederick Bailey had made his escape, had been stormed and captured by the Red Army just two months before Roy's arrival in Tashkent.

The grizzled amir had been forced to flee for his life, 'dropping favourite dancing boy after favourite dancing boy in his flight,' according to one who was there.

Roy now established a revolutionary government in the former emirate and fired everyone associated with the deposed amir. But one vestige of the old regime remained in place: the amir's four hundred concubines refused to leave the sanctuary of the palace.

Roy sent them a message informing them that 'the revolution had freed them from the bondage of the harem and they could go wherever they liked.' But still none of them showed any inclination to leave the safety of that bondage. Eventually, Roy ordered the harem to be stormed by a band of his most loyal troops.

The young men launched their assault with considerable relish, as well they might: Roy had said that each soldier who took part in the attack could take home one of the concubines as 'booty.'

He presided over the division of the spoils like a benevolent uncle, claiming (but offering no evidence) that the ladies of the harem had enjoyed the attack as much as the men. '[It] was a new experience to women whose erotic life naturally could not be satisfied by a senile old man.'

The reality was almost certainly more sinister. Even Roy admitted that the concubines 'behaved like scared rabbits'. They must have been absolutely terrified to have their secluded existence shattered by a band of ill-disciplined and sexually frustrated soldiers.

Roy's ultimate goal was British India, but first he had to break the resistance in the mountainous Ferghana region. This was dangerous territory – a string of high-altitude valleys that lay one hundred miles to the east of Tashkent. The

Turkman rebels hiding out there proved highly skilled in guerrilla warfare, for they were toughened by years of fighting and were also familiar with the terrain.

The assault was led by the Red Army, which struck in two fighting columns. 'While the frontal attack pushed the rebels back over a much longer distance,' wrote Roy, 'the other columns struck at their main base only a few miles from the Indian frontier.'

He was there to witness their victory and he was also there when the army swept southwards and ceremoniously planted the red flag on the highest summit of the Pamir Mountains. It was an emotional moment; Roy now stood at the gates of India and the subcontinent was stretched out before him like a vast oriental carpet.

'Standing on the roof of the world,' he wrote, 'I looked at India through a field glass.'

But unbeknown to Roy, India was also watching him.

CHAPTER EIGHTEEN

WINNER TAKES ALL

Manabendra Roy had been under observation for nearly five years by the time he pitched up in Tashkent.

He was known to hide behind a number of aliases, including Mr White, Father Martin and Roberto Allen, his most recent incarnation. He was also known to have been involved in illicit gun-running during the First World War.

The viceroy, Frederick Thesiger, the 3rd Baron Chelmsford, was seriously alarmed by the danger posed by Roy and the Comintern. He knew that their initial goal was the North-West Frontier Province, an increasingly volatile region whose Muslim tribesmen were certain to extend a warm welcome to Roy's soldiers.

If the Army of God successfully captured Peshawar, which was by no means impossible, then Roy would have a base from which to advance south-eastwards towards the Punjab, a distance of some 250 miles. Here, he was equally certain to be welcomed by the local population. The Punjab was suffering serious and continued unrest in the wake of the Amritsar Massacre.

The viceroy's initial response to the crisis was to order an immediate increase in expenditure on espionage. This led to a boost in the number of staff in the Peshawar intelligence bureau 'which is specially charged with the detection of Bolshevik agents.'

The viceroy also established a new bureau in Quetta, less than fifty miles from the Afghan border. This, too, was to deal directly with the Bolshevik threat.

His next step was to send agents directly to Tashkent, in order that they could monitor Roy's activities at close quarters. It was to prove extremely dangerous work. One of these agents had the misfortune to be captured by Roy and was summarily executed.

In spite of the risks, such operations were deemed vital to the security of India. 'All authorities concerned are alive to the importance of intercepting Bolshevik agents and literature,' wrote the viceroy.

This could not be done from India itself. 'With our vast frontier we must rely in the main on the evil being tapped at its source by means of intelligence systems at all chief centres of Bolshevik activities.'

As news of the Army of God filtered back to India, the viceroy took the decision to establish a specialist anti-Bolshevik unit that was primarily involved in dirty tricks. As such, its work was remarkably similar to that which had been undertaken by Wilfrid Malleson and his agents.

'Work has now been co-ordinated by officers specially appointed for counter-propaganda, co-ordination of intelligence, both internal and external and organisational measures to keep Bolshevik emissaries and propaganda out of India.'

It was not long before this unit intercepted the first delivery of weapons to India – a consignment of 150 automatic pistols.

Shortly afterwards, a large quantity of revolvers and ammunition was also seized. Unbeknown to Roy, the net was closing in on his Army of God.

★

The net was also closing in on the Comintern, although no one inside Zinoviev's organisation was aware that Mansfield Cumming was eavesdropping on its activities.

Even government ministers in London were unaware of the extent and reach of Cumming's espionage operations. The work of his agents had become so clandestine in the previous months that only members of his own staff were privy to what was taking place.

In the aftermath of Paul Dukes's return to London, Cumming had moved into a new, more secretive headquarters. He relocated his offices from Whitehall Court to an anonymous villa at Number One, Melbury Road in Holland Park, West London.

With its bay windows and giant chimneys, Number One looked like any other house in the street. But Cumming, its ostensible owner, was to receive far more colourful visitors than any of his neighbours. Curious residents must have twitched their curtains and wondered how this eccentric old gentleman came to have such an eclectic collection of friends.

Cumming had his living quarters on the upper floor of the house, while the downstairs rooms were turned into offices and workshops. It was the perfect set-up: here in Melbury Road he could create 'new extensions to my organisation as can be kept separate and distinct from the Main Bureau and to work from this central office any scheme or project that requires absolute secrecy.'

Secrecy had always been of paramount importance to Cumming. '[The] first, last and most necessary essential of a S[ecret] S[ervice] is that it should be SECRET,' he wrote in one of his notes on espionage. He said that this was 'the first thing to be forgotten in any scheme and the last thing to be remembered in putting it into practice.'

Ever since his appointment to the job in 1909, Cumming had made secrecy the guiding principle of his life. Indeed, he had delighted in wrapping himself in a cloak of anonymity. He continued to hide behind his acronym, C, and never wrote publicly about his work. He once joked that if he ever published his autobiography, it would be quarto, bound in vellum and consisting of 400 pages – all of them blank.

His office diary offers few clues about his daily routine in the troubled period that followed Dukes's return to London. It contains little more than a list of meetings with Whitehall civil servants. But a couple of the entries are more beguiling and hint at the clandestine work that was still being undertaken by his agents.

'Promised Jack £750 down, £750 on his return from Moscow, £500 if his report [is] exceptional, on the understanding that he attends the conference of the 3rd International [the Comintern]'. So reads one of the cryptic entries in Cumming's diary.

The identity of 'Jack' remains a mystery, yet he was clearly an agent who was able to move freely within the Soviet regime. The ability to attend meetings of the Comintern was of vital importance, given that this was the organisation in charge of spearheading the global revolution.

Agent George Hill, now back in London, also hinted at the existence of an undercover team working inside Russia. In his memoirs he spoke of 'a score of other names in this silent service who could tell of tasks done and obstacles overcome which would read like fairy stories and yet contain not a sylla-ble of exaggeration.'

It is possible that Hill himself had recruited one of these mysterious 'names' at some point during 1919. If so, it was a brilliant coup: this anonymous agent was to work like a conju-ror for years to come, plucking top-secret documents from under the very noses of the Soviet elite. He would transform the quality (and, indeed, the quantity) of information being received at Number One, Melbury Road.

His identity – and the clandestine work he undertook – would not be revealed for another decade. At the time when Roy was training his Army of God, Cumming's most enig-matic spy was carrying out his work in the deepest of shadows.

One of the documents acquired from Moscow was written by Lev Karakhan, the Vice Commissar for Foreign Affairs. It concerned the Soviet-backed Comintern agents who were 'actively engaged in organising a revolution in India.' It revealed that they were also fomenting unrest in other British-held territories in a bid to stretch defences to the limit.

'We have already succeeded in linking up different groups . . .' wrote Karakhan, 'and harmonising their move-ment with that of Egypt, Arabia and Turkey.'

He remained convinced that the overthrow of British India would play a key role in destroying the already shattered economies of the West. '[It] will have enormous effects on the whole of Europe,' he said, '[and] is regarded as a means by itself of bringing about the triumph of Bolshevik world policy.'

Karakhan's memo provided Cumming with irrefutable evidence of the links between the Soviet leadership and the Comintern. Such links were consistently denied by Lenin's commissars, who insisted that the Comintern was an international organisation and wholly independent of the Soviet government. This was an important deceit to maintain, for it enabled them to distance themselves from any direct role in Roy's planned invasion of British India.

Cumming kept in regular communication with his colleagues in Indian intelligence, sharing information on the growing nature of the threat. When his documents were collated with those from India, the complete dossier ran into hundreds of pages. It also made for highly disturbing reading. Roy's Army of God was in a state of high alert and would soon be ready to cross the frontier of Northern India.

★

It was one thing to gather intelligence, quite another to know how to exploit it. Wilfrid Malleson had proved that espionage could be used to devastating effect: his Machiavellian exploits had seriously undermined Soviet plans for an alliance with Afghanistan in the summer of 1919.

But subtlety, too, could reap rich dividends. In the dangerous game of Russian Roulette, playing an unexpected hand could upset the best laid plans.

It so happened that the establishment of Roy's Army of God coincided with economic collapse inside Soviet Russia. The country found itself in meltdown, with a slump in industrial production and a catastrophic decline in grain supplies. The much heralded policy of War Communism had proved a disaster, one that left millions of Russians on the verge of starvation.

In the spring of 1921, Lenin replaced War Communism with his New Economic Policy. Limited private trade was to be sanctioned and enterprise encouraged. So, too, was international trade. It was this quest for trade that brought two of Lenin's senior commissars to London: Leonid Krasin (Commissar for Trade and Industry) and Lev Kamenev (Head of the Congress of Soviets).

The ensuing talks were to preoccupy British ministers for many months. They were often acrimonious and broke down completely on several occasions. The British had good reason not to trust the Russian negotiating team: they were eavesdropping on every wire, telegraph and communication that was passing between Moscow and London.

'That swine Lloyd George has no scruple or shame in the way he deceives,' said Lenin to Krasin in one telegraphic exchange. 'Don't believe a word he says and gull him three times as much.'

The message was decoded and placed on Lloyd George's desk within hours of it being sent. It was one of numerous intercepts that shed light on Soviet methods and intentions. Lloyd George confessed to his Cabinet colleagues that eavesdropping was providing 'real insight into Bolshevik interests and policy.'

By the spring of 1921, the Soviet economy was in such dire straits that Lenin was desperate for the agreement to be signed. International trade was deemed to be the only way to lift Russia from its economic woes.

In a speech to the Congress of Soviets, he publicly voiced his fears that the British Government was divided between those who wanted an agreement and those who vehemently opposed it.

'It is in our direct interest, and it is our direct duty to give all our support to whatever can help to fortify those parties and groupings [in London] who are striving for the signature of this treaty with us.'

Lord Curzon had long been urging his colleagues to seize the golden opportunity presented by Lenin's need for an agreement. 'We know from a great variety of sources that the Russian Government is threatened with complete economic disaster,' he said, 'and that it is ready to pay almost any price for the assistance which we . . . are in a position to give.'

The price that Curzon wanted them to pay had nothing to do with trade: his thoughts were focused on the Army of God. 'It seems to me that [the] price can far better be paid in a cessation of Bolshevik hostility in parts of the world important to us than the ostensible exchange of commodities.'

He wanted the immediate disbanding of Roy's army.

There was one drawback to this strategy. The only way to force a showdown with the Soviet Government was to reveal intelligence that had been obtained by espionage. But this carried the risk of compromising the British agents still working undercover in Moscow and Tashkent.

An additional sticking point was the fact that the British public remained wholly unaware of the existence of Mansfield Cumming's organisation. Nor did people have any inkling of the extent of the espionage and eavesdropping that had been taking place over many years.

The Cabinet Secretary, Maurice Hankey, warned his colleagues that the undercover work had been so secret that even many in Whitehall had no notion of what had been taking place. 'Public opinion may experience a shock if it realises what has been going on,' he said.

Winston Churchill urged ministers to throw caution to the wind. He favoured confronting the Soviet commissars with all the secret information that had been obtained by British agents. He wanted to disclose decrypted telegrams as well, even though it would alert the Soviet government to the fact that their codes had been cracked.

In the end, wiser counsel prevailed. Ministers decided to use carefully selected morsels of intelligence in their quest to force the Soviet Government into a climb-down.

A blistering covering note was attached to the proposed trade agreement, one which revealed that British ministers had 'for a long time past been aware of the intrigues in which the Soviet Government, with their agents, subordinates and associates have been engaged.'

They admitted to knowing a great deal about the Indian revolutionaries in Central Asia; they even named Roy as the principal conspirator. 'Were nothing known of the present activities of these self-convicted traitors, the fact of their employment by the Russian Government would be enough to cast the gravest suspicion on the good faith of the Soviet government towards Great Britain in the East.'

A few choice items of intelligence about Roy's military training camp were also dropped into the covering note. 'At Tashkent is established the advance base for Indian work, with a political department and a military technical centre: here is provided instruction in revolutionary tactics for all Indians arriving in Turkestan from whatever direction.'

And so it went on. Carefully selected examples of Soviet treachery were cited, all of them gleaned from operators working for either Mansfield Cumming or for his colleagues in Simla.

Such activities would now have to cease, and cease with immediate effect, if the British were to sign the trade agreement. The planned invasion of India had to be permanently put on ice. The complete cessation of hostilities was to be 'an essential corollary of the conclusion of any agreement between the two countries.'

The British revelations left no one in Moscow in any doubt that the Soviet plot against India stood compromised and hopelessly exposed. It was hard to see how Roy's invasion could now take place, given that the British had been alerted to so many strategic details. Besides, in the final reckoning Lenin needed trade with Britain more than he needed Roy's Army of God.

After much debate, Moscow reluctantly concluded that it had been forced into a corner: it had no option but to abandon its planned assault on British India's North-West Frontier. It also consented to all the other terms of the British covering note. Lenin and his senior commissars promised to refrain 'from any attempt, by military or propaganda, to encourage any of the peoples of Asia in any form of hostile action against British interests or the British Empire, especially in India.'

News of the Russian climb-down was the cause of private jubilation in Whitehall: it was a triumphant vindication of the value of professional espionage. The threat to the Raj had been trounced not by armed force, nor by aerial bombardment, but by a small team of spies and code-breakers working undercover in Moscow and Tashkent.

The Anglo-Soviet Trade Agreement was finally signed on Wednesday, 16 March 1921, a typically damp and overcast day in London. There was no fanfare of trumpets and precious little publicity: *The Times* relegated its report to page eleven of the following day's newspaper.

Yet ministers in both London and Moscow had no doubts as to the importance of what had just been agreed. 'This diplomatic document, though modest in scope, is of truly historic significance,' wrote the Soviet diplomat, Ivan Maisky, who would later serve as ambassador to London.

It was a formal acknowledgment that a vicious undeclared war had been ongoing between Soviet Russia and Great Britain for more than three years. It also made public Russia's intention of destroying British India, the first step in its quest to engulf the world in violent revolution. Although it was not a peace treaty, it was tantamount to one.

The dry prose of the agreement gave little hint of the deception, subterfuge and intrigue that lay behind it. Undercover agents, infiltrators and code-breakers hiding out in the Pamir Mountains had all played a role in unmasking the Soviet plot to sow mayhem and revolution in British India.

Both sides would claim victory in the aftermath of the agreement, for both sides had to justify it to the sceptics at home. But there was one definite loser and that was the Army of God.

Roy knew that there was no hope of pressing on with his planned invasion. There were too many hidden eyes watching his every movement. Besides, he was sent a curt order from Moscow to abandon his training camp and disband his army.

Roy himself broke the news to his troops. At a specially convened meeting he informed them that all of the various battalions were being dissolved with immediate effect.

The news came as a bombshell to the soldiers. The hardship, camaraderie and gruelling military training had all come to nothing. The dream of carrying armed revolution deep into India was over before it could become a reality. It was the cruellest defeat. The Army of God, established with such bravado, had been vanquished without a single shot being fired.

A few of the soldiers ventured to ask what the future held for them. Roy could do little more than shrug his shoulders. In truth, he did not know the answer. He promised each one a small sum of money and told them to go on their way.

Most drifted off to Persia or Afghanistan while others remained in Turkestan. A few struggled across the dangerous territory to the east of Bokhara and eventually managed to re-enter the Raj by way of the North-West Frontier.

One of these, Abdul Qadir Khan, was later interviewed about his attempt to return home. He explained how he and a few companions had scaled the freezing Baroghil Pass in the teeth of a biting gale and entered India near the frontier town of Chitral. They were immediately arrested.

'It is clear that the authorities in India knew for weeks that we were making for the Indian frontier,' said Khan. 'The Political Officer showed no surprise at our arrival . . . He said that the Intelligence Department had issued instructions regarding the possibility of Russian agents entering from that side of the border.'

By the time of Abdul Khan's arrest, Roy had packed his bags and headed back to Moscow, along with a handful of his most promising recruits. He was depressed by the fact that all his dreams of invading India had come to such an inglorious end. 'A year and a half ago, I had left Moscow with great expectations,' he wrote.

Now, those expectations had come to nothing. 'So I closed an exciting chapter of my life with the experience of failure, but without regret. Now, I must discover other ways to my goal and to help the Indian Revolution.'

Roy would persist in his revolutionary dreams for years to come, but they became increasingly desperate and forlorn. Spurned by the Comintern and ditched by the Soviet leadership, he would launch a final bid for revolution in 1930, slipping back across the frontier into India.

Intelligence agents were soon on his trail. On 21 July 1931, he was arrested in Bombay. Soon afterwards, he was charged under Section 121A of the Indian Penal Code with 'conspiring to deprive the King-Emperor of his sovereignty in India.'

His attempt to overthrow British India, begun with such high hopes, ended in a squalid Indian jail.

EPILOGUE

TOP SECRET

In the aftermath of the disbanding of the Army of God, Lord Curzon took the opportunity to reflect on the role played by the spies and code-breakers.

They had infiltrated Soviet organisations, eavesdropped on communications and played a skilful game of cat and mouse in the citadels and back-lands of Central Asia, often in situations of extreme danger. More than this, they had transformed the means by which the government could now operate. Old-fashioned diplomacy had been shown to have serious limitations in times of crisis. A spy, working undercover and in disguise, could achieve more in a day than a frock-coated ambassador could hope to do in a year.

Lord Curzon was deeply impressed by their work; it had proved a highly efficient way to neutralise a serious threat. Now he wrote to the viceroy asking if Indian intelligence operations needed to be expanded yet further. If so, money would be made available.

'I should emphasise the importance of selecting the very ablest and most discreet investigating agents . . .' he wrote. 'The matter is of worldwide interest to all governments and this explains my anxiety that all that is possible should be done.'

Winston Churchill agreed with Lord Curzon on the value of espionage. He attached particular importance to a newly established organisation whose purpose was the interception of secret telegraphic transmissions.

The Government Code and Cipher School, as it was known, had already been tapping communications between Moscow and London during the trade negotiations. It was to play a key role in future espionage operations and would eventually move to Bletchley Park, where its brilliant code-breakers would (in the years to come) decrypt Nazi Germany's Enigma enciphers. But even at this early date, its work was proving critical in directing government policy.

'I attach more importance to them [intercepts] as a means of forming a true judgement of public policy ...' wrote Churchill, 'than to any other source of knowledge at the disposal of the State.'

Few ministers believed that the Comintern was serious about abandoning its goal of global revolution and they were soon proved correct. Within months of the Anglo-Soviet Trade Agreement being signed, Moscow's commissars were once again engaged in secret talks about attacking British India.

These discussions were picked up in London within a matter of hours, for Mansfield Cumming was by now receiv-ing intelligence from the very heart of the regime.

This intelligence was of an extraordinary nature, for it included the actual minutes of Politburo sessions and verba-tim accounts from the Soviet inner circle. Cumming even received the transcript of a heated discussion between Trotsky, Stalin and other senior commissars. This was particularly noteworthy, because the meeting had been held behind closed doors at Chicherin's private residence.

A number of the surviving typescripts still bear their Secret Intelligence Service cover notes. 'The following information has been obtained at first hand by a highly reliable agent,' reads one of these notes. 'It is requested that VERY SPECIAL PRECAUTIONS AS REGARDS SECRECY AND SAFE CUSTODY be taken with regard to the information and documents.' The documents revealed the Soviet leadership's ongoing links with Indian revolutionaries.

Lord Curzon was incensed by Moscow's duplicity and told his Cabinet colleagues that unless something urgent was done, the lies would continue 'until the dark-haired among us become grey, the grey-haired white and the white bald.'

In the spring of 1923, the Prime Minister gave him the green light to issue his famous Curzon Ultimatum. This was an uncompromising demand that the Soviet government and the Comintern refrain forever from fomenting revolution against British interests.

The British once again released selected snippets of intelligence to bolster their case. Indeed Lord Curzon taunted his Soviet counterparts with the transcripts of intercepted communications. 'The Russian Commissariat for Foreign Affairs will no doubt recognise the following communication dated 21 February, 1923 . . . The Commissariat for Foreign Affairs will also doubtless recognise a communication received by them from Kabul, dated the 8th November, 1922 . . .'

The left-wing British newspaper, the *Daily Herald*, was appalled by Lord Curzon's ultimatum. 'Such a note sent by one Great Power to another would, before 1914, have meant war.'

The Soviet Government also expressed surprise at the aggressive tone of the ultimatum and went so far as to accuse Lord Curzon of inventing the transcripts. But Moscow had no desire to sever the hard-won trade relations at a time of continued economic chaos. It backed down once again, only this time it promised to abandon forever its designs on British India.

'The Soviet Government undertakes not to support with funds or in any other form persons or bodies or agencies or institutions whose aim is to spread discontent or to foment rebellion in any other part of the British Empire.'

After all the setbacks, a line had finally been drawn in the sand. Even Lord Curzon himself felt that the danger was finally over. 'I think that I may claim to have won a considerable victory over the Soviet Government,' he wrote in a private letter to a friend. 'I expect them to behave with more circumspection for some time to come.

★

As the dust slowly settled, one question remained unanswered: who was supplying Mansfield Cumming with the top-secret intelligence from Moscow?

One clue to his identity was the fact that he could procure the actual minutes of Politburo meetings. This, coupled with his reports of verbatim conversations between commissars, strongly suggests that Cumming's finest agent was a Russian mole by the name of Boris Bazhanov.

If so, this represented a sensational coup. Bazhanov was one of Soviet Russia's most senior functionaries, who rose to become secretary to both Joseph Stalin and to the Politburo.

Unbeknown to Moscow, Bazhanov was also a fifth-column insider. As Lenin's inner circle discussed tactics for destroying

British India, they had no idea that the man taking the minutes was sending them directly to London.

Bazhanov would later publish his memoirs in French under the title, *Avec Staline dans le Kremlin*. He confessed to having been a double agent from the very moment he joined the Communist Party in 1919, describing himself as a 'Trojan horse' who infiltrated 'the Communist fortress' in order to undermine the system from within.

'It was an undertaking of the greatest peril,' he wrote, 'but I did not allow myself to be deterred by the thought of risk. I had to be constantly on my guard. I had to watch every word I spoke, every move I made, every step I took.'

Those steps took him to the top of the Soviet ladder. Within a year, he had become one of the regime's key secretaries with access to all the top-secret reports being produced by Stalin and the Politburo.

'As a soldier of the anti-Bolshevist army, I had set myself the difficult and dangerous task of penetrating to the very heart of enemy headquarters. I had achieved my goal.'

This was to prove of vital importance for British intelligence. As Bazhanov said, the Politburo was responsible for all major decisions respecting the government of the country, as well as questions of world revolution.

'I held in my hands the key to the secret bureau where the dark destiny of Russia was being planned, along with the plot against the peace of the civilized world.'

Bazhanov's behaviour eventually aroused Stalin's suspicions. In fear of his life, he made an exhilarating flight from Russia to Persia with the secret police hot on his trail. After contacting British intelligence in Meshed, Bazhanov was smuggled to British India by car, camel caravan and the viceroy's private train. Once he arrived in Simla, he supplied intelligence chiefs with yet more valuable information about the inner workings of the Soviet regime.

Bazhanov would continue to work sporadically for British intelligence until the outbreak of the Second World War, when Britain's alliance with Stalin proved more than he could stomach.

Bazhanov's story is as remarkable as it is full of twists. When his autobiography was translated from French into English, all the lines about his work as a mole were mysteriously expunged. Bazhanov does not explain who ordered them to be deleted. Nor does he say why.

He would eventually settle in Paris, a hunted man with a $5 million price on his head. He was to survive no fewer than a dozen assassination attempts, including one notable occasion when a hired thug tried to knife him to death in his garage. The fact that Stalin made such efforts to have him killed is strong evidence that he was telling the truth about his life as a mole.

When first interviewed by the French authorities, Bazhanov warned them that he would be hunted for the rest of his life. 'I must tell you straight away that if I am suddenly tapped on the shoulder in the street by a stranger in civilian clothes and pushed towards a car, I shall simply shoot him down with the pistol I now always carry with me.'

Stalin's assassins never succeeded in their quest to kill him: Bazhanov died peacefully at a ripe old age.

★

By the time of Bazhanov's heady ascent up the Soviet hierarchy, many of Cumming's old players had moved on to new games. George Hill undertook a brief intelligence mission to the Middle East, only to be left destitute when Secret

Intelligence Service funds dried up. He returned to England and moved into a caravan in Sussex with his wife.

He was recalled into service at the outbreak of the Second World War and given employment in his original field of expertise: sabotage and destruction. One of his most able students was a young Cambridge graduate named Kim Philby, later to become infamous as one of the Cambridge Five. Philby referred to Hill as 'Jolly George'.

Hill's final and most extraordinary mission came in 1941, when he led a team to Moscow in order to set up a joint Allied operation that brought together Britain's Special Operations Executive and Stalin's secret police. It was the point at which his life had turned a full circle. He had started out his career working with Russia as an ally. Now, twenty-five years later, he found himself doing the same thing.

George Hill's undercover work in the turbulent early years had cemented his friendship with Sidney Reilly. The two men continued to socialise together and Hill acted as best man at Reilly's third wedding, in 1923, to the actress Pepita Bobadilla.

Reilly had thoroughly enjoyed life as a spy and was keen to continue serving Mansfield Cumming. But when his offer to work against the Soviet regime was rejected, Reilly turned instead to Boris Savinkov, who remained the most credible opponent to the Russian Government. In 1925, Reilly was lured back to Moscow in the hope of making contact with Savinkov's supporters inside Russia.

'I would not have undertaken this trip,' he wrote to Pepita, '. . . if I was not convinced that there is practically no risk attached to it.'

Reilly walked straight into a trap. He was arrested by the Soviet secret police and subjected to a long and gruelling interrogation. He had already been sentenced to death in absentia back in 1918. Now that sentence was carried out. He was executed in November 1925, and buried in the inner courtyard of the old Cheka headquarters, the Loubianka.

Robert Bruce Lockhart had always enjoyed the dangers and intrigues that came with espionage. He also happened to be a gifted raconteur. In the early 1930s, he began working on his autobiography, *Memoirs of a British Agent*. Published in the following year, it became an international bestseller and was turned into a Warner Brothers movie. Lockhart went on to write a string of successful books and also became editor of the *Evening Standard's* gossip column, Londoner's Diary.

He would be recalled to service in the Second World War, helping to produce propaganda against Nazi Germany. But his best days were passed: he never again matched the fame and notoriety he had achieved for his role in what had become known as the 'Lockhart Plot'. He was still a controversial figure when he died in 1970: one of the last people to visit him at his deathbed is said to have been his beloved Moura.

Moura would herself earn a posthumous fame of sorts as the great-great-aunt of Britain's Deputy Prime Minister, Nick Clegg.

Paul Dukes, knighted in 1920, chose a very different path from his fellow agents. In the aftermath of his return to England he was increasingly drawn to Eastern mysticism. In 1922, he joined a tantric community at Nyack, near New York, led by an eccentric doctor known as Omnipotent Oom.

Dukes would also develop an enduring fascination for yoga, which he introduced to the Western world in a series of successful books.

The final significant member of Cumming's team, Arthur Ransome, had left Russia with Evgenia in 1919. After spending several years cruising around the Baltic coastline in his beloved yacht, *Racundra*, he eventually married Evgenia in 1924. The couple then moved into an old stone cottage above Windermere in the Lake District. Here, Ransome began writing *Swallows and Amazons*, the first in a series of highly successful children's books.

His work for Mansfield Cumming – and the controversies that surrounded it – was quietly forgotten for many years. The intelligence file on his activities in Russia, including MI5's reports about his pro-Bolshevik sympathies, was only released into the public domain in 2005.

Some agents found it difficult to settle down after the excitement of their undercover work. Frederick Bailey returned to British India after brushing the Karakum sand from his boots. But he was soon off in search of new adventure, heading to Gangtok in the state of Sikkim, where he lived with his new wife, Irma.

He made frequent travels to Tibet and became close friends with the thirteenth Dalai Lama. He also added to his already extensive collection of butterflies, Nepalese birds and stuffed mammals. These were eventually bequeathed to the British Museum in London and the Metropolitan Museum in New York.

Bailey died in 1967, along with Paul Dukes and Arthur Ransome. George Hill died shortly afterwards, in 1968. It was the end of an era for British espionage.

And what of Mansfield Cumming himself? He remained a workaholic to the end, even though he was suffering from increasingly severe angina. He suffered his first heart attack just before Christmas Day, 1922. A second one followed a few days later.

He returned to his offices in Holland Park as soon as he was recovered, but he knew that he could not continue forever.

Reluctantly, he decided that it was time to pack up his gadgets and secret inks and retire to Bursledon.

He never got the chance. He was still hard at work when a third heart attack killed him on 23 June 1923.

He had just had a valedictory drink with one of his former agents, Valentine Williams, who had come to wish him a happy retirement. Shortly after Williams left the building, Cumming sat down on the sofa in his office. A few minutes later, he was dead.

'He died in harness,' wrote Williams, 'as he would have wished.' Work had brought meaning to his life: it was appropriate, perhaps, that it also brought about his end.

He was buried close to his beloved home in Bursledon, just a short distance from the First World War tank in which he liked to tour the Hampshire countryside. There was no obituary, nor even any announcement of his death. He simply disappeared without trace. It was exactly as he would have wished.

His successor had been chosen before his death: it was to be Rear Admiral Hugh Sinclair, the cigar-smoking, pleasure-seeking former head of Naval Intelligence. Cumming had been delighted when he learned of Sinclair's appointment, describing him as 'in every way qualified and suitable.'

Sinclair was also made director of the Government Code and Cipher School, bringing code-breaking and deciphering into the orbit of the Secret Intelligence Service.

A few months before his retirement, Cumming had told Samuel Hoare, his former bureau chief in Petrograd, that the service was destined to have an illustrious future under Sinclair. 'In his capable hands, this organisation will grow to be very useful – it is not too much to say essential – to the Govt. Departments we serve.'

In fact, Winston Churchill had made it clear that its work was already deemed essential by government ministers. The Secret Intelligence Service had begun as a ramshackle network of 'rascals', 'scallywags' and public school adventurers. In little more than a decade, it had become a slick and highly skilled organisation that could penetrate to the very heart of enemy governments. Mansfield Cumming had successfully overseen the creation of the world's first professional secret service.

By the time of Cumming's death, a new team of special agents was at work in Moscow and Petrograd. Their principal task was to infiltrate the Soviet regime's new chemical weapons programme.

This was a whole new story, one that was once again to involve deception, subterfuge and secret intelligence. Mansfield Cumming, of course, was no longer at the helm. But he would have been pleased to know that by the time the first game of Russian Roulette had come to an end, the second one had already begun.

NOTES AND SOURCES

The material for *Russian Roulette* is derived from two principal sources: published accounts written by the agents themselves and their unpublished intelligence reports and letters. Most of the reports were written for either Mansfield Cumming or for his colleagues in the Indian Bureau (in Simla) and Indian Political Intelligence in London.

The original material is stored in two principal repositories: the National Archives (NA) in Kew and the India Office Collection in the British Library.

MI6 files remain closed, a source of continual frustration to historians. There is the occasional (and exceptional) release of material. Documents relating to Arthur Ransome were placed in the public domain as recently as 2005.

The story of *Russian Roulette* largely concerns British India, and the records of Indian Political Intelligence were released en masse in 1997. They are a treasure trove of information, not least because they contain some duplicate copies of original MI6 records that are still kept under lock and key.

These records reveal the close working relationship between the Secret Intelligence Service and Indian Political Intelligence.

When the files were initially placed in the public domain, the historian Patrick French commented that 'an ambitious PhD student could have a field day.' So, indeed, can anyone with a British Library reader's ticket and plenty of time on their hands.

Espionage is by its very nature secret, but the 751 files and volumes of Indian Political Intelligence, coupled with the thousands of once-classified documents at the National Archives, provide a fascinating glimpse into the murky world of espionage and deception that took place inside Soviet Russia in the aftermath of the 1917 revolution.

In the notes below, full references to each book are given unless they are listed in *Selected Reading.*

Prologue

The eyewitness account of Lenin's arrival at Finlyandsky Station, as recorded by an unnamed Russian journalist, can be found at http://bigsiteofhistory.com/lenins-address-at-the-finland-station

Paul Dukes's account of Lenin's arrival is recorded in his book, *The Story of ST 25.* William Gibson's impressions were published in his book, *Wild Career: My Crowded Years of Adventure in Russia and the Near East.*

Sir George Buchanan's memoirs were published under the title *My Mission to Russia.* Lord Hardinge's account was published in *The Reminiscences of Lord Hardinge of Penshurst* (London, 1947). Sir George Molesworth, who was later to play a key role in the Anglo-Afghan War and the defence of the Raj, wrote up his experiences in *Afghanistan, 1919.*

PART ONE: SHOOTING IN THE DARK

1: Murder in the Dark

Samuel Hoare wrote extensively about his experiences in Russia in *Fourth Seal: The End of a Russian Chapter* (London,

1930). His time as Mansfield Cumming's bureau chief is also analysed in Michael Smith's excellent study, *Six: A History of Britain's Secret Intelligence Service* (London, 2010). Smith also discusses the unlikely secret service career of Oswald Rayner.

The traditionally accepted account of Rasputin's murder is derived from Prince Feliks Yusupov's highly coloured autobiography, *Lost Splendour.*

Yusupov's account has been convincingly picked apart by Richard Cullen in his fascinating book, *Rasputin: The Role of Britain's Secret Service in his Torture and Murder.*

Cullen's book revisits all the surviving accounts, published and unpublished, including the autopsy report written by Professor Kosorotov.

With the help of experts in ballistics, he presents a highly convincing scenario for Rasputin's murder, implicating not only Oswald Rayner, but several other members of Mansfield Cumming's team inside Russia.

Cullen's work has sparked a vigorous debate on the Internet: this can be followed at: http://forum.alexanderpalace.org/index.php?action=printpage;topic=1363.0

Rasputin's death was the subject of a BBC Radio 4 documentary, *Great Lives: Rasputin* (January 2013). This is on-line at: http://www.bbc.co.uk/programmes/b01phgjs

2: The Chief

The best recent biography of Mansfield Cumming is Alan Judd's *The Quest for C.* There is also much information to be found in Keith Jeffrey's *MI6*. I also consulted Christopher Andrew's *Secret Service* for a wealth of background material.

Other anecdotes about Cumming are to be found in Compton Mackenzie's *Greek Memories*, Valentine Williams' *The World of Action* (London, 1938), Samuel Hoare's *The Fourth Seal* (London, 1930) and Edward Knoblock's *Round the Room: An Autobiography* (London, 1939).

Hoare's account is adapted from his book, *Fourth Seal*; Harvey Pitcher, *Witnesses of the Russian Revolution*; Smith, *Six*; Yusupov, *Lost Splendour*; Chambers, *Last Englishman*. The story about William Gibson is from his autobiography, *Wild Career*. Knox's reminiscences can be found in his book, *With the Russian Army*.

3: The Perfect Spy
The most detailed account of Lenin's arrival at Torneå is to be found in Michael Pearson's *Sealed Train*. See also Helen Rappaport's fascinating *Conspirator*. The story about Harry Gruner is explored in Smith, *Six*; there are also anecdotes about Gruner in William Gerhardie's *Memoirs*.

The story of Trotsky's arrest is to be found in 'Englishmen in New York: The SIS American Station, 1915–21' by Richard B. Spence, *Intelligence and National Security*, vol. 19, no. 3 (2004). Another interesting article is 'Interrupted Journey: British Intelligence and the Arrest of Leon Trotsky, April 1917', by the same author, published in *Revolutionary Russia*, vol. 13, no. 1 (June 2000). I also consulted *Leon Trotsky in New York City* by I. D. Thatcher, *Historical Research*, vol. 69, no. 169 (June 1996).

Trotsky's interview with the *New York Times* was published 16 March 1917. See also Guy Gaunt's *Yield*.

George Hill, *Go Spy* and *Dreaded Land*; Hector Bywater, *Strange Intelligence*; Smith, *Six* (contains the story of Frank

Stagg); Judd, *Quest*; Andrew, *Secret Service*. I also drew much information from a National Archives file of recipes for secret inks: KV3/2 *Invisible Ink and Secret Writing*.

Meriel Buchanan, *Ambassador's Daughter*; Pitcher, *Witnesses*; Pipes, *The Russian Revolution*; Price, *Reminiscences*.

There are several good accounts of Maugham's mission to Russia. Maugham wrote a series of articles about it and my own account is largely derived from these articles: *Sunday Express*, 30 September & 7 October 1962; Maugham's trip is dealt with in some detail by Selina Hastings in *Secret Lives*. Also consulted were Maugham, *Writer's Notebook* and Voska, *Spy*.

See also Keith Neilson's ' "Joy Rides"? British Intelligence and Propaganda in Russia, 1914-1917,' published in *Historical Journal*, XXIV (1981) for an analysis of the early years of Cumming's Russian bureau and Maugham's mission.

4: Know Thy Enemy

Buchanan, *My Mission*; Pitcher, *Reminiscences*; Pipes, *Russian Revolution*; Hill, *Go Spy*.

The internal organisation of Cumming's office is covered in detail by Jeffrey, *MI6*. Freddie Browning's obituary was published in *The Times*, 15 October 1929. Inter-departmental rivalries are dealt with in considerable detail both in Jeffrey's *MI6* and Judd's *Quest*. There is also much on Macdonogh in Andrew, *Secret Service*.

Lockhart; *Memoirs*. Lockhart's time in Russia is dealt with in some detail by Gordon Brook-Shepherd, *Iron Maze*. See also Hill, *Go Spy*; Chambers, *Ransome*; Brogan, *Signalling*. Wardrop's account of Lockhart's employment is in FO/371/3331.

Extracts from Cumming's *Notes on Instruction and Recruiting of Agents* are published in Jeffrey, *MI6*.

The most accessible general book on the Cheka remains George Leggett's *Cheka*. See also Lockhart, *Memoirs*.

PART TWO: MASTERS OF DISGUISE

5: The Man with Three Names

Much has been written about Reilly: see Reilly, *Master Spy*; Cook, *Ace of Spies*; Bruce Lockhart, *Ace of Spies*; Thwaites, *Velvet*; Brook-Shepherd, *Iron Maze*; Smith, *Six*; Service, *Spies*.

Reilly was also the subject of a popular 1983 television mini-series called *Reilly: Ace of Spies*, starring Sam Neill.

Lockhart, *Memoirs*; Hill, *Go Spy*. Smith's *Six* has information about Boyce and operations inside Russia. The account of the Congress of Soviets is derived from the eyewitnesses who were there, as well as Chambers, *Double Life*.

6: A Double Life

George Hill's lengthy report into his undercover work in Russia, with details of safe houses and the courier system, can be found in the National Archives: FO/371/3350. See also Hill, *Go Spy*; Reilly, *Master Spy*; Cook, *Ace of Spies*; Bruce Lockhart, *Ace of Spies*; Brook-Shepherd, *Iron Maze*; Smith, *Six*.

The question of how best to deal with Russia is dealt with in considerable detail in Brook-Shepherd, *Iron Maze*. Lockhart sets out his own position in FO/371/3337 and *Memoirs*.

Moura's life has been the subject of a 2005 biography by Nina Berberova entitled: *Moura: The Dangerous Life of the Baroness Budberg* (New York, 2005). I am grateful to one who knew Moura for background information about her life.

The story of Ransome's trip to Vologda occupies an entire chapter of his autobiography. It is also dealt with in some detail by Chambers' *Last Englishman,* as well as by Lockhart's *Memoirs.* Lockhart's request for help for Evgenia is to be found in NA: KV2/1903. This file contains much fascinating and hitherto unknown information about Ransome. The MI5 file on Ransome has also been released into the public domain: it can be found at KV2/1904.

There is a great deal of information on the internment of British nationals in the NA. See FO/371/3336 for a list of prisoners and more.

7: Mission to Tashkent

This chapter is derived from a number of sources: Bailey, *Mission*; Hopkirk, *Setting the East Ablaze*; Swinson, *Bailey*; and records in the India Office Collections. I found the following particularly useful: IOR/L/PS/10/722, Bailey's report on his missions to Tashkent (2 vols.) and IOR/L/PS/10/741, a massive collection of material pertaining to Bailey's mission.

There is also a wealth of information in Daniel C. Waugh's excellent monograph *Etherton at Kashgar: Rhetoric and Reality in the History of the Great Game*, Bactrian Press (Seattle, 2007). This is on-line at: http://faculty.washington. edu/dwaugh/ethertonatkashgar2007.pdf

There is a fascinating account of life in Tashkent at this time in Brun, *Troublous Times*. Also of interest is George Macartney, 'Bolshevism as I saw it at Tashkent' published in the *Journal of the Royal Asia Society*, vol. 7, nos. 2–3 (1920).

8: Going Underground

George Hill's account is in *Go Spy* and also in his fascinating long report to London, National Archives: FO/371/3350. See also Smith, *Six*.

The so-called Lockhart plot has received extensive coverage, not just by the players themselves but also in secondary accounts. First-hand published accounts include: Lockhart, *Memoirs*; Hill, *Go Spy*; Reilly, *Master Spy*.

There are several key documents in the NA. FO/371/3348 includes Lockhart's own report; FO/371/3337 has much additional information, including many documents from the Russian point of view. See also FO/371/3336, in which Zinoviev calls the British 'a disgusting stinking lump of filth.'

The fullest secondary account is in Brook-Shepherd, *Iron Maze*, although not everyone will agree with the author's conclusions. The plot has also been the subject of a BBC Radio 4 documentary: *Document: The Lockhart Plot* (March 2011), on-line at http://www.bbc.co.uk/programmes/b00zlfkt

9: Vanishing Trick

This chapter is derived from a number of sources: Bailey, *Mission*; Hopkirk, *Setting the East Ablaze*; Swinson, *Bailey*, and records in the India Office Collections, notably as above, IOR/L/PS/10/722, Bailey's own report (2 vols.) and IOR/L/PS/10/741.

10: The Plot Thickens

Reilly's account of events is in *Master Spy*; Brook-Shepherd, *Iron Maze*, also has details of the embassy raid. Nathalie Bucknall's dramatic account of Captain Cromie's death, dated

1 September 1918, is in NA: FO/371/3336. There are relevant documents in FO/371/3337, including Wardrop's report into the incident and reports by Lockhart and Mr Kimens of the Dutch Legation. This file also contains many Russian newspaper reports, notably those from *Pravda*.

The story of the aftermath of the raid – notably what happened to George Hill's female couriers – is detailed in Cook, *Ace of Spies*. This includes previously unknown material from the Russian archives. Hill, *Go Spy*; Reilly, *Master Spy*, and Brook-Shepherd, *Iron Maze*, also have accounts of the aftermath. Important new information is to be found in Orlov, *March*. Lockhart, *Memoirs*, gives a full account of his own predicament. There is much additional information in NA: FO/371/3334 and FO/371/3337.

11: A Deadly Game

Paul Dukes, *Red Dusk*, provides details about Merrett (whom he refers to as Marsh). There is much information of interest in the NA. Mr Woodhouse's report is in FO/71/3975. Paul Dukes's reports are in ADM/223/637. This includes such notable intelligence successes as intercepts between Trotsky and Admiral Altavater (CX062092). See also T/161/30 for letters and memoranda.

The internal battles fought by Cumming are detailed by Jeffrey, *MI6*; Judd, *Quest*; and Andrew, *Secret Service*.

Hill, *Go Spy*; Smith, *Six*; Judd, *Quest*. Dukes's story of his induction into the secret service is recounted in his two books, *ST 25* and *Red Dusk*.

Ransome, *On Behalf* and *Autobiography*; Chambers, *Last Englishman*; Smith, *Six*. In particular, see the recently released intelligence files on Ransome in the NA: KV2/1903 and KV2/1904. This latter contains the MI5 files on Ransome.

12: Toxic Threat

Bailey's own account is in *Mission*; see also Swinson, *Beyond*, and Hopkirk's excellent *Setting the East*. Much of the information about Bailey's mission has been gathered from original reports, letters and memos. These are scattered through the India Office collections, but the most important files are: IOR/L/PS/10/722, Bailey's report on his missions to Tashkent (2 vols.) and IOR/L/PS/10/741. This latter is a massive collection of material about Bailey's mission and also about Malleson's work.

I consulted dozens of files on British espionage activities in Central Asia. The most pertinent were the following files: IOR/L/PS/825 (Kashgar Diaries 1912–20) and IOR/L/PS/976 (Kashgar Diaries 1921–30); IOR/L/MIL/17/14/91/2 (Bolshevik activities in Central Asia 1919), IOR/L/PS/10/836 (Bolshevik Activities in Central Asia, Dec 1919–Feb 1920); IOR/L/PS/11/159 (Bolshevik Propaganda in Central Asia) IOR/L/PS/10/741 (Bolshevik Activities in Central Asia).

There are many documents relating to Afghanistan in the above files. The most detailed published account of the Afghan offensive and the British Indian defence is written by Molesworth, *Afghanistan*. A copy of the treaty (and negotiations) can be found on-line: http://www.iranicaon-line.org/articles/anglo-afghan-treaty-of-1921-the-outcome-of-peace-negotiations-following-the-third-anglo-afghan-war

PART THREE: THE PROFESSIONAL SPY

13: Master of Disguise

Dukes writes about his mission in *ST25* and *Red Morrow*. A number of his intelligence reports are to be found in the NA. See ADM 223/637 and ADM 1/8563/208. See also FO/371/4375; it contains many documents from the Political Intelligence Department on the situation inside Russia. FO/608/195/7 has many reports on conditions inside Soviet Russia. FO/236/59 contains Mr Woodhouse's report on conditions in Petrograd.

Ransome, *Autobiography*; *Six Weeks*; *Signalling*; Chambers, *Last Englishman*. Ransome's principal intelligence report, 'Report on the State of Russia', can be found in NA: FO/371/4002A. This file also contains several reports by ST 25 (Paul Dukes) on conditions inside the country. Dukes later wrote numerous reports for *The Times*, all of which are now indexed on *The Times* database. The most informative are 'Bolshevism at Close Quarters' (15 October 1919 – part of an eight-part series) and 'Designs for Asia: Bolshevist Interest in the East' (15 January 1920). This latter article quotes an important memo written by Karakhan.

14: The Lethal M Device

There is an excellent account of Churchill's policy towards Soviet Russia in Gilbert, *Churchill* (vol. 4). This also explains internal divisions within the government. More detailed – and equally fascinating – is Antoine Capet's ' "The Creeds of the Devil": Churchill between the Two Totalitarianisms, 1917–1945.' This sets out Churchill's rabid anti-communist views. It is available on-line at: http://www.winstonchurchill.org/

support/the-churchill-centre/publications/
finest-hour-onlineon-line/725-the-creeds-of-the-devil-chur-
chill-between-the-two-totalitarianisms-1917-
1945#sdfootnote34sym

See also Ullman's *Anglo-Soviet Relations* for detailed coverage of the war in Russia.

Hill, *Go Spy* and *Dreaded Hour* cover his mission to General
Denikin. But there is also much of interest in the NA, notably
FO/371/3962 and FO/371/3978 which contain Sidney
Reilly's despatches and reports about General Denikin and
his advisors, sent from Sebastopol, Ekaterinodar and
elsewhere.

The story of Churchill's deployment of chemical weapons is
little known. The best scholarly article was published by the
Imperial War Museum Review, 12 (1999): '"The Right
Medicine for the Bolshevist": British Air-Dropped Chemical
Weapons in North Russia, 1919' by Simon Jones. But the full
story of the research and development of chemical weapons
in the immediate aftermath of the First World War remains to
be told.

Many of the original documents, including reports by the
War Office and medical reports into the effects of the chemical gas, are to be found in NA. There are also a number of
photographs contained in the NA files. I found the following
most useful: WO/32/5749, 'The Use of Gas in North Russia';
WO/33/966 *European War Secret Telegrams*, Series H, vol. 2,
Feb–May 1919; WO/32/5184 and WO/32/5185 (Churchill
and the use of chemical gas); WO/158/735; WO/142/116;
WO/95/5424 and AIR/462/15/312/125 (these all contain
reports about the dropping of gas); WO/106/1170 (the case
of Private Leeposhkin); T/173/830 (Grantham's evidence).

See also J.B.S. Haldane, *Callinicus: A Defence of Chemical Warfare* (London, 1925).

15: Agent in Danger

The best general account of Agar's rescue mission is in Ferguson, *Operation Kronstadt*.

The material about Dukes is gathered from his published accounts, *ST25* and *Red Dusk*, and from his intelligence reports to London, some of which are in the NA: ADM/223/637.

Agar wrote three books about his adventurous life. The most relevant to the Paul Dukes rescue mission is *Baltic Episode*. There is also an account of Admiral Cowan's service: *Sound of the Guns: Being an Account of the Wars and Service of Admiral Sir Walter Cowan* by Lionel Dawson (Oxford, 1949).

The NA has several files on Agar's mission: ADM/1/8563/208 and ADM/137/16879 (an account by Agar of his raid). The files also contain maps of the Baltic.

16: Dirty Tricks

Published accounts include Bailey, *Mission*; Hopkirk, *Setting the East*; Swinson, *Beyond*. There is also a wealth of material in the India Office Archives. See IOR/L/PS/10/722 and IOR/L/PS/10/741. Bailey's papers are also in the IOR: see Mss EurD 658 and Mss EurD 157/178, 157/180, 157/182, 157/183, 157/232 and 157/275.

The principal published account of Malleson's mission is Wilfrid Malleson, 'The British Military Mission in Turkestan, 1918–1920' published in the *Journal of the Central Asian Society*, vo. 9, no. 2 (1922). There is also useful background material: 'British Secret Missions in Turkestan' by L.P. Morris in the *Journal of Contemporary History*, vol. 12, no. 2 (1977); Alexander Park's *Bolshevism in Turkestan* (New York, 1957); G.L. Dmitriev, *Indian Revolutionaries in Central Asia* (India, 2002); *The Transcaspian Episode* by C.H. Ellis (London, 1963) and *British Military Involvement in Transcaspia* by Michael Sergeant (Camberley, 2004).

But most of the material is unpublished and kept in the India Office Records at the British Library. I found the following the most useful: IOR/L/MIL/17/14/91/2 'Bolshevik Activities in Central Asia'; IOR/L/PS/10/836 'Bolshevik Activities in Central Asia'; IOR/L/PS/10/886, this file includes the important 'Report of Interdepartmental Committee on Bolshevism as a menace to the British Empire'; IOR/L/PS/11/159, containing Bolshevik propaganda; IOR/L/PS/11/201 'Bolshevik Activities in Central Asia'; IOR/L/PS/10/741 contains lots of reports from Malleson and Etherton. The Kashgar consular diaries (IOR/L/PS/825 and IOR/L/PS/976) give Etherton's perspective.

See also the aforementioned on-line monograph by Waugh, *Etherton at Kashgar.*

17: Army of God

M.N. Roy's time in Moscow and his designs on India are detailed in his autobiography, *Memoirs*. There is a great deal of additional information about the threat to be found in the India Office (see notes pertaining to Malleson, above) and in two books published for internal distribution by the Intelligence Bureau in Simla: *Communism in India* by Sir Cecil Kaye and its sequel *Communism in India* by Sir David Petrie. The latter is particularly useful and gives a real insight into the scale and reach of the Intelligence Bureau in Simla.

Of interest, too, is IOR/L/PS/10/886, the aforementioned report into the threat of Bolshevism to India. This incorporates a great deal of material obtained from the Secret Intelligence Service.

L/PJ/12/99 is one of the many files on Roy and his various aliases.

The Baku conference is well documented. For general background, see Hopkirk, *Setting the East*. For documents, transcripts of speeches and background material, see Eudin and Fisher, *Soviet Russia*, and Degras, *Communist International*. H.G. Wells also wrote about the congress in his *Russia in the Shadows* (London, 1920).

The speeches of the congress are on-line at http://www. marxists.org/history/international/comintern/baku/ch01. htm

18: Winner Takes All

Roy, *Memoirs*; Judd, *Quest*; Jeffrey, *MI6*; Andrew, *Secret Service*; Smith, *Six*. I also found Paul Dukes's reports in *The Times* a useful source: his report published on 15 January 1920, 'Bolshevik Interests in the East', contains a copy of one of Karakhan's memoranda.

The best general discussion of the Anglo-Soviet trade talks is in Andrew, *Secret Service*. Andrew has written extensively (and informatively) on the subject. See 'The British Secret Service and Anglo-Soviet Relations in the 1920s: Part 1: From the Trade Negotiations to the Zinoviev Letter' published in *The Historical Journal*, vol. 20, no. 3 (1977).

Also of great interest is 'The Anglo-Soviet Trade Agreement, March 1921,' by M.V. Glenny, *Journal of Contemporary*

History, vol. 5, no. 2 (1970); 'Engaging the World: Soviet Diplomacy and Foreign Propaganda in the 1920s' by Alistair Kocho-Williams, on-line at http://www.academia.edu/720588/Engaging_the_World_Soviet_Diplomacy_and_Foreign_Propaganda_in_the_1920s1

Kocho-Williams also wrote the interesting 'Comintern Though a British Lens', also on-line at http://www.academia.edu/720580/The_Comintern_through_a_British_lens

Beyond the scope of this book, but worthy of further reading, is the work of the cryptologists. Andrew, *Secret Service*, provides an outline of their work. See also *Action this Day*, edited by Ralph Erskine and Michael Smith (London, 2001) and an article on the work of Brigadier John Tiltman in 'Brigadier John Tiltman: One of Britain's Finest Cryptologists', published in *Cryptologia*, vol. 27, no. 4 (October 2003).

Abdul Qadir Khan's experiences with Roy were published in a three-part series in *The Times*, 25, 26 and 27 February 1930.

The trade agreement was published in *The Times* under the headline 'Trade with Red Russia' on 17 March 1921.

Epilogue

Information on espionage and intelligence gathering in the aftermath of the trade agreement can be found in IOR/L/PJ/12/117; this includes Lord Curzon's memo to the viceroy. There is a wealth of information in Popplewell, *Intelligence and Imperial Defence*, especially pp. 308–12.

Perhaps the most important intelligence file covering the period immediately after the trade agreement is IOR/L/PJ/12/119; it contains a large amount of top-secret documents acquired by Mansfield Cumming's Secret Intelligence Service. Boris Bazhanov's own account of his work as an inside agent can be found in *Avec Staline*. Information about Bazhanov can also be found at the NA: see KV3/11 and KV3/12. For more on Bazhanov's flight from Russia, see Brook-Shepherd, *Storm Petrels*. Bazhanov's story was published in the *Sunday Telegraph*, 19 and 26 September and 3 October 1976.

The concluding paragraphs about all the main players in *Russian Roulette* are drawn from three principal sources: their own accounts, their obituaries and the *Dictionary of National Biography*. Judd, *Quest*, provides an excellent account of Cumming's final months.

SELECTED READING

The books listed below will prove of interest to anyone who wishes to explore further Britain's espionage operations inside post-revolutionary Russia.

A full list of books, articles, unpublished documents and Internet resources can be found in the *Notes and Sources* section.

Agar, Augustus, *Baltic Episode: A Classic of Secret Service in Russian Waters* (London, 1963).

Footprints in the Sea (London, 1959).

Showing the Flag (London, 1962).

Andrew, Christopher, *Secret Service: The Making of the British Intelligence Community* (London, 1985).

Bailey, Frederick, *Mission to Tashkent* (London, 1992).

Bazhanov, Boris, *Avec Staline dans le Kremlin* (Paris, 1930).

Brogan, Hugh, *Signalling from Mars: The Letters of Arthur Ransome* (London, 1997).

The Life of Arthur Ransome (London, 1992).

Brook-Shepherd, Gordon, *Iron Maze: The Western Secret Services and the Bolsheviks* (London, 1998).

The Storm Petrels: The First Soviet Defectors (London, 1977).

Bruce Lockhart, Sir Robert, *Memoirs of the British Agent* (London, 1932).

Diaries, ed. Kenneth Young (London, 1973).

Bruce Lockhart, Robin, *Reilly: Ace of Spies* (London, 1983).

Brun, Alf Harald, *Troublous Times: Experiences in Bolshevik Russia and Turkestan* (London, 1931).

Buchanan, Meriel, *Ambassador's Daughter* (London, 1958).

Buchanan, Sir George, *My Mission to Russia* (London, 1923).

Bywater, Hector, *Strange Intelligence* (London, 1931).

Calder, Robert, *Somerset Maugham and the Quest for Freedom* (London, 1972).

Chambers, Roland, *The Last Englishman: The Double Life of Arthur Ransome* (London, 2009).

Cook, Andrew, *Ace of Spies: The True Story of Sidney Reilly* (London, 2004).

Cross, J.A., *Sir Samuel Hoare: A Political Biography* (London, 1977).

Cullen, Richard, *Rasputin: The Role of Britain's Secret Service in His Torture and Murder* (London, 2010).

Deacon, Richard, *Spyclopedia: The Comprehensive Handbook of Espionage* (New York, 1988).

Degras, Jane, *The Communist International, 1919–1943: Documents*, 3 vols. (London, 1956–65).

Dukes, Paul, *The Story of ST 25: Adventure and Romance in the Secret Intelligence Service in Red Russia* (London, 1938).

Red Dusk and the Morrow: Adventures and Investigations in Red Russia (London, 1922).

The Unending Quest: Autobiographical Sketches (London, 1950).

Ellis, Charles, *Transcaspian Episode, 1918-1919* (London, 1963).

Eudin, Xenia and Harold Fisher, *Soviet Russia and the West*, vol. 1; *Soviet Russia and the East*, vol. 2 (Stanford, 1957).

Ferguson, Harry, *Operation Kronstadt* (London, 2008).

Gaunt, Guy, *The Yield of the Years* (London, 1940).

Gerhardie, William, *Memoirs of a Polyglot* (London, 1973).

Gibson, William, *Wild Career: My Crowded Years of Adventure in Russia and the Near East* (London, 1935).

Gilbert, Martin, *Winston S. Churchill*, vol. 4 (London, 1977).

Hastings, Selina, *The Secret Lives of Somerset Maugham* (London, 2009).

Hill, George, *Go Spy the Land: Being the Adventures of I.K.8 of the British Secret Service* (London, 1932).

Dreaded Land (London, 1936).

Hoare, Sir Samuel, *Fourth Seal: The End of a Russian Chapter* (London, 1930).

Hopkirk, Peter, *Setting the East Ablaze* (London, 1984).

The Great Game (Oxford, 1991).

Jeffrey, Keith, *MI6: The History of the Secret Intelligence Service, 1909–1949* (London, 2010).

Judd, Alan, *The Quest for C: Sir Mansfield Cumming and the founding of the British Secret Service* (London, 2000).

Kettle, Michael, *Russia and the Allies, 1917–1920*, 4 vols.; *The Road to Intervention* vol. 4 (London, 1981).

Sidney Reilly: The True Story (London, 1983).

Knox, Major-General Sir A., *With the Russian Army, 1914–1917*, 2 vols. (London, 1921).

Leggett, George, *The Cheka: Lenin's Political Police* (Oxford, 1981).

Ludecke, Winfred, *Behind the Scenes of Espionage: Tales of the Secret Service* (London, 1929).

Selected Reading

Malleson, Major-General Sir Wilfrid, 'The British Military Mission to Turkestan, 1918-1920,' *Journal of the Central Asian Society* (London, 1922).

Maugham, Somerset, *Ashenden, or The British Agent* (London, 1928).

A Writer's Notebook (London, 1949).

Molesworth, George, *Afghanistan, 1919: An Account of Operations in the Third Afghan War* (London, 1962).

O'Brien-Ffrench, Conrad, *Delicate Mission* (London, 1979).

Occleshaw, Michael, *Armour Against Fate: British Military Intelligence in the First World War* (London, 1988).

Dances in Deep Shadows: Britain's Clandestine War Against Russia, 1917–20 (London, 2006).

Orlov, Alexander, *The March of Time* (London, 2004).

Pearson, Michael, *The Sealed Train* (London, 1975).

Pethybridge, Roger, (ed.) *Witnesses to the Russian Revolution* (London, 1964).

Pipes, Richard, *The Russian Revolution, 1988–1919* (London, 1990).

Pitcher, Harvey, *Witnesses of the Russian Revolution* (London, 2001).

Popplewell, Richard, *Intelligence and Imperial Defence: British Intelligence and the Defence of the Indian Empire* (London, 1995).

Price, Morgan Philips, *My Reminiscences of the Russian Revolution* (London, 1921).

Ransome, Arthur, 'On Behalf of Russia', *New Republic* (1918).

Six Weeks in Russia in 1919 (London, 1919).

The Autobiography of, ed. Rupert Hart-Davis (London, 1976).

Rappaport, Helen, *Conspirator: Lenin in Exile* (London, 2009).

Reilly, Sidney, *The Adventures of Sidney Reilly, Britain's Master Spy* (London, 1931).

Ronaldshay, Earl of, *The Life of Lord Curzon* (London, 1928).

Roy, Manabendra Nath, *Memoirs* (Bombay, 1964).

Service, Robert, *Lenin: A Biography* (London, 2000).

Spies and Commissars (London, 2011).

Trotsky: A Biography (London, 2009).

Smith, Michael, *Six: A History of Britain's Secret Intelligence Service* (London, 2010).

The Spying Game: The Secret History of British Espionage (London, 2003).

Soutar, Andrew, *With Ironside in Russia* (London, 1940).

Swinson, Arthur, *Beyond the Frontiers: The Biography of Colonel F. M. Bailey, Explorer and Special Agent* (London, 1971).

Teague Jones, Reginald, *The Spy Who Disappeared* (London, 1990).

Thwaites, Norman, *Velvet and Vinegar* (London, 1932).

Tyrkova-Williams, A., *Cheerful Giver: The Life of Harold Williams* (London, 1935).

Ullman, Richard, *Anglo-Soviet Relations, 1917–1921*, vol. 2; *Britain and the Russian Civil War, November 1918–February 1920* (Princeton and London, 1961–72).

Voska, E. and Irvin, W., *Spy and Counterspy: The Autobiography of a Master-Spy* (London, 1941).

Walpole, Sir Hugh, *The Secret City* (New York, 1943).

Wells, H.G., *Russia in the Shadows* (London, 1920).

West, Nigel, *MI6: British Secret Intelligence Service Operations, 1909–45* (London, 1983).

Yusupov, Prince Felix, *Lost Splendour* (London, 1953).

PERMISSION ACKNOWLEDGEMENTS

Pictures
akg-images/RIA Novosti: 3 above left. The British Library, Bailey Collection: 4. Corbis: 1 above right and below, 2 above right, 3 above right, 7 below right. Paul Dukes *The Story of "ST 25" Adventure and Romance in the Secret Intelligence Service In Red Russia*, 1938: 5. Imperial War Museums/© IWM Q20636: 6 above. Michael Kettle *The Road to Intervention, Russia and the Allies 1917-20* Vol 2, Routledge 1988: 8 below. Gustav Krist *Alone Through The Forbidden Land, Journeys In Disguise Through Soviet Central Asia*, 1938: 7 above. Reproduced with the permission of Leeds University Library: 2 below left and right. The National Archives/WO 106/1170: 6 below left and right. M. N. Roy *Memoirs*, 1964: 8 above left and right. TopFoto/RIA Novosti: 1 above left.

Text
Grateful acknowledgement is made to the following for permission to reprint previously published material:

Ian Fleming quote reproduced with permission of the Ian Fleming Estate (taken from Sidney Reilly, *The Adventures of Sidney Reilly, Britain's Master Spy*, London, 1931).

Oxford University Press: *Mission to Tashkent* by F. M. Bailey, © F. M. Bailey 1946 and renewed 1992. Reprinted by permission of Oxford University Press.

The Marsh Agency Ltd and Frontline Books: *Memoirs of a British Agent* by Robert Bruce Lockhart. Reprinted by permission of Frontline Books on behalf of print rights and The Marsh Agency, on behalf of The Estate of Sir Robert Bruce Lockhart, on behalf of electronic rights.

The Arthur Ransome Estate and Random House UK: *Autobiography* by Arthur Ransome. Reprinted by permission of The Arthur Ransome Estate and Random House UK on behalf of print and electronic rights.

Every reasonable effort has been made to trace the copyright holders, but if there are any errors or omissions, Hodder & Stoughton will be pleased to insert the appropriate acknowledgement in any subsequent printings or editions.

INDEX

Index

Index

Index